❧The Ethics of Human Rights❧

The Ethics of Human Rights

Contested Doctrinal and Moral Issues

Esther D. Reed

BAYLOR UNIVERSITY PRESS

Scripture quotations are from the New Revised Standard Version Bible, copyright 1989, Division of Christian Education of the National Council of the Churches of Christ in the United States of America. Used by permission. All rights reserved.

Cover Design: Pamela Poll
Cover image: "Ecce Homo or Christ Carrying the Cross" by Hieronymus Bosch (c. 1450–1516). Consignment: COA0049634. Museum voor Schone Kunsten, Ghent, Belgium. Photo Credit: Scala/Art Resource, NY. Used by permission of Art Resource.

Library of Congress Cataloging-in-Publication Data

Reed, Esther D., 1965-
   The ethics of human rights : contested doctrinal and moral issues / Esther D. Reed.
      p. cm.
   Includes bibliographical references and index.
   ISBN 978-1-932792-97-3 (alk. paper)
   1. Civil rights--Religious aspects--Christianity. 2. Human rights--Religious aspects--Christianity. 3. Human rights--Moral and ethical aspects. I. Title.

BT738.15.R44 2007
261.7--dc22

2007026452

Printed in the United States of America on acid-free paper with a minimum of 30% pcw recycled content.

Contents

Acknowledgments and Abbreviations

The author and publisher gratefully acknowledge permission to reprint "Richard Hooker, Eternal Law and the Human Exercise of Authority" in *Journal of Anglican Studies* 4.1 (2006), and sections from "Revelation and Natural Rights: Notes on Colin E. Gunton's *Theology of Nature*," in Paul Louis Metzger, ed., *Trinitarian Soundings in Systematic Theology* (London: T&T Clark International, 2005), chap. 5, pp. 203–15.

Unless otherwise stated, scriptural quotations in this publication are from the New Revised Standard Version (NRSV). The following list of abbreviations indicate the alternative versions that are used occasionally.

AV	Authorized Version
NKJV	New King James Version
NASB	New American Standard Bible

Introduction

The legacy of Western dyophysitism extends into the Enlightenment in two essentially Christian heresies: deism and the rights of man. In deism, God is removed from his creation, and the incarnation is denied, implicitly if not explicitly. In the concept of the rights of man, humanity gains an autonomy that a consistently incarnational faith will not permit.

—Vigen Guroian (emphasis added)[1]

Since the Second World War the reach of the rule of law has been expanded by the lessons of the Holocaust and the growing recognition that human rights must be effectively protected. . . .

[T]he recognition and development of human rights law is the best guarantee there is of creating a world order in which countries, hopefully democratic, can flourish in peace, and the best guarantee of promoting a just and tolerant society in our pluralistic democracy.

—Johan Steyn[2]

Toward a Christian Ethic of Human Rights

Heresy or one of the best available means of promoting the rule of law alongside standards of decency and justice? Alien to biblical witness or compatible with human dignity as created in the image of God? These dilemmas entail some of the most demanding issues facing Christian ethics in the twenty-first century. Theologians of liberation, notably from Latin

1

America, have reminded us since the 1970s of the ideological biases that human rights contain.[3] Tied historically to the interests of private property and, arguably, the logic of imperialism, modern liberal discourses are often said to be biased in favor of Western interests and property owners. Abstract notions of human rights quickly become instruments of oppression rather than liberation.[4] Yet, today, many disciples of Christ undertake human rights advocacy because of an intuited affinity between this work and Jesus' command to love. Even among some theologians of liberation, there has been a move away from condemnation of rights discourse towards critical appropriation of the kind that gives priority to the rights of the poor.[5]

The global and interdisciplinary dimensions of the topic mean that it is potentially huge and that we must delimit ourselves to the most important themes: why and how the theological foundations for Christian engagement with human rights might be specified more adequately; why and how human rights have a role to play in Christian social action; why and how a Christian account of human rights yields results different from today's modern, secularist notions; why and how better to support Christian human rights advocates, activists, and policymakers who work with these legal instruments every day. Mindful that theological controversies about the ethics of human rights have been running for more than two generations, and show no sign of flagging, this book offers a theological account of Christian engagement with human rights that seeks to shed light from faith in the gospel of God on the promise and problems of a human rights culture. It addresses a lack in present-day Protestant theology and ethics for dogmatic, biblically rooted engagement with human rights and seeks to move beyond the common impasse in present-day Protestant ethics between defenders and critics of the human rights tradition.[6] It seeks to learn from the witness of diverse practitioners in the field while attempting to recognize and support their work. If successful, it should further ecumenical dialogue about the tasks of moral reasoning, albeit in modest ways, and help readers to analyze better the problems of secularist approaches to human rights and also the retreat from human rights that is evident in some liberal democracies today.

Human rights still have the highest importance for political thought in our time. We must emphasize at the outset, however, that if Christians are to speak in defense of human rights, the rationale is likely to be *indirect*. How to act in obedience to God's command is the key question of all Christian ethics: "What must I do because God is?"[7] The priority of this means that human rights cannot be treated first and foremost as general moral truths derivable from intuitions or legal principles, or as rationalizations of what it is to be human, but as one kind of response (temporal, relative, and contingent) to God's graciousness toward humankind. Christian commitment to human rights will always be indirect and functional, derivative of prior doctrinal convictions and determined by "baseline" assumptions about God's preserving providence in ordering creaturely realities to their proper ends (Job 38; Acts 17:24-28; Rom 8:28-30; Eph 1:11). If the phrases were more catchy and less pious-sounding, "acts of human righteousness for the sake of Christ present among sinners" or "claims recognized for the sake of Christ and his coming kingdom" might be more adequate expressions than "human rights" in a Christian ethic of rights. Thus a primary theological conviction running throughout this book is that "right" is not primarily a liberty or zone of non-interference that sets one individual apart from another but that which is owed to a person by virtue of his or her existence within divine providence. "Right" understood in this way *might* equate to a liberty or a claim that *might*, in turn, be expressed in human rights as we know them today, but the transition from "right" to "rights" is multistepped and contestable. Epistemologically, the meaning of "right" rests in God and is thus prior to subjective rights. The meaning of "right" is found in God as revealed preeminently in Christ. Subjective rights—whether expressed as natural rights or human rights—are context-bound and contingent moral and/or legal instruments. God's commands to all humanity, as recorded in Holy Scripture, are not conveyed in the language of rights. Nor is it necessary that Christ's claim upon us in and through our neighbor is expressed in the terms of rights. Nonetheless, our thesis is that the recognition of human rights is often today an appropriate response to divine command. The recognition of subjective human rights is a possible, albeit not a required or indispensable, way of expressing love of God and neighbor (Matt 22:36-40) under the God-given authority of national and international institutions (Matt 22:21; Acts 25:10; Rom 13:1-6).

This is not to suggest that human rights require some kind of theological or religious grounding in order to be coherent. That would be to claim too much; today's human rights legislation functions without the invoking of any theistic authority. In pluralistic societies, communities of all faiths and none must work out their own critique of, as well as rationale for, the kind of respect for others that human rights instruments express and facilitate. Our aim is more modest—to offer theological thinking with and for Christian people working in the field. Before God, all human law falls short of the requirements of his justice: "we know that society's supreme law not only can sometimes be its supreme injustice, but before God it always is."[8] The challenge is to think ethically about subjective natural and/or human rights on Christian theological grounds, for the sake of God's coming kingdom. This means, we may anticipate, that human rights will look different in Christian perspective than when treated postmetaphysically as liberties conferred on human beings by philosophical principle, discursive consensus, positive law, or Convention/convention. Part of our work (see chaps. 2 and 3 below) is to explore the various tensions between theological conceptions of "right" and/or "natural right" understood with reference to God and modern, liberal notions of subjective rights, and to help equip Christian people for dialogue with those who come to the discussion from other perspectives. Part of our work is to seek a route between accommodationism on the one hand and failure to engage in everyday politics on the other, between sect and compromise, what Tillich called "correlation" and impotence with respect to political judgment. The most innovative aspect of the book is, arguably, the tropological reading of Genesis 9:1-17, God's covenant with Noah (see chap. 4), as a means of asking how Scripture challenges, directs, and gives substance to critical Christian engagement with rights discourse.

Ecumenical Gift Exchange

In addition to engagement with philosophical and political debates concerning the meaning and function of human rights, there is an ecumenical dimension to our work.[9] To a limited extent, human rights look different when viewed from different Christian traditions due to different construals of "natural law." As Carl E. Braaten observed recently, "It is a longstanding commonplace in Christian thought that Protestantism distinguishes its moral theology from that of Roman Catholicism by its rejection of natural law."[10] As with most generalizations, this oversimplifies the matter—though Braaten himself usefully tells the story of "the inner Protestant struggle" over the question of natural law, from supposedly complete rejection in Barthian covenant theology to qualified acceptance in a Lutheran theology that draws a proper distinction between law and gospel, creation and redemption.[11] He alludes to a history of conflict, misunderstanding, and problems associated with thinking about "nature" and "the natural" outside of Christ, that is, in ways detached from the church's confession that Jesus Christ is Lord. As Jean Porter also comments:

> [U]ntil recently, work on the natural law among Christian theologians has tended to divide along broadly denominational lines, insofar as Protestant scholars have generally focused on the theological significance of the natural, widely construed, while Catholic scholars have given more emphasis to the rational character and normative content of the natural law.[12]

Disputes about the place and role of natural reason in theology, the extent to which humans still have a natural inclination toward God and his goodness, and how the divine law completes in Christ what the natural law intends have shaped ecumenical debate for many years. Any attempt to talk theologically about human rights must do so in awareness of this history. It is relatively easy for Protestants especially to accept outdated and mistaken assumptions about Roman Catholic construals of natural law in ways that hinder ecumenical exchange. But the cost is high in terms of mutual understanding and cooperative work for social justice. Robust dialogue is needed to prepare us all for the service of God in postmodern, pluralistic societies.

Mindful that Protestants have often struggled to perceive the inherently Christological character of traditional Roman Catholic theologies of "right" and "natural right," we may note that significant ecumenical progress has been made in recent years toward better mutual understanding and unity. Important moves were made at Vatican II, and subsequently, toward a more explicitly Christologically determined theology of natural law in which teleological ethical thinking is brought into livelier contact with the mysteries of faith. So, for instance, the intellectual basis of *Veritatis Splendor* §1 is the confession that Jesus Christ is "the true light that enlightens everyone" (John 1:9). Natural law is still understood as the law that God has inscribed in the hearts of his human creatures whereby he orders them to their final end (Rom 2:15), that is, what *Veritatis Splendor* describes as "nothing other than the light of understanding infused in us by God, whereby we understand what must be done and what must be avoided" (§12). This light has its meaning and fullness in Christ. Roman Catholic scholars, notably Fergus Kerr, have done much to demonstrate that Aquinas's *Summa Theologia* is christologically informed throughout and Trinitarian in essence from start to finish. Kerr represents the whole structure of the *Summa Theologia* as that of a "movement towards the promised enjoyment of divine beatitude which Thomas expounds in the *secunda pars*, located between the mystery of the Godhead in the *prima pars* and the mystery of Christ's humanity in the *tertia pars*."[13] The third part of the *Summa* where Aquinas includes most christological material is the capstone of theological commitments that pervade the whole project. The Christology in the *tertia pars*, says Kerr, is the consummation of Aquinas's whole theological endeavor—the implication being that it is a mistake to separate the Christological content of the later sections from Aquinas's earlier focus on the divine nature. Aquinas might not begin the *Summa Theologia* with Christology, but it is through the incarnation that human nature is saved and in Christ Jesus that human nature is truly known: "In Christ the human nature has its proper form and power whereby it acts."[14]

The territory indicated by these debates is vast and much delimitation is required. What follows are brief comments on how selected Roman Catholic authors have made recent and notable theological contributions to the bridging of denominational differences where human rights are concerned. In 1992 the Jesuit scholar Kieran Cronin made overt moves to reclaim the relationship between Christian theology and human rights. His book *Rights and Christian Ethics* pursues a covenantal approach in which the central claim is that humans have rights because God himself has prior rights or justifiable claims upon humanity. God ventures into covenantal relations with humankind. Consequently, human beings are required by virtue of their creaturely status to "give God his due." This includes recognition of the justifiable claims of human neighbors. Curiously, perhaps, Cronin does not appeal directly to Aquinas and/or natural law traditions but to Old Testament accounts of covenant. Even so, he argues that Christian theorists should try to identify what they can hold in common with secularist theorists, especially with reference to morality and human rights, because morality is a vital part of the relationship that every person has with God: "God gives rights to human beings against one another because of his providential care for his children, whether they believe in him or not. This allows for the protection of human dignity."[15]

In 2003 another Jesuit scholar, David Hollenbach, took a different approach in *The Global Face of Public Faith: Politics, Human Rights, and Christian Ethics*. He argues for a theological reconstruction of rights that turns on the traditional natural-law conviction that humans are essentially social beings. The church, he claims, offers a communitarian alternative to liberal human rights theory that better serves the common good. Religious persons should therefore be vigorous advocates of politics for the common good, human rights, and democratic governance, thereby becoming more effective peacemakers. In continuation of earlier work including *Claims in Conflict: Retrieving and Renewing the Catholic Human Rights Tradition* (1979) and *The Common Good and Christian Ethics* (2000), much of Hollenbach's recent work is directed toward articulation of the role of religious communities in the public square, and how inter alia their engagement with human rights can help "strengthen the public life of a free society in democracies."[16] Part of this effort involves rethinking the practical import of the civil right of all persons to religious freedom. On the basis of the right to freedom of religious expression, he defends the role of religious communities in advancing faith-based arguments in the public forum, urging that this right should mean the right of religious communities "to be seen and heard in public and to propose their visions of the common good for deliberation in public."[17] Lamenting the unnecessarily factious nature of much liberal debate, he argues that it should be neither assumed by Christians that direct appeal to faith-based convictions is appropriate in the public square nor asserted by secularists that direct appeal to faith-based convictions is inappropriate in liberal democracies.[18] Essential to his work is demonstrating why and how secularist and religious persons alike can meet around human rights agendas oriented toward the common good.

In 2005 Jean Porter concluded *Nature as Reason: A Thomistic Theory of the Natural Law* with chapters on historical and conceptual links between Thomistic concepts of natural law and modern ideas of subjective rights. Her central claim is that the idea of subjective natural rights has been shaped decisively by theological perspectives on the human person and the moral order.[19] "[E]arly assertions of natural rights emerged as a reasonable, albeit not a necessary, development of the Scholastic concept of the natural law, and correlatively, central elements of later natural rights theories can be shown to stem from the theological commitments informing this context."[20] This aspect of her work centers around the universality of the natural law and how the Scholastics themselves dealt with issues of law and justice in both theological and juridical terms, and also the diversity among Scholastic thinkers with respect to a doctrine of subjective natural rights. The conclusion reached is that the Scholastic period comes very close at points to a doctrine of subjective rights as freedoms of action that an individual properly enjoys. Aquinas himself does not advance such a doctrine; that is, he does not assert the existence of subjective natural rights, but comes close to asserting that individuals properly have freedoms that can be asserted against others and defended in a court of law.[21] Thus, for Porter the transition from natural law to human rights is marked more by continuity than discontinuity; it is a development rather than a break. Her claim consequently is that Christian people need not worry on historical grounds that the origin of the doctrine of rights is problematic.

Writing from a Protestant perspective, there is much to be gained from ecumenical gift exchange where a Christian ethic of human rights is concerned. Our attempt to give a critical theological account of Christian advocacy of human rights owes much to these authors, and more besides. In particular, it shares many features of Cronin's work, especially his focus on covenant. Yet, the dialogue partners and objectives are different, and our concern is not to establish the genesis of modern secular rights in the Judeo-Christian tradition. With Cronin, we affirm that the task of outlining a theological ethic of rights falls primarily within the realm of dogmatics: "Dogmatics aims at the conceptual clarification of the Christian gospel which is set forth in Holy Scripture and confessed in the life and practices of the church."[22] The task of a Christian ethic of rights is only ever to enquire into the entailments of the gospel for Christian action in the world. One of our motivating concerns, however, is the urgent need in Protestant theology and ethics for renewed encounter with the gospel and the reasonableness of God's revealed moral law. The challenge is to give a theological account of critical Christian engagement with human rights while analyzing why—often for good reasons—it remains such a difficult thing for Protestant ethics to do. Of particular interest is how a strong Christological focus can engender teleological conceptions of human nature and "the natural," of "right" and human rights, and, more especially, of the operations of reason in the framing of good law.

Hollenbach's work is significant to this project for many reasons, not least because it seeks to demonstrate that prioritizing the common good need not threaten individual rights in ways that procedural liberals sometimes fear. His theologically grounded conviction is that the relation between the common good and the peace and unity of society embraces both public and private good, including its various manifestations in friendship, social stability and order, social traditions, families, personal freedom, law, justice and health, and so on. Drawing on Aquinas especially, he argues that "God is the origin of all good and that divine goodness, which is without limit, orders all things toward their perfection."[23] This does not mean radicalizing the contrast between the natural and the divine, church and state, sacred and profane, and so on, to the extent that this kind of contrast cannot be overcome. Rather, the contrast can be challenged by concentration on what framing law for the common good might entail in a human rights culture. Hollenbach's work relies on theological convictions that we share, namely, that God's goodness is the ultimate end of every "whole" and "part" in creation; God's transcendent unity of being and purpose draws all created things toward concord and fulfillment; "it belongs to Him to make all things best."[24] Theological reflection on how all human goods are related to the *Summum Bonum* that is above and anterior to them all, holding all within a cosmic, metaphysical, and ontological unity of divine purpose, is, arguably, one of the finest gifts of Roman Catholicism to twentieth- and twenty-first-century ecumenism. Hollenbach's work is especially significant in the ecumenical exchange, though we hesitate over his reading of the smoothness of continuity between modern rights discourse and Christian tradition.

Similarly, historical apologetics of the kind undertaken by Porter is informative, corrective, dogmatically provocative, and essential to an adequate theological ethic of rights. In particular, her work is useful in the historical debate about points of transition between Scholastic understanding of "right" (*ius*), as having an objective status independent of subjective claims, and modern, subjective notions of "right" residing in individuals as such. A more explicitly theological approach is required if we are to distinguish doctrinal discussion of "right" with reference to God from historical observations. More needs to be done in framing an ethic of rights explicitly in Christological, pneumatological, and eschatological terms. It is not enough to show that subjective rights are amenable to historical demonstration in the Scholastic period; doctrinal judgments should not be confused with historical considerations or substituted for them, although both are necessary. Porter herself is highly sensitive to such concerns and is careful to distinguish the various aspects of her project. Indeed, her earlier work has done much to show that Karl Barth's challenge to the Scholastics about their non-Christological framing of natural law fails because they never claimed to speak of "unaided natural reason" outside of a Christian theological context. The Scholastics, she demonstrates, never presented natural law as the deliverance of pure moral reason. Rather, natural law was always "a theological concept, grounded in a particular reading of Scripture."[25] In reply to Barth, she urges Christian ethicists to look again at the theological commitments that enabled the Scholastics to affirm natural reason and to conclude that, typically, they never fell outside of affirmations of God as Creator and Redeemer. This sets an important challenge to Protestant theology and ethics not only to learn more about the Scholastic period but to build on better historical research by emphasizing the critical function of a dogmatic approach to the various dimensions of an ethic of rights.

Human Rights in Protestant Discourse

All this said, the need for ecumenical colloquy remains considerable. While it is not our primary purpose to tell the history of recent Protestant approaches to human rights, a few pointers might be helpful. Of particular note is John Nurser's recent account of the contribution of Christian people, not least members of Protestant churches, to formulations of the 1948 United Nations Declaration of Human Rights (UNDHR).[26] His fascinating historical study is of how, in the ten years after 1937 when church leaders agreed to found the World Council of Churches (WCC), a group of men and women from diverse Protestant traditions was able to "play a significant role in including what became a 'universal declaration' of human rights within the post-World War II attempt to construct a new order of international affairs in the United Nations."[27] Nurser traces the involvement of members of the Reformed tradition (e.g., Dr. Joseph Oldham), those with YMCA experience (e.g., John Mott and Galen Fisher), those influential in the North American Federal Council of Churches and Foreign Missions Council (e.g., Otto Frederick Nolde), those with connections to the World Student Christian Federation (e.g., the Dutch clergyman Visser't Hooft), and many more, in working behind the scenes to bring the UNDHR to fruition. His summary judgment is that "the churches of the Protestant ecumenical movement played a significant role in giving the international settlement after World War II in the United Nations its 'soul' in human rights. It was their intention."[28] In other words, Protestant involvement with the early post–World War II human rights movement was noteworthy. The men and women involved knew, he implies, that the Word of God cannot be identified with any "ism," mode of governance, political movement, cultural trend, or set of natural or human rights. Nevertheless, their faith required and sustained ecumenical involvement with preparations for the UNDHR as integral to their prayers of invocation "for the healing of the nations" (Rev 22:2).

In the years following 1948, the WCC was vocal in affirming those human rights that protected religious liberty especially. Witness, for instance, the "Statement on Religious Liberty" in *The New Delhi Report: The Third Assembly of the World Council of Churches, 1961* which stated: "God's redemptive dealing with men is not coercive. Accordingly, human attempts by legal enactment or by pressure of social custom to coerce or eliminate faith are violations of the fundamental ways of God with men. The freedom which God has given . . . implies a free response to God's love."[29] James E. Wood Jr. argues, for instance, that the concept of "liberty of conscience" is deeply rooted in Protestant thought. Tracing this idea back to the Westminster Confession of Faith, Section XX, "Of Christian Liberty and Liberty of Conscience," and beyond, he examines similarities between early Protestant affirmations of God's lordship over the conscience of the individual and early WCC support for UNDHR-recognized rights to freedom of religion.[30] His apologia for religious rights finds a special connection between religious rights and UNDHR affirmations regarding human dignity, even to the extent of regarding religious rights as basic to all other human rights because of the inviolable sacredness of the conscience before God. Moreover, these Protestant believers, he suggests, were clear at this time that they had sufficient reason to support rights to religious freedom and to welcome national and international instruments to this effect. Civil society should ensure that persons are free to worship God.

Similar convictions are found in diverse statements issued by Protestant churches in the 1970s. Following the lead given by Pope John XXIII in *Pacem in Terris* (1963), which gave the recognition of universal human rights a central place in Roman Catholic social teaching, a variety of statements were issued in the 1970s by churches in the Calvinist tradition, the Lutheran World Federation, the World Baptist Alliance, and more besides.[31] Martin Shupack draws attention to Protestant agreement with Roman Catholic social teaching with respect inter alia to human dignity inhering in the creation of human beings in the image of God, and the God-given role to exercise dominion thereby "representing God within history,"[32] noting similarity between diverse Protestant churches and Pope John XXIII regarding the importance of religious liberty as the norm of other freedoms. The inviolability of every person's answerability before God permits, or even requires, recognition of the "negative" human rights to freedom of thought, conscience, and religion.[33] He interprets the emphasis on liberty in human rights instruments as resonating harmoniously with growing emphasis across the denominations on the so-called "preferential option for the poor" and discerns agreement among the churches that states should facilitate the goal of human solidarity by ensuring freedom from oppression and minimal material welfare. Considerable agreement existed among the churches with respect to the importance of understanding human rights in the context of human sociality. Witness the World Alliance of Reformed Churches' declaration that human rights "point to a universal community."[34] Lutherans emphasized that all humans are equally sinners before God; Baptists emphasized God's love for all apart from personal merit; and Calvinists emphasized the covenant framework within which God's claim on human beings is the ultimate source of rights.[35] Yet all affirmed a possible role for human rights in Christian social teaching and action.

Not all post-World War II Protestant support for human rights was as theologically secure. Paul Tillich's 1965 contribution to the International Convocation called to examine the encyclical *Pacem in Terris* of Pope John XXIII is a case in point.[36] Albeit brief, his article betrays a search for philosophical, rather than theological, reasons to sustain human rights engagement.[37] Affected deeply by the repudiation of civil liberties and the rights of man by both National Socialism and Communist-dominated countries, Tillich had turned to the kind of protection offered by the existentialism of Heidegger, Jaspers, and Sartre with respect to the "finite freedom" of individuals. The result was a doctrinally minimalist defense of human rights that accorded harmoniously with Kant's unconditional imperative to respect every person "as the highest criterion of *humanitas*."[38] Protestants, Jews, and humanists may agree with the basic principle of the encyclical, Tillich urges, namely with the principles of justice and the dignity of every human as a person from which follow rights and obligations: "There is no difference in this point of view among Jews, Protestants and Humanists."[39]

Where differences emerge among persons with respect to human rights, they are due to divergent utopian expectations, and this is as true for Christians as for anyone else.

Today, those closest to Tillich's method of correlation—whereby theologico-spiritual answers are sought to questions that arise from human situations—are, arguably, those who ask: "What is the social and political relevance of faith to human rights?" The assumption hidden in this question is that Christian ethics must somehow relate its task to human rights in order to draw out its own relevance for present-day sociopolitical concerns, thereby correlating aspects of the social witness of the gospel with secularist human rights ideals. This approach tends to imply that Christianity can be shown to be relevant for today. So, for instance, Max Stackhouse, a theologian from Princeton with interests in public affairs, argues that human rights need reference to the transcendent to explain and support their very existence. At the least, he says, human rights have needed God historically; the modern humanist movement was nourished more definitively by theological ideas than by neo-Kantian philosophy, and Christianity is better able to sustain appeals to the universality of human rights than philosophically grounded, abstract notions of human dignity. "Without the impetus of theological insight, human rights concepts would not have come to their current widespread recognition, and . . . they are likely to fade over time if they are not anchored in a universal, context-transcending metaphysical reality."[40] Only reference to God explains why human beings have the right to have rights. Similarly, the legal philosopher Michael J. Perry argues a case for allowing religion into politics, not least human rights politics, especially in America where the Declaration of Independence famously asserts that "all men are created equal . . . with certain inalienable Rights" with which they are "endowed by their Creator."[41] The idea of human rights is "ineliminably religious."[42] How strange it would be, he suggests, if a nation whose very birth was rooted in belief in a Creator God should now treat the introduction of religion into the public sphere as, "at best, 'bad taste'" and, at worst, a danger to free society.[43]

An advantage of this approach is its witness to the serious state of everything human isolated from the divine. Its danger is the potential reduction of Christian ethics to a pragmatic response to secularist needs, and its downplaying of the primary work of Christian ethics as dogmatics. In his response to the papal encyclical *Pacem in Terris* cited above, Tillich identified genuine bases for hope as inter alia the technical union of humankind in the conquest of space, increasing numbers of cross national fields of cooperation (e.g., relating to food and medicine), and a growing consensus with respect to legal protection of these fields of cooperation.[44] Despite his embedding of faith within the political, Tillich's method of correlation downplays divine revelation to a dimension of "ultimate concern" within human existence, and reduces faith from a relationship with God to the attitude of the subject toward the ground of being. Today, we find comparable emphases in, for instance, the editorial stance in the recent collection of essays entitled *Does Human Rights Need God?* The title supplies the question around which the book centers and is understood to inquire whether human rights "require some sort of theological or religious grounding to be coherent, valid, or otherwise sustainable—both in theory and in practice."[45] The book comprises responses from Jewish, Christian (Protestant and Orthodox), Muslim, Confucian, and secularist scholars and concludes with Jean Bethke Elshtain's afterword, which draws our attention to "the many intricate features of the interplay between our religions and our politics."[46] Significantly, however, the editors leave the meaning of the term "god" unspecific and contested, claiming that this facilitates debate and allows space for dialogue with partners outside a Western Judeo-Christian and Islamic framework. In effect, it suggests that the editors deem human nature to be somehow more fundamental than the beliefs of the major world religions, thereby denying the basis on which many believers enter the debate. It would be unfair to press the point overmuch because it is not strongly emphasized by the editors. Nonetheless, the book betrays a contentious assumption that the concept of "human nature" provides the possibility of idea exchange among the religious and nonreligious, thereby undercutting the kind of theological account of engagement with human rights that treats Christian ethics and moral reasoning as part of dogmatics. The risk is that human rights becomes an ethic by which Christian theologians seek to reconcile religion and the modern world, and/or that a Christian ethic of rights is squeezed into gaps left by other disciplines.

At the other end of the spectrum are those concerned that the notion of inalienable human rights is antithetical to Christian faith. Stanley Hauerwas's objections to many aspects of a human rights culture are well known. "America," he says, "is the only country that has the misfortune of being founded upon a philosophical mistake—namely, the notion of inalienable rights."[47] (We look further at his objections in chap. 2 below.) Nor is Hauerwas alone. Witness the recent debate in the UK about the employment status of clergy, which illustrates an anxiety within many churches about rights and rights claims because they are not integral to the Christian ethos. We consider the matter briefly. Traditionally, clergy have not normally enjoyed "employee" or even "worker" status for the purposes of statutory employment rights. As a result, they are generally excluded from basic employment protections, including unfair dismissal protection, family-friendly rights (e.g., the right to maternity or paternity leave and pay), and collective rights. Typically, clergy do not have a contract of employment or an employer, and are often treated similarly to those who are "self-employed." Today, for tax purposes, they are "office holders" and are taxed in the same way as employed persons. But the employment status of the clergy and their access to employment rights has been under review. Under Section 23 of the UK Employment Relations Act of 1999 (ERelA), the UK Government has the power to extend the scope of employment protection legislation to those not previously classed as employees, including clergy, and to confer rights on those who are currently excluded. Kevin Maguire of *The Guardian* newspaper wrote: "The Trade and Industry Secretary, Patricia Hewitt, yesterday intervened between vicars and God by holding out the prospect of extending employment rights to the clergy."[48] Ruth Gledhill, religion correspondent, picked up the issue for *The Times*: "Sacked clergy might soon be able to sue the Church of England for wrongful dismissal."[49]

Debate was sparked by the case of the Reverend Raymond Owen, who submitted a petition to the European Parliament in April 2001 appealing against the decision of his bishop to terminate his tenure as the team rector in the parish of Hanley, Stoke-on-Trent, as of July 18, 1999. The petition turned on the church's failure to protect fundamental human rights. The case was referred to the European Human Rights Commission where it was denied initially on the grounds that where clergymen do not have the status of employees according to national law the provisions of the relevant directive cannot apply.[50] The church authorities sought a possession order for his tied house, the rectory, and at the time of writing a counterclaim before the courts is pending based on Articles 6 and 8 of the European Convention on Human Rights (ECHR). These details were publicly available on the trade union Amicus's Web site, and we are not party to information other than that available publicly. According to Amicus, three things are of note. First, Articles 6 and 8 of the ECHR were the foci of attention. (Article 6 concerns the right to a fair trial "within a reasonable time by an independent and impartial tribunal established by law." Article 8 concerns the right to respect for private and family life.) Second, Amicus lobbied hard on Rev. Owen's behalf and recorded significant membership gains from the ranks of the clergy. Third, a growing number of the clergy no longer have "the parson's freehold," or right of free occupancy, and although they have some influence in any replacement of the parsonage, they have no interest in the capital value. Licenses especially have relatively little security.[51] The issue of employment rights for clergy resurfaced more recently in the context of the application of antidiscrimination laws prohibiting discrimination on the grounds of sexual orientation. A legal challenge was brought by unions within the UK to test the application of new EU laws on sexual orientation to faith-based organizations.[52] Once again the courts refrained from requiring faith-based organizations to provide equal treatment rights for clergy.

The matter of setting a good example with respect to minimum standards in the workplace is significant. Discussion about extending employment rights to the clergy does not happen in a vacuum but amid much larger struggles to ensure minimum standards of protection for casual workers, home workers, temporary-agency workers, labor-only subcontractors, and others who bear the brunt of casualization and increased flexibility in the workforce. Resistance on religious grounds might appear protectionist and regressive in ways that hinder rather than help public witness to the gospel. Why, for example, should the churches be exempt from antidiscrimination legislation? Public opinion might see little difference between the armed forces removing obstacles to gay and lesbian soldiers and the Roman Catholic Church removing obstacles to the ordination of women.[53] Yet, objections may also be raised. Albeit not in today's idiom, it is at least arguable that Jesus taught his disciples to refrain from claiming any "rights" they might have, thereby implying a resistance to the acquisition or assertion of rights: "Do not resist an evildoer. But if anyone strikes you on the right cheek, turn the other also; and if anyone wants to sue you and take your coat, give your cloak as well; and if anyone forces you to go one mile, go also the second mile" (Matt 5:39-41). Similarly, Jesus' advice to his disciples is to come to terms with an accuser while on the way to court (Matt 5:25). It could be argued from these teachings that a rights-oriented way of living falls below that expected of Jesus' disciples. Paul's teaching is equally, if not more, uncompromising (1 Cor 6:1-7). It is a "defeat" (Gr *hetton*) for members of the body of Christ to disagree among themselves publicly. The nature of the bond between members of the body of Christ is not mediated through the law courts; they should bear witness to divine eschatological judgment rather than going to court against one another.[54]

Consider further Article 8 of the Human Rights Act (1998), which concerns the right to respect for family and private life and states:

1. Everyone has the right to respect for his private and family life, his home and his correspondence.

2. There shall be no interference by a public authority with the exercise of this right except such as is in accordance with the law and is necessary in a democratic society in the interests of national security, public safety or the economic well-being of the country, for the prevention of disorder or crime, for the protection of health or morals, or for the protection of the rights and freedoms of others.

If statutory employment protection is extended to members of the clergy, then it might become legally possible for them to rely on this article in any dispute over unfair dismissal. This raises the question of whether the church has duties to recognize and protect the right to private and family life, or whether recognition of the "right" of respect to private life runs counter to mainstream Christian tradition. We note section 30(1) of the Anglican *Clergy Discipline Measure 2003*:

> 30(1) If a person who is a priest or deacon—
> (b) has a decree of divorce or an order of separation made against him following a finding of adultery, behaviour in such a way that the petitioner cannot reasonably be expected to live with the respondent or desertion and, in the case of divorce, the decree has been made absolute, he shall be liable without further proceedings to the penalty of removal from office or prohibition (whether for life or limited) or both.[55]

This measure provides for the possibility that a member of the clergy could be removed from office on the grounds of divorce or other conduct unbecoming. No temporal employer could dismiss an employee on the grounds of divorce or enforce morality in ways provided for by the Church of England. Such an action would be deemed illiberal and impermissible. Mindful of the needs of the families of clergy, it is not clear that there is, or should be, a right to respect for family and private life in the church in the same way as in the wider society. The freedom enjoyed in covenantal relationships is not the same as the "maximization of freedom" that individuals with a superficial or distorted awareness of human rights might seek. A Christian vision of a good private and family life arguably exceeds any rights-based notion of respect for the private and should not be reduced to it.

What, then, are we to say? The above illustrates that there are good reasons for wariness in the Christian community with respect to overt Christian engagement with human rights agendas—not least because the new human rights culture is inherently individualistic and can encourage an aggressive, protectionist, and/or acquisitive mind-set. Moreover, there is no denying that human rights are often construed as an ethic independent of theology, based on the human body alone. Fifty years after its proclamation, Elie Wiesel described the UNDHR as the sacred text of what has been called a "world-wide secular religion."[56] In other words, it requires no religious commitment. Secularizing the gospel amid a fervor for social work neglects the truth that only God can save the world and potentially distracts the church from matters spiritual and ecclesial. Yet, this is not all that needs to be said. Failure to engage with secularist human rights agendas can leave Christian people with professional, workaday responsibilities for such matters underresourced. Undue wariness leads to the risk of not heeding the God-given restlessness that stirs the heart of the believer to understand the meaning of our times in God and, consequently, of failing to mobilize assistance for the most vulnerable, or neglecting to allow the hope of eternity to influence our life on earth in every part. As Barth writes: "The unrest which God gives us must bring us into critical contact with 'life.'"[57] Believers await the redemption of the body (Rom 8:23), but until that time God himself meets us in history and calls us to faith and action. Earthly laws have no ultimacy, but "[w]hen the *soul* remembers that its origin is in God, it places the origin of *society* there as well."[58]

Hence the need, in some respects at least, to seek the meaning of obedience to divine command anew every day amid changing situations, including human rights discourse. To draw back from appropriate reflection on "the Christian's place in society" risks what Barth denounced as "the new temptation of ecclesiasticism."[59] The truth of the gospel in a believer's life causes such an unrest that apathy with respect to the sufferings of others is rendered impossible. Church members are lulled to sleep by the siren tones of ecclesial business and forget that "*all life* must be measured by Life."[60]

Project Outline

This book urges critical engagement with human rights agendas not because they are the "only game in town," the last vestige of moral argumentation present in Western culture, but because human rights feature significantly in the contexts in which we find ourselves today. We seek a route between, on the one hand, the kind of reconciliation with the world that risks abandonment or compromise of substantive theological doctrines in favor of secularist modes of rationality and, on the other, the kind of ecclesiasticism that leaves church members ill equipped to be active citizens who can engage critically with human rights instruments and institutions for the practical benefits that they might achieve.

To this end, the first five chapters outline an ethic of human rights in terms of response to the command(s) of God. We attempt to conceive of "right" theologically with reference to God's self-revelation of righteousness, divine law, sovereign mercy, providential care of the created order, and so on, and from here to engage critically with present-day notions of human rights. Primary definitions of "right" are measured with reference to what has been revealed of God's eternal law—though in ways that are mindful of the provisionality of all human law, ethics, and moral reasoning. We draw especially on the work of Protestant scholars who, broadly speaking, treat "the natural," "natural law," and "natural reason" as subsets of the doctrines of creation and Christology. Our main dialogue partners are significant Protestant theologians who have engaged constructively with questions about the relation between divine providence, the law of nature and the law of reason, and human governance. Chapter 2 sets the scene politically, ethically, and theologically. Chapter 3 probes *why* the relation between divine and human law should concern Christian people today. It considers Richard Hooker's (1554–1600) account of what characterizes good human law. Our social and cultural contexts self-evidently differ from those of Hooker's day. The "sacred canopy" under which the church was the people of the nation, and the people of the nation was the church, has long since gone. It has been many years since the practice of religion was prescribed by the state in England or elsewhere in Europe. In the United States, the First Amendment provides in part that "Congress shall make no law respecting an establishment of religion, or prohibiting the free exercise thereof." In the eyes of secularist liberalism, there is no working assumption that God is the basis of all law. Yet central arguments in Hooker's theology of law remain valid. All human law has a share in divine wisdom to the extent that "right," or what is "due" to a person or thing within divine providence, belongs to justice, and justice is a virtue directed to good that "observes the mode of reason in all things."[61] For these reasons, Hooker remains a useful focus for our thinking about present-day Christian engagement with jurisprudence and the relation between divine and human law in a human rights culture. More specifically, he offers distinctively theological *reasons for* and pointers with respect to the *characteristics of* Christian engagement with lawmaking, providing for his own age the kind of serious theological questioning that we need again today.

Our more immediate context is the twentieth-century problem of "the natural" in Protestant ethics and attempts to overcome it. Chapter 4 thus examines the openings provided by Karl Barth and others for renewed interest in theology of the natural, and natural rights, and how Protestant theologies of "nature" and "the natural" (notably from Dietrich Bonhoeffer and Colin Gunton) have opened ways of thinking pneumatologically and eschatologically about human ends and interim goals. It addresses the topic of a revelatory theology of natural rights and examines theological reasons for affirming that natural rights are a way of expressing the dignity and liberties bestowed on humanity by God—marks of the Author upon his creation that form the basis of claims that humans can and should make on one another. The working assumption is that secularist human rights as we know them today are essentially *human* and part of everyday life in present-day societies regulated by legislative and penal power. Human rights belong to the autonomy of earthly governance within divine providence. As

such they fall under the concept of reconciliation or the kingdom of Christ
among sinners, rather than under the concept of creation, as if to Adam
and Eve in the garden before sin. Like all human law, "if God is present
in it, it is as Christ among *sinners*."[62] No Tillich-esque correlation is thus
possible between divine law and human rights. We need instead the kind
of analogy that preserves proper distinctions between divine and human
action while requiring that human moral action corresponds to what has
been revealed of the work of God in Christ.

Building on the argument developed in Chapter 4, namely, that the
commands of God the Creator are restored to believers in Christ, Chapter
5 attempts to describe a biblical basis for critical Christian engagement
with rights discourse. By means of a tropological reading of Genesis 9:1-17
(God's covenant with Noah), it begins to probe what kinds of questions
Scripture poses to Christian engagement with human rights, and what is
properly the consequence of faith in God and his sustaining grace toward
us. This reading of God's covenant with Noah provides the basis and direction for the case studies treated later and functions as a bridge between the
first five chapters (which establish a theological framework within which to
consider a Christian ethic of rights) and those that follow (which address
selected topics pertaining to rights-related issues: reproduction, animal life,
and the administration of law). It is never enough for a Christian ethic of
rights to make easy allusions or uncritical jumps between biblical teaching and secularist notions of human rights. As Miroslav Volf explains, it is
not possible to arrive at a Christian ethic (in his case an ethic of work) by
analyzing and combining individual passages of the Bible.[63] Discrete biblical passages cannot be fitted together, like pieces in a jigsaw, to comprise
a complete theology or ethic. Yet nothing substitutes for attentive engagement with Scripture. The tropological reading of Genesis 9:1-17 serves to
"map" or delineate moral space within which to consider selected practicalities of moral reasoning with respect to human rights, and it is intended
as indicative of the need for the continuous submission of human moral
reasoning to the judgment of God's living word.

Chapters 6–8 have a practical focus on learning from and assisting
Christian people whose work involves engagement with human rights
instruments. It addresses selected rights-related topics that, arguably, set
priorities for Christian engagement today. Following the agenda set by the
tropological reading of Genesis 9:1-17, chapter 6 asks whether there is a
right to reproduce and, if so, why and how the biblical account of God's
covenant with Noah requires attention to its global and transgenerational
perspectives. Chapter 7 asks whether moral and legal rights should be
accorded to nonhuman species. Chapter 8 discusses the right to person-

hood at law in the face of terrorism and the retreat from human rights
in supposedly "benign" Western democracies. Consideration of biblical
imperatives beyond Genesis 9:1-17 could lead us to discussion of other
rights-related issues; our particular delimitation of topics is more practical
than doctrinal. Continuous reminders in Scripture to care for the stranger
might, for instance, spur Christian people to rethink the responsibility of
states to assist asylum seekers and refugees: "You shall not oppress a stranger,
for you know the heart of the stranger—you yourselves were strangers in
Egypt" (Exod 23:9 *NKJV*); "When a stranger lives with you in your land,
do not ill-treat him. The stranger who lives with you shall be treated like
the native born. Love him as yourself, for you were strangers in the land
of Egypt. I am the LORD your God" (Lev 19:33-34). At a time when the
1952 UN Convention Relating to the Status of Refugees is surrounded by
controversy,[64] shared traditions of hospitality to the stranger among the
Abrahamic religions could form the basis for interfaith initiatives on the
ethics and politics of asylum. For the moment, our work is restricted to
the claim that the command of God still encounters all humanity through
the covenant with Noah, and that meditation on this covenant can both
generate and help sustain reflection on natural and human rights in the
twenty-first century.

Perhaps an ethic of rights is a Christian heresy, then, and, without
doubt, it is a potentially arbitrary and oppressive phenomenon that is vulnerable to abuse. But also, sometimes, it may be an appropriate response
to God's command and the evangelical imperative to love our neighbor.
Those for whom following Christ involves human rights advocacy have
little option but to negotiate this tension daily. This book is dedicated to
those working with human rights instruments as one means by which God
might yet be pointing his creatures away from total destruction.

❧ 1 ❧

The Question of Rights

Despite the increasingly litigious character of Western societies, the topic of law remains relatively unpopular. Images of law courts in novels by Franz Kafka haunt literary imaginations. In the film *The Devil's Advocate*, the world's most powerful law firm is the setting in which the devil of Judeo-Christian tradition finds opportunity to tempt the corruptible.[1] In John Steinbeck's novels, we see the incapacity of the law to distribute wealth and power equitably. *The Grapes of Wrath* recounts how a farmer, whose land is being taken away from him, confronts at gunpoint the tractor driver who is knocking down his house. The farmer is confused when the driver tells him not to shoot because he takes his orders from a banker in Oklahoma City, who takes his orders from a banker in New York. "Then who can I shoot?" the farmer cries out in distress. "The law distributes wealth and poverty through taxes but in such complicated and indirect ways as to leave this farmer bewildered and afraid."[2] The unpopularity of the law is long-standing—Dick the Butcher in Shakespeare's *Henry VI* proposes the following solution to society's problems: "The first thing we do, let's kill all the lawyers."[3]

The Promise of Human Rights

Paradoxically, it is the law—more specifically, human rights law—that carries the burden in the twenty-first century of much cultural anxiety about how individuals and societies can live together peaceably.[4] In some quarters, a quasi-religious belief in human rights and individual freedoms is fast becoming what Agnes Heller calls "*the* rational language of the human race

21

beyond space, time and history."[5] Human rights provide the language and conceptuality around which theorists and politicians unite, even if they do not agree about their reasons for unity. Degrees of enthusiasm for recent developments with respect to human rights vary. Theorists like Francesca Klug have claimed that human rights are the only vehicle with the potential to provide a common set of values for a diverse, multiethnic society.[6] Human rights values are "not a Ten Commandments for the twenty-first century. Nor do they represent a clear ideology on a par with Socialism or free-market economics."[7] Nevertheless, human rights discourse supplies a framework for debating the difficult issues of our age. Human rights need not be associated with selfishness and general social dislocation. If allowed to inform notions of the common good, they need not be irredeemably individualistic.[8] Klug claims rather that the ethical force of human rights legislation resides in a positive concept of humanity that gives rise to norms of justice that inform regulative procedures. If she is correct, human rights have served, and should continue to serve, to awaken and inspire a proper sense of justice and to give content to the common good.

The promise of human rights is that they provide a language that all can speak and that can be used to "do things" to improve people's living conditions. Evidence suggests, for instance, that the United Nations Convention on the Rights of the Child (1990) has made life better for children in different parts of the world.[9] The Convention protects a child's right to survival and development; freedom of thought, conscience and religion; right to education, and so on. The United Nations Committee on the Rights of the Child monitors how well member states are meeting their obligations under the Convention on the Rights of the Child. Similarly, the Convention against Torture and Other Cruel, Inhuman, or Degrading Treatment or Punishment (1987) provides political leverage and monitoring mechanisms with respect to minimum acceptable standards of human behavior. Governmental and nongovernmental agencies, such as Amnesty International, make frequent appeal to the Convention against Torture when attempting to transform the lives of political prisoners and their families around the globe. Since 1919 the International Labor Organization (ILO) has promoted workplace rights and responsibilities. It has mechanisms for supervising and reporting on measures taken to put into effect the provisions of the international labor standards.

Practically minded lawyers and politicians frequently find that human rights provide focal points for campaigning. As ideals and principles that form the basis of liberal democracy, human rights have a moral value and authority without precedent in the history of the world.[10] As norms of justice that inform regulative procedures, we must surely agree that human rights can morph into invaluable legal instruments for the protection of the weak against the strong. After World War II, and in the absence of unifying political ideologies or religious belief systems to bind the vast majority of individuals together, human rights gained force as a source of ethical value in and of themselves. Experiences of dictatorship, mass atrocities, and brutality had made European countries conscious of the value of democracy and reinvigorated faith in the rule of law. The universality of human rights was a tremendous idea whose time had come. In the years following 1950 it became increasingly apparent that the values inherent in the "first wave" of human rights legal procedures could not be realized unless social and economic conditions were of a sufficiently high standard for social and political rights to be meaningful. Now, as we begin the twenty-first century, human rights are established as the dominant ethic on the international political scene. Controversy remains intense around innumerable issues including the relation between civil and political, social and economic rights; how better to translate human rights standards into reality around the globe; how to retain corporate memories of the need for such safeguards; why societies need a common language of law that functions around shared, albeit disputed, principles and values; why rights cannot be reduced in political manifestos to allusions to "choice" without significant loss. Nevertheless, respect for human rights is the language of the international community—even if, in some countries, human rights are honored as much in the breach as in the observance. Human rights are finding acceptance in cross-cultural perspectives, including the Islamic and Buddhist.[11] Regardless of disputed foundations and interpretations, human rights function increasingly to provide a transcultural and normative discourse under which international affairs can be conducted and global commerce regulated.

Secular Reasons for Skepticism

The promise of human rights remains considerable, yet there are reasons for skepticism. Bookshops now contain collections of skeptical essays that cast doubt on the adequacy of individual rights as a means of securing communal and global goods. Two books stand out for special comment: *Understanding Human Rights* (1996) and *Sceptical Essays on Human Rights* (2001).[12] Collectively, the several authors expose how human rights legislation has functioned to protect vested power interests, to encourage litigiousness, to squeeze out consideration of the common good from public discourse, and to reduce the relationships between citizens and the state and between citizen and citizen to those of regulation by contract. Studies in labor law, antidiscrimination law, criminal justice law, and diverse studies of legal protection for minorities, all express caution, concern, and doubt. Skeptics from a variety of academic disciplines and ideological perspectives claim that the symbolic value attaching to modern, liberal concepts of rights often fails to meet some of the greatest needs facing us today.

K. D. Ewing's highly respected work in labor law illustrates the point as he recounts how human rights legislation has served to dilute other legislative attempts to control corruption and bad practice on the part of employers. Only the naive, claims Ewing, will be surprised that attempts have been made by corporate interests to "capture" the UK Human Rights Act of 1998. Similar attempts were seen in Canada.

> Nothing new here. Similar instruments have been used in other jurisdictions by similar interests for similar purposes. In Canada it was a corporation (not workers or consumers) which used the freedom of religion guarantees in the Charter of Rights to strike down Sunday trading legislation; it was a corporation (not consumers or health professionals) which used the freedom of speech guarantees of the Charter of Rights to strike down restrictions on tobacco advertising; and it was a corporation (not voters or candidates) which used the same guarantees of the Charter of Rights to strike down election spending rules previously introduced in the interests of political equality.[13]

The symbolic value attaching to modern, liberal concepts of "the rights of man" does not serve automatically to effect change on behalf of the poor, the marginalized, and the dispossessed, or even the average consumer. Merely to incorporate international human rights instruments into domestic legislation is not enough to ensure judgment on behalf of the oppressed and vulnerable.

Skepticism with respect to what human rights can achieve in Western societies arises from at least two conflicting issues: politicization and loss of political accountability. First, in modern liberal democracies, human rights are the outcome of political processes. These processes are necessarily uncertain and open-ended, and contribute to the kind of social context in which the normative claims of ethics cannot be assumed. In a free-choice, free-market economy, politics is always at risk of becoming a power struggle between competing interests in which priority is accorded typically to liberty—especially economic liberty—over equality or mercy, cosmopolitanism, hospitality, or other such values. Second, the shift of political authority from normal political processes of representative government to the judiciary entails a loss of accountability for human rights legislation in democratic forums. In Western contexts, skeptical observers claim that human rights legislation is failing to achieve the neutrality sought by modern liberalism and that the jurisprudence of the courts provides little guidance about the meaning of the common good beyond the protection of individual liberties. At the time of the French Revolution and into the early years of the nineteenth century, the idea of "the rights of man" might have terrified the rich and powerful. Today, the vision of human rights is so often distorted by electorally-led government manipulation that fine-sounding rhetoric panders to public desire for "individual choice" but fails to facilitate good governance. In other words, rights claims are justified ultimately in liberal democracies by some conception of democracy but jurisprudential evidence often reveals an unpleasant underside of the beneficial processes of democracy, not least the use of human rights legislation to effect the tyranny of minorities by the majority. Rights claims must be respected in liberal democracies because they command general support. As Martin Loughlin notes, however, "if rights are rooted in consensus, how can entrenched rights that restrict the power of democratic majorities be defended?"[14] What will prevent majorities from passing laws that oppress minorities? What is to prevent the reduction of ethics to politics, as politics becomes the recording of aggregate preferences and modern rights claims collapse into some form of game within democratic political systems democracy? The onus rests on politicians to justify restraint on individual liberties before they justify actions for the common good. Public opinion, however, often justifies only the minimal state.

To put it bluntly, we have an overpoliticization of human rights legislation on the one hand, and a loss of political accountability on the other. This latter problem is especially acute in countries that have enshrined human rights conventions into domestic legislation, thereby constraining the political power of parliamentary majorities. New Zealand, Canada, and the UK have recently entrenched human rights legislation in domestic law, thereby shifting primary responsibility for articulating human rights from the processes of democratic government to the courts. An upside of this integration of constitutional rights into domestic law is that widely accepted human rights principles become normative for the conduct of politics. A possible downside is that it puts considerable influence into the hands of the judiciary. There is a shift in the balance of power between parliament and the judiciary. Minority interests can become subject to a different power (normally upper-middle-class, white, male) as the balance tips away from representative parliamentary institutions to the courts. Observers of the American experience of living with a bill of rights identify a relatively conservative effect on political outcomes.[15] Arguments for the public interest are difficult to take to court unless "victims" are readily and immediately identifiable. The right of liberty is often exalted over substantive commitments to equality and solidarity, and the rhetoric can serve to undermine rather than enhance freedom.

It seems a "no win" situation! If legitimate law rests on the principle of popular sovereignty, then the ethical worth of rights is at danger of collapsing into democratic processes. So, for instance, the UK has seen a steady erosion in recent years of civil liberties protected by human rights legislation as electoral pressures on the government to be "tough on crime" increase. Helena Kennedy's *Just Law: The Changing Face of Justice and Why it Matters to Us All* includes a catalog of attacks against the rights of many citizens: internment without trial for noncitizens suspected of terrorist links; serious limits on access to justice because of cuts to legal aid; severe limitation on the right to silence; the streamlining of extradition processes so that British citizens can be removed abroad with insufficient protections; the removal of judicial review in asylum cases.[16] Prime Minister Tony Blair has been reported as intending to revise the Human Rights Act of 1998 (HRA), which incorporated the European Convention on Human Rights into domestic law. He was outraged by a High Court ruling that nine Afghan hijackers should be allowed to stay in Britain because there are substantial grounds for believing that they will be subjected to torture,[17] and he is concerned that the wrong balance was being struck between public safety and individual rights—though this attitude is surprising given that the HRA was a flagship statute of his own Government. Commitment to human rights weakens in the face of electoral pressure to be seen doing something about public safety. The balance between security and liberty is deeply contested. Swings in public opinion can endanger the protection of minorities and individuals. *Yet,* when attempts are made to put the brakes on this politicization of rights, a different problem develops as power reverts to the judiciary. Some interpretations in the courts reflect what many regard as "the moral intuitions of the average, male, middle-class member of a modern Western society."[18] Reasons for skepticism pile up as human rights prove sometimes to be unreliable mechanisms for change on behalf of the poor, the marginalized, and the dispossessed.

Skeptics thus decry human rights as humanly constructed political "fictions" that will remain as long as socially useful to the most powerful. This is hardly surprising when the record of modern liberal democracies—including those nations that played a leading role following World War II in drafting and mustering support for the Charter of the United Nations (1945) and the Universal Declaration of Human Rights (1948)—evidences a retreat from human rights. Thirty years ago, Peter Novick described human rights as regulative fictions whose illusion or pretense is swallowed as long as it remains socially useful.[19] This observation has proved to be remarkably prescient. Evidence is mounting that the most powerful nations in the world disregard human rights conventions and international rules of justice when they no longer suit them. Consider the case put by international lawyer Philippe Sands against the United States, in particular concerning its opposition to the International Criminal Court (ICC). The need for a permanent international criminal court that would act only if national procedures had failed has been discussed since the 1940s and 1950s though practicable proposals for such a court were not drafted until the 1990s when the Clinton administration was broadly supportive. Sands records the concern of George W. Bush's administration that the Court's jurisdiction was too broad, and that the checks and balances were insufficient to prevent the politicized prosecution of, notably, U.S. armed services personnel. He accuses the Bush administration of double standards: appealing to ICC standards when convenient (e.g., in October 2003 when Charles Taylor, former president of Liberia, had been indicted for war crimes and claims were advanced in his defense that he was entitled to immunity from the Liberian courts) but not otherwise.[20] The authority of the Court is recognized only when politically expedient. Reasons for skepticism with respect to what human rights can achieve reach to the very heart of power.

A different genre of reasons for skepticism is found in philosophical debates about whether the concepts of humanity and universality are strong enough to support the desired objectives and sustain momentum. This has been discussed at length elsewhere—for example, in Michel Rosenfeld, *Just Interpretations: Law between Ethics and Politics*—and so we shall not delay.[21] Briefly, theorists such as Richard Rorty, who regard as outmoded and improbable all talk about human rights as founded in human nature, deny philosophical or theological truths about what it is to be a human being and opt instead for novels and stories that move us emotionally. Rorty is mistrustful of references to "human nature" as if it were a single entity and cites the perpetuation of slavery in the eighteenth century as an example of the uselessness of the concept to effect change when people's hearts and minds are affected more by profit than by the thought of shared humanity. Thomas Jefferson, the third president of the United States, did not regard himself as violating universal human rights in perpetuating slavery. Philosophical claims to universality are a fiction, says Rorty. What really matters is whether another person's experience of pain or distress evokes as strong a response as if it has happened to oneself. The sentimentality evoked by novels comes closer, he claims, to Christ's suggestion that love matters more than knowledge.[22] Immanuel Kant's *Foundations of the Metaphysics of Morals* should be regarded as but a "placeholder" for *Uncle Tom's Cabin*—the latter being likely to have done considerably more than the former to deepen mutual understanding between persons of human experiences.[23] By refusing to look beneath or beyond language and sentimentality, Rorty regards human rights as but one of many contested alternatives that must be considered and discussed.

How, then, is change for the better to be achieved against such a diverse and multilayered backdrop of skepticism? How is judgment possible amid such complexity? Such questions often divide "idealist" from "realist" strands of political thought.[24] Human rights idealists present themselves as the champions of rationality and equal applicability of human rights across the globe. International labor standards, for instance, are deemed to be the necessary means of enforcing a *uniform minimum* of law to safeguard the bare essentials of workers' well-being. By contrast, realist approaches are sometimes so beset by the awfulness of how things are that reasoned and strategic engagement becomes impossible. Somber "realists" are, says O'Donovan, those who are downcast and shameful in the face of necessity and whose sense of tragedy cuts short "reasonable interaction" or adequately reasoned engagement with social problems.[25] The trouble with idealism is that it sometimes underestimates the complexity of a given country's affairs, such as the fragility of a developing economy, and downplays why laws differ from one society to another, and why they ought to do so. Enforcing a uniform minimum of law risks idealism in the vicious sense of the word: "it supposes some other kind of society, with other problems and possibilities, than the one it actually has to serve."[26] Conversely, the trouble with unabated realism is that reasoned political action can be undermined. Skepticism with respect to human rights discourse since the heyday of the postwar years might weigh so heavily that we become dispirited and fail to pay due attention to what has been achieved.

Christian ethics is *not* a middle way between idealism and realism but the church's formation and conformation to Christ as claimed by God's word, and a response in faith to God's self-revelation and will. The primary purpose of Christian ethics is not to provide a bulwark against secularist skepticism. Amid upbeat accounts of what a reasoned approach to social problems can achieve and downcast assessments of the unavoidable injustices embedded in the underside of free-market capitalism, the goal of Christian ethics is only ever obedience to God's merciful self-manifestation in love. This does not equate, however, to the claim that human rights advocacy is necessarily and antagonistically at variance to a Christian ethos. To the contrary, many material goals will be shared with persons working from other perspectives in pushing forward certain human rights agendas. The voice of God might sound from traditions, cultures, and perspectives not our own. With Tom Campbell, we adopt a working definition of skepticism as not only about disbelieving all that one is told but also about wanting to continue searching.[27] In their introduction to *Sceptical Essays on Human Rights*, he and his coauthors describe skepticism as searching for a better way. We, too, regard our task as searching for a better way to define, specify, and apply human rights—the big difference being that our task in this book centers around a theologically derived definition of "right" within the divine ordering of creation.

Ambivalence in the Christian Community

In the meantime, ambivalence, if not skepticism, runs deep in the Christian community with respect to human rights today. And for good reasons. Many warn against individualism and the inevitable inadequacy of "noninterference" as a basis for societal existence in the new human rights culture. So, for instance, Stanley Hauerwas is concerned for the following reasons:

> [A]n appeal to rights cannot provide the kind of basic moral presuppositions needed for the social and political life of a good society. When rights are assumed to be basic there seems to be no way to avoid an arbitrariness in the list of alleged rights and/or how conflicts of rights can be adjudicated. . . . . When rights are taken to be the fundamental moral reality we are encouraged to take an ultimately degrading perspective on society. No real society can *exist* when its citizens' only way of relating is in terms of noninterference. The language of "rights," especially as it is displayed by liberal political theory, encourages us to live as if we had no common interests or beliefs.[28]

The social atomism that characterizes a rights-based society falls far short, he believes, not only of a kingdom way of living but of the kind of community that sustains human well-being. Some identify a chasm between a God-centered vision of human rights and contractarian ideologies that have dominated modern Western debate.[29] Some warn against "a naïve and facile appropriation of the language of rights" in which we slip too easily from theological affirmations that humankind is created in God's image to assertions about the universal possession of rights.[30] Some have worked for decades with professional bodies in formulating codes of conduct that deliberately cast ethical discussion in terms of duties, interests, and liberties, rather than rights.[31] An ethic of human rights is regarded by many as inherently conflictual and tending toward the engendering of a culture of blame rather than of mutual respect, as moral reasoning is reduced to arbitration between competing claimants. Even the Vatican is worried about the proper implementation of human rights, because they are seen as more and more bound up with the self-assertion of the individual, obsessed with the idea of freedom from interference by others, "demanding my rights."

On the occasion of the fifty-fifth anniversary of the Universal Declaration of Human Rights, Msgr. Celestino Migliore affirmed that human rights are "one of the highest expressions of the human conscience of our time" and "a real milestone on the path of the moral progress of humanity."[32] He also said that "there is . . . a tendency of some to choose self-serving rights." "One of the greatest threats today to the integrity of the universal rights . . . comes from exaggerated individualism."[33] According to the Roman Catholic Church, a split is emerging between the original vision of the UNDHR and present-day implementation of human rights. The original vision of the UN declaration is one in which political and civil rights are indispensable for social and economic justice, and vice versa, and in which a resounding affirmation of human freedom is held together with an insistence on the oneness of the human family for which all bear common responsibility. The church today, said the Vatican representative, must hold together the two halves of the divided soul of the human rights project and counter excessive individualism with concern for the common good.

This wariness must be seen against the backdrop of a more positive assessment of human rights in diverse Protestant and Roman Catholic social teaching where secular theories of rights are viewed as rooted in the soil of Christian teaching about the *imago Dei*, the grace of reason, the providential orders of society, the doctrine of vocation, and so on.[34] Much Vatican teaching promotes respect for human rights because it is linked to the dignity of life.[35] The neo-Thomist John Finnis argues that modern rights talk can be viewed as amplifying "undifferentiated reference to 'the common good' by providing a usefully detailed listing of the various aspects of human flourishing."[36] Some Protestants also claim that the weight of Christian teaching falls in support of the human rights movement. Richard Harries, the bishop of Oxford, for instance, affirmed in the House of Lords during debate on the incorporation of the European Convention on Human Rights into domestic legislation: "The Churches are deeply committed to human rights, both in theory and practice, and support the incorporation of the European Convention [on Human Rights] into United Kingdom law."[37] The World Council of Churches recognizes human rights as compatible with thanksgiving for the life and dignity that God has bestowed on all creation.[38] George Newlands has recently completed a theology of human rights that focuses on the Christ of the vulnerable viewed from the margins of society and makes his solidarity with the powerless a criterion for moral judgment.[39] Even so, ambivalence still besets Christian (especially Protestant) engagement with human rights.

Behind the Ambivalence

Behind this ambivalence lie complex historical, semantic, and interpretive issues, especially those concerning the relation between terms (e.g., liberty, freedom, "natural rights," "rights of man," "rights of the citizen," and "human rights") as well as conceptual differences between liberty as defined in many secularist philosophies of rights and the human freedom to which God's grace gives rise. We must probe these issues at least minimally if we are neither to overemphasize the radically new nature of modern, subjective concepts of rights as powers, qualities, or entitlements pertaining to an individual as such, nor to assume too readily that modern concepts of human rights are the product of Christian natural law thinking as if in a smooth line of historical continuity from one to the other. Responsible theologico-ethical engagement with human rights requires at least some awareness of historical research into questions of continuity and discontinuity with medieval theological doctrine.

Consider, for instance, a historical debate that concerns points of transition between Scholastic understanding of "right" (*ius*), as having an objective status independent of subjective claims, and the modern, subjective sense of "right" residing in individuals. This debate concerns the extent to which modern liberal conceptions of rights have their roots in Scholastic teaching about law or emerged at a later, identifiable point in European history. Some claim, for instance, that human rights as we know them today may be used as synonyms for the natural rights alluded to by Aquinas and his fellows. John Finnis posits that modern rights-talk is compatible with Aquinas's treatment of *ius* within a theology of the *ratio Dei* (God's reason or rationality) and *ordo* (order or place within that order).[40] Assuming that the modern grammar of rights "provides a way of expressing virtually all the requirements of practical reasonableness," he minimizes differences between Aquinas's concept of "right" as "the just thing" and modern analyses of claim- and liberty-rights.[41] Rights-talk, he says, is simply the modern way of talking about how persons benefit from the fulfillment of duties and receive what is due to them. This equates to Aquinas's primary meaning of *ius*, albeit with the difference that it relates primarily to the beneficiary of the just relationship.

Several studies have been devoted to this question. Michael Villey's *Questions de saint Thomas sur le droit et la politique* (1987) draws a sharp distinction between Aquinas's notion of natural right and modern conceptions of subjective, individual right, arguing that the latter was rooted in the nominalist philosophy of the fourteenth century. William of Ockham (ca.

1287–1347), he claims, inaugurated a new way of thinking about natural right that facilitated its transition into subjective powers or claims. Ockham moved beyond classical thought in which, typically, a right was an incorporeal thing within a given set of metaphysical premises. The ancient Greeks and Romans, Villey claims, could speak of each person being entitled to a just share, or their just due, within a particular set of social relationships—the point being that this classical perspective fits ill with modern conceptions of rights inhering in persons as such; Ockham did something new.

In *The Idea of Natural Rights: Studies on Natural Rights, Natural Law, and Church Law, 1150–1625* (1997), Brian Tierney takes issue with the weight that Villey puts on the novelty of Ockham's theory of quasi-subjective rights and argues that the whole Western tradition stretching back before Ockham to the ancient world is more diverse than Villey allows. There are at least some conceptual equivalents in the ancient world to modern concepts of subjective rights, he claims. More specifically, Tierney argues that Villey pushes his case too far when positing that the novelty of Ockham's theory arose from nominalist philosophy rather than earlier juridical concerns that arose in disputes about Franciscan poverty. Tierney denies the logical link between nominalism and subjective rights and disputes Villey's suggestion that the concept of subjective right is logically incompatible with the classical concept of natural right.[42] A related claim is that Villey fails to take account of passages in which Aquinas appears to equate *ius* (right) and *lex* (law), thereby failing to take account of flexibility in Aquinas's usage where he interchanges these terms freely. "Thomas followed the common usage of his age in which *ius* and *lex* could sometimes be used interchangeably and sometimes differentiated from one another in their more specialized meanings."[43] In other words, Aquinas's writings include at least the possibility of a more fluid or nuanced relation between *ius* and *lex* and thus an, albeit minor, subjective sense.[44]

To illustrate the point, consider the following passage in which Aquinas hints that "rights" do inhere in persons. Aquinas is discussing whether human law prescribes acts of all the virtues, and he refers to an occasional need "for upholding the rights of a friend":

> Now all the objects of virtues can be referred either to the private good of an individual, or to the common good of the multitude: thus matters of fortitude may be achieved either for the safety of the state, or for upholding the rights of a friend, and in like manner with the other virtues. But law, as stated above (90, 2), is ordained to the common good. Wherefore there is no virtue whose acts cannot be prescribed by the law. Nevertheless human law does not prescribe concerning all the acts of every virtue: but

only in regard to those that are ordainable to the common good—either immediately, as when certain things are done directly for the common good—or mediately, as when a lawgiver prescribes certain things pertaining to good order, whereby the citizens are directed in the upholding of the common good of justice and peace.[45]

Aquinas seems to imply that the friend is entitled to a just share, or just due, in some respect. There is an apparently smooth transition from the claim that law must be framed for the common good to the claim that one friend can defend the legitimate entitlements of another, and that this kind of "right" (*ius*) could be attested in a court of law. The concept of right is equivalent to the concept of the just thing or action owed to someone; it permits a judge to pronounce that a just thing or action is owed (*debitum*) to someone, and it is intrinsically social in character. We must remember, however, that Aquinas's acceptance of Roman law and its definition of justice would probably have included this willingness to give to others what is due to them, or what is their right. The meaning of right would have been very different from that implied by the modern idiom. Tierney cites Villey's point that the *ius* of an ancient Roman might be punishment: "the *ius* of a parricide was to be tied up in a sack of vipers and thrown into the Tiber."[46] The fact that dealings with others are characterized by "what's fair" (*juste partage*) does not imply a subjective meaning of rights. An act of justice is doing what is right, as prescribed by the virtues and with reference to the private good of an individual and/or the common good of the many, as measured with reference to the eternal law.

This debate is finely nuanced and cannot be pursued here in more detail. Yet, we may take from it three points. First, we cannot assume that medieval theologians and modern theorists express the same demands of justice, albeit in different contexts and using different terminology; the worldviews are too different for any such assumption. Second, nor can we assume that there is radical discontinuity between Scholastic teaching on natural law and later doctrines of subjective rights; the historical issues are more complex. Third, when insufficiently supported on historical grounds, claims of synonymity between Scholastic and modern idioms justify at least some of the ambivalence described above. There might be continuity between the different discourses, as Porter suggests (see the introduction above), but it is doubtful that present-day Christian engagement with human rights maps directly onto Aquinas's theological notions of natural right(s), and thus the latter cannot be taken as synonymous with present-day human rights.

Modernity and "Natural Right" without Reference to Divine Law

Related reasons for ambivalence in the Christian community become apparent when we consider the gradual detachment of modern talk about "rights" from theological influences. Others have traced this story more fully than is possible here, but it might be helpful to note a few major figures and themes.[47] After Aquinas and his fellow Scholastics, philosophers such as Hugo Grotius (1583–1645), Samuel von Pufendorf (1632–1694), John Locke (1632–1704), Jean-Jacques Rousseau (1712–1778), and Immanuel Kant (1724–1804) slowly effected changing definitions of "right" and "natural right." Grotius, for instance, held that the law of nature exists beyond both human and divine volition: "Natural right is the dictate of right reason, shewing the moral turpitude, or moral necessity, of any act from its agreement or disagreement with a rational nature, and consequently that such an act is either forbidden or commanded by God, the author of nature."[48] A given action, he says, is either binding or unlawful in itself, depending on its agreement or disagreement with nature. From this agreement or disagreement with a thing's rational nature follows its agreement or disagreement with God's law. God himself would not command by divine right that which fails to accord with reason. The law of nature is so unalterable that it cannot be changed even by God himself; it antedates not only human but also divine power and is intellectually independent of revelation. Hence Grotius's infamously impious thesis that "what we have been saying would have a degree of validity, even if we should concede that which cannot be conceded without the utmost wickednesses, that there is not God" (*Etiamsi daremus, quod . . . non esse Deum*).[49] It marks a methodological shift toward the purely rationalist natural law theories of the seventeenth and eighteenth centuries in which natural right is defined with reference not to God's law but to pure reason. Law denotes a rule of moral action that obliges us to do what is proper, according to the best counsels of reason. All law, including divine law, should stem not from mere power or will, arbitrariness and whim, but from reason.[50] After Grotius, Locke treats law less as what God has given to his creatures and more as that which the people have given to themselves. The end of law is no longer the common good and discernment of the will of God but the maintenance of society via the preservation of individual freedom: "The end of law is not to abolish or restrain but to preserve and enlarge freedom."[51] Despite using quasi-theological arguments (notably to refute the doctrine of the divine right of kings and to advocate the principle of popular sovereignty) the vision of a cosmic hierarchy of law in which "the good of the one" is drawn toward becoming "common to many" is diminishing. Increasingly important is the contract between the individual and the state, for its own sake.

Jean-Jacques Rousseau offers another understanding of natural and civil rights. Becoming a social being, says Rousseau, entails giving up one's natural rights in exchange for civil rights. An exchange takes place in which citizens acquire rights based on law. Contra Locke and Hobbes, he does not think that individuals alienate their liberty upon entry into civil society, because the kind of contract that he envisages is grounded in assent and therefore consistent with liberty. All legitimate rights in civil society are based on agreement. The purpose of the social treaty is to preserve the contracting parties and to protect their freedom and equality. Indeed, individuals gain civil liberty by virtue of participation in the social contract wherein each person is united with others while remaining obedient to himself alone. Entry to this kind of civil society means leaving behind the unlimited natural right to everything that he or she can appropriate by labor: "What man loses by the social contract is his natural liberty and the absolute right to anything that tempts him and that he can take."[52] What the individual gains is participation in a civil society held together by convention and laws, and also the mastery of goods as given and protected by law: "what he gains by the social contract is civil liberty and the legal right of property in what he possesses."[53] The important point for our purposes is that the state is the basis of all rights for all members of it. The state holds its powers only by virtue of the powers of all its members, but it is master of all their goods as a result of the social contract. Individual ownership is, in effect, acknowledged trusteeship of part of the public property. Natural freedoms and potentially unlimited rights to life, liberty, health, and property have been relinquished in favor of submission to the general will.

Grotius, Locke, and Rousseau all confess belief in God but argue on increasingly nontheological grounds for the defense of natural rights. There is a drift in their writings from natural law and natural right defined with reference to God's law to natural rights possessed by virtue of our existence as human beings (with God diminishing into the background), and then to natural rights defined by the state through its exercise of government. This is the problem of God in the political philosophy of the Enlightenment; the God who remains relevant in the private affairs of faith and devotion disappears from political argument and finally becomes irrelevant. Rousseau tracks this drift as follows:

> All justice comes from God, who alone is its source; and if only we knew how to receive it from that exalted fountain, we should need neither governments nor laws. There is undoubtedly a universal justice which

springs from reason alone, but if that justice is to be admitted among men it must be reciprocal. Humanly speaking, the laws of natural justice, lacking any natural sanction, are unavailing among men. In fact, such laws merely benefit the wicked and injure the just, since the just respect them while others do not do so in return. So there must be covenants and positive laws to unite rights with duties and to direct justice to its object. In the state of nature, where everything is common, I owe nothing to whom I have promised nothing, and I recognize as belonging to others only those things that are of no use to me. But this is no longer the case in civil society, where all rights are determined by law.[54]

Rousseau has no intention to undermine belief in God as the source of all goodness and law. He is no atheist but is concerned that God's laws are not self-evident, that civil society requires forms of authority in which individual liberty is preserved and protected within arrangements of recip-rocal submission. Hence his emphasis is on mutually agreed covenants and positive laws as the means of binding society together. Rousseau adamantly repudiates Grotius's and Locke's notions of natural law as too readily "estab-lished from fact."[55] Grotius, we recall, had allowed for the possibility that some are born for slavery and others for domination. Such a notion of natural law, says Rousseau, favors tyrants and refuses to recognize that the exercise of human power should be for those governed. Similarly, he repu-diates Locke's belief that, in the state of nature, the right to liberty means the right to as much of nature as one can make use of before it spoils, and that labor fixes a right of property in things. This understanding of natu-ral right, says Rousseau, benefits the wicked, injures the just, and creates societies characterized by greed and inequality. Better to substitute socially agreed notions of justice for notions of original, unlimited common owner-ship of the earth. For this, no explicit reference to God is required.

Immanuel Kant's *Metaphysic of Morals* (1797) warrants special men-tion as one of the most significant modern texts on the topic. "What is right?" he asks in a text that represents his mature work and deals with the conditions whereby the freedom of every human being is respected. The question would, he says, probably embarrass many jurists who deal with the practical questions every day. It should be addressed carefully, however, because it concerns the practical relations between persons that are required in order to protect human freedom. All the more reason, he says, to probe the rational conditions for legal justice that provide the grounds on which a judge may pronounce a verdict in a court of law. The doctrine of right concerns the conditions for the day-to-day regulation of human life and answers the question "What is right?" in terms that translate into legal justice: "Right is . . . the sum of the conditions under which the choice of one can be united with the choice of another in accordance with a universal law of freedom."[56]

The doctrine of right (or the universal law of right) specifies obligations that are required so that every person's free choice can coexist with the free choice of everyone else. Every person's freedom is limited only by the freedom of others. Thus:

> One can locate the concept of Right directly in the possibility of connecting universal reciprocal coercion with the freedom of everyone. . . . Strict Right rests on the principle of its being possible to use external constraint that can coexist with the freedom of everyone in accordance with universal laws.[57]

The "doctrine of right" makes possible legal coercion; it authorizes coercion and may be laid down as a legal right and brought before a civil court. The equally important "doctrine of virtue" concerns free rational choice, in conformity with duty, rather than in response to coercion. Right relates to a narrower form of obligation than can be laid before a court of law. Justice unites virtue and right in a positive (or statutory) notion that can carry both legal and moral obligation.

After the revolution in France, the French National Assembly promulgated its Declaration of the Rights of Man and of the Citizen. It was translated into English by Thomas Paine (1737–1809) and published in 1792 in his *Rights of Man*. The preface begins:

> The representatives of the people of France . . . considering that ignorance, neglect, or contempt of human rights, are the sole causes of public misfortunes and corruptions of the natural, imprescriptible, and inalienable rights. . . . in the presence of the Supreme Being, and with the hope of his blessing and favour, the following sacred rights of men and of citizens . . .

On August 22, 1795, another declaration was prefixed to the French Constitution. It defined the following rights:

2. Liberty consists in the ability to do that which does not harm the rights of others.

3. Equality consists in that the law is the same for all, whether it protects or punishes. Equality does not admit any distinction of birth, any inheritance of power.

4. Security results from the co-operation of all in assuring the rights of each.

5. Property is the right to enjoy and to dispose of one's goods, one's revenues, the fruits of one's labour and industry.[58]

This declaration provides some of the clearest designations of the terms "liberty," "equality," "security" and "property" from the period and illustrates the interconnectedness of subjective rights to liberty with rights to the enjoyment and disposal of private property. Paine picked up these definitions and asserted that these "rights of man" are an expression of the being, meaning, and worth of every human being that should be recognized and protected by governments; rights are not privileges to be granted and revoked but self-evidently part of that great order of humankind that precedes particular governments and would exist if all governments were abolished.

By contrast, Karl Marx said that the freedom protected by all these rights is that of individuals treated as isolated monads and withdrawn into themselves:

> . . . the right of man to freedom is not based on the union of man with man, but on the separation of man from man. It is the right to this separation, the rights of the limited individual who is limited to himself. The right of property consists in "the right of selfishness."[59]

Marx reacted against the rights discourse that viewed society as an association of individuals and that was closely intertwined with the protection of civil status, private property, and economic growth, linking the growing utilization of rights discourse to the growth of commodity production and the increasing importance of the bourgeoisie.

Mind the Gap

This glance at historical and conceptual issues, albeit cursory, begins to explain why there are good reasons for ambivalence in the Christian community, given the gradual detachment of modern talk about "rights" from theological convictions. It reminds us that modern liberal notions of rights became one of the most significant means by which Western democracies disconnected their legal systems from cosmic visions of divine governance. Throughout the modern period, assertions of individual liberty have come to replace an essentially hierarchical worldview in which justice is the moral virtue that gives to God and neighbor their due within divine providential ordering of the universe; subjective rights are now original and not derived.[60] Jeffrey Stout summarizes as follows: "The linguistic innovation was to use the old word 'rights' to stand for statuses involving . . . new sorts of legitimate claims."[61] As Agnes Heller describes, such modern concepts of rights comprise a phenomenon that *enabled* Western societies to renounce religious worldviews and accompanying social hierarchies in their lawmaking: "For it is the idea of 'human rights', the archetype of natural rights, that upsets the time-honoured balance of asymmetric reciprocity by challenging it head-on."[62] Belief in subjective rights and the freedoms that they protected usurped the very place once occupied by belief in divine judgment, thereby becoming almost an object of faith in themselves. Modern, subjective notions of rights played a role in ousting medieval worldviews in which divine sovereignty was supreme. Religion had to be abolished, or at least curtailed, if the new tradition of liberal thought with its foundations in the dignity of individual freedom was to flourish.

What, then, are we to say? Does this history of opposition to theological worldviews by proponents of modern concepts of subjective rights put a Christian ethic of rights antagonistically and necessarily at variance to secularist ethics of human rights? Alternatively, should it render a Christian ethic of rights indifferent to secularist discourse? Put bluntly, does it mean that the task of theological ethics vis-á-vis secularist approaches is always to end in negation and condemnation, or that Christian people should not really care about the archaeology of human rights advocacy as undertaken within secularist approaches? How "alien" need Christian practitioners feel when engaged in human rights advocacy in contexts where no reference is made to the existence or will of God?

Working Assumptions

In response to these questions, this book proceeds with several working assumptions. First, it assumes that a Christian ethic of human rights must be clear about the theological grounds on which it is based and from which it argues. Hence the importance of affirming that "right" has an objective meaning with reference to God's gracious self-communication and providential ordering of the universe. Hence our recourse in chapters 3 and 4 to significant thinkers in (especially Protestant) Christian traditions who have grappled with questions about the relation between divine and human law, divine and natural "right," and so on. Our approach is to give an account of Christian engagement with human rights that is predominantly theological, that is, which falls within the realm of dogmatics. We presuppose with Aquinas and subsequent Roman Catholic theorists that "right" has an objective meaning with reference to God and because every good belongs within a cosmic continuity and is drawn toward higher things and union with God.[63] "Right" preexists in the mind of God and is, by the grace of God, grounded in humanity's rational nature and apprehensible by reason.[64] The meaning of "right" can be understood only with reference to the objective righteousness of God as revealed preeminently in Christ—the thesis being that subjective or natural rights may be recognized as a means of expressing that every person is a creature of God and beloved by God. As Bonhoeffer wrote, and as we examine further in chapter 4 below, subjective or natural rights may be understood as God-given such that their curtailment constitutes an attack on natural life itself and thus dishonors its Creator. The body's claim to joy, or to food and shelter, is not grounded in mutual obligation but in God's will and purpose; "it is in the first place God who stands up for these rights."[65] The human body has a claim to food and shelter not first and foremost because someone else has an obligation to feed and house it but because both are required for the preservation of its God-given life. The human body has a claim to joy because God created it for joy.[66] "It follows from the will of God, who creates individuals to give them eternal life, that there is a natural right of the individual."[67]

Second, and relatedly, it is important to be clear that there is no essential reason why the evangelical command to love must be expressed in the language of rights. Indeed, there is a sense in which Christian social theory "must articulate Christian difference in such a fashion as to make it strange."[68] Christian theologians and moralists must posit a radical discontinuity between the substance, if not the material aims, of Christian and any other form of ethics and morality, not least modes of reasoning with respect to rights. So, for instance, it is important to be clear that a Christian ethic of rights does not appeal to a mythic natural state (à la Locke) where all persons were equal and free to pursue life, health, liberty, and possessions, as their natural right. A Christian ethic of rights does not appeal to the rational ideals of equality and the moral autonomy of individuals, to the dynamic between rights and duties, or to the universally valid requirements of practical reason or categorical imperatives in ways that rest on formal principles of practical reason (à la Kant). Nor does a Christian ethic of human rights originate in the positive law of a nation-state (à la Bentham). A Christian ethic of rights does not appeal (primarily at least) to the fact that human beings in all countries and cultures are simply that, human beings. The essential dignity of all humanity might be an axiom shared by Christian and non-Christian alike, but it is not the foundation of a Christian ethic of rights. The intrinsic universality of human existence does not supply the only necessary recourse for knowledge of basic human goods. Human rights legislation belongs to human law and the secular vocation of the state as God's servant for good until Christ comes again (Rom 13:4).

To illustrate the point, we note that modern notions of subjective liberty have often been conceived as principles of autonomy or independence, the setting aside of constraints or obstacles to self-expression, a breaking free of hierarchical modes of governance, and suchlike. This contrasts radically with theological accounts of human freedom as the gift of God to live in obedience for God and others. As John Webster puts it in his commentary on Barth's moral theology:

> Christian freedom is freedom from . . . false necessity, and takes a twofold form. Its first form is the freedom to call upon God, in which "may be seen the limit which is set for the kingdom of human disorder." This freedom is a given freedom; and it is a freedom to call upon God to act himself in this matter by manifesting the restoration of order which has been accomplished in Jesus Christ. But it is also, second, a freedom to act in accordance with this restored reality, to act as "born counter revolutionaries," by claiming freedom from necessity and living in analogy to "the proclamation of the order of right, freedom, and peace which is given to man."[69]

True human freedom is not neutrality, indeterminacy, indefinite self-possibility, a zone of noninterference by others, being one's own judge of good and evil in refusal of God's word, and so forth, but a way of describing creatureliness within limits set by divine grace. The meaning of true freedom before God is different from the exercise of those freedoms that secularist human rights instruments seek to protect. Yet, it does not follow from these fundamental differences that a Christian ethic of rights should necessarily denounce or resist claim- and liberty-rights of the kind described by diverse secularist theorists. Similarities in *material* goals are sufficient warrant for dialogue and cooperation with secularist approaches even when *formal* differences are hugely significant. Indeed, this project is committed to cooperation with others where practical, material objectives are shared. Even so, it is important to be clear that the truth claims of faith do not translate directly into any particular form of ethics or moral reasoning, nor any form of earthly governance, even the desirability of respect for human rights across the globe.

Third, we must refuse absolutely any use of analogy that threatens the qualitative difference between liberal-individualist notions of rights and confession of God's saving righteousness. There is no suggestion that subjective human rights can be compared intrinsically with the righteousness of God in any sense that compromises divine transcendence or the truth that any and every perfection that belongs to creatures is given by grace and perceived in faith: "[A]s creation it has no knowledge of the ways which God will take with it as it exists, and no control of the part which He will allot it. . . . We must be clear that it is God's faithfulness alone if creation in its totality is in fact always involved in this receiving and becoming, and may have this function, *telos* and character, and be this servant and instrument, this theatre, mirror and likeness."[70] The history of analogy in Protestant thought from Luther onward reminds us that it is not enough merely to rely on natural knowledge of God for critical interaction between theologically derived notions of "right" and natural or human rights. Yet, neither is it true to the gospel of Christ to deny that the proper connection between human creatureliness, human determination as God's covenant partner (Gen 9:1-17), and the history of both takes place under divine lordship and his provision as Creator and Reconciler. A dogmatically responsible analogical approach will be cast in terms of divine initiative and human response, "*Gott spricht—der Mensch entspricht*," and rooted in the events of revelation. Such an approach is needed both to safeguard the difference between divine and human action and to enable the work of Christian moral reasoning.[71]

Fourth, the challenge is to specify in practical terms why and how analogical thinking of this kind makes a difference to Christian engagement with human rights instruments. We cannot counterbalance secularist reasons for skepticism with a theologically buttressed metaphysically realist ethic of natural and/or human rights that trumps any and all opposition with appeal to biblical truth or divine revelation. Badly expressed in this way, a Christian ethic of rights would be closed, assertive, and positivistic, and very far indeed from the dialogic work of moral reasoning required by practitioners. The claim in what follows is that faith in God provides stronger reasons for the defense of fundamental human rights than secularist groundings in contract, positive law, universal human experience, custom, and so on. Christian ethics (and faith communities more generally) has a role to play alongside, and as an alternative to, secularist theories of human rights rooted in global liberal or utilitarian theorizing. This is all the more important at a time of retreat from human rights in some liberal democracies and elsewhere. On reading the Universal Declaration of Human Rights in braille soon after its formulation, Helen Keller is reported to have said: "My soul stood erect, exultant, envisioning a new world where the light of justice for every individual will be unclouded."[72] Today human rights advocates might be tired and jaded. Despite their cause having become a kind of legal Esperanto, horrendous human abuses are far too often a reality. Like any legal instruments, human rights can be turned into "swords of vengeance" or "injurious pretexts for self-aggrandizement."[73] The nations most deeply involved with the United Nations Human Rights Commission in 1946–48, when the Universal Declaration of Human Rights was drafted, are now oftentimes guilty of undermining its legacy and hindering progressive interpretation.[74] Difficult times lie ahead. In readiness for these challenges, theology remains "tragically too important."[75]

❧2❧

On the Relation between Divine Law and Human Law

To deny God and God's commandments, to conquer the whole world in the sign of a future-oriented ideology, to harness nature absolutely—these are all interpretations of freedom. There are almost infinite interpretations of freedom!

—Agnes Heller[1]

ALMIGHTY and everlasting God, we be taughte by thy holy word, that the hartes of Princes are in thy rule and governauce, and that thou doest dispose, and turne them as it semeth best to thy Godly wysedome: we humbly beseche thee, so to dispose and governe the harte of Elizabeth, thy servaunte, our Quene and governour, that in all her thoughtes, wordes, and workes she may ever seke thy honoure and glorye, and studye to preserve thy people committed to her charge, in welth, peace and godlynes. Graunt this O merciful father, for thy deare sonnes sake Jesus Christ our Lorde. Amen.

—*Book of Common Prayer*, 1559

Questions about the relation between God's eternal law and the human exercise of jurisprudential authority are not new to Protestant thinkers. In this chapter, we consider Richard Hooker's (1554–1600) conception of the nature of divine authority and relation between divine and human law. The social and cultural context in which we live is self-evidently different from that of Hooker's day, yet central arguments in his theology of law remain valid. God's law, as revealed to Moses and others, is not confined to the people of Israel but spills over into creation more widely in positive law framed for the common good. Israel received guidance that holds good for those outside the Old or New Covenant. Human law has a share in divine wisdom to the extent that "right," or what is "due" to a person or thing within divine providence, belongs to justice, and justice is a virtue directed to good that "observes the mode of reason in all things."[2] For his investigation into these truths, Hooker remains a useful focus for our thinking about present-day Christian engagement in jurisprudence. He helps us to specify the conditions that will both give rise to and constrain our work.

The suggestion in what follows is that Hooker's discussion of the fallible and discursive nature of lawmaking might yet help Christian people, even in secularist democracies, to rethink the benefits of God's gift of the law in restraining sin and orienting creation toward its proper ends. Much has changed since Hooker wrote, not least social attitudes toward what constitutes legitimate law. The pyramid of traditional, ethical, and social hierarchies that was familiar to early Anglicanism has been replaced by a trampoline on which the legitimacy of governments goes up and down depending on their performance in the eyes of the electorate or the extension of democracy to new groups.[3] Today, in modern liberal democracies, the norms recognized by the political legislature have to prove their "rationality" by means of procedures and communicative presuppositions.[4] Legitimate political decisions are those where citizens have freely consented to the exercise of power.[5] Yet, the authority of God remains constant, and Christian people still need an account of the relation between divine and human law within which to consider the interaction of questions about the authority of God and authority from God.

In this chapter, we tread a narrow path between Hooker as "villain" because of his role in preparing for the modern separation of ethics from metaphysics and as "unqualified hero" whose ethically substantive and teleological theology of law took inspiration inter alia from the angels living in perfect obedience to God "whom they adore, love, and imitate."[6] Despite reasons for caution, however, he bears witness to the ontological and ethical priority of divine law over human law, the virtues that Christian faith brings to public life, and the theological imperative to continue Aquinas's project of subjecting all human laws to the Decalogue. For these reasons, his theology of law provides a fertile environment in which to think practically today about questions such as: What is human law for? How might we envisage the relation between divine law and human law? What kind of witness to God's law might be appropriate in modern liberal democracies?

The project is different from Christopher J. Insole's use of Hooker's writings in *The Politics of Human Frailty: A Theological Defence of Political Liberalism*, where he argues that there are similarities between Hooker's resistance to the use of public power for theological reasons and both Edmund Burke's early liberalism and John Rawls's later political liberalism. Insole's agenda is to offer a Christian defense of political liberalism across the centuries, to which end his reading of Hooker emphasizes "a certain relativism and particularism in political arrangements" and a healthy distinction between the visible and invisible church.[7] While agreeing with Insole about Hooker's aversion to any identification of the visible church with God's perfect will, and having some sympathy for his suggestion that Hooker might yet provide resources for present-day Christian engagement with liberal pluralism, we are concerned that sufficient attention be given to the theological reasons for Hooker's stance with respect to reciprocity, toleration, the importance of consensus, and so on. Insole is surely correct that Hooker resisted simple divisions of society into good and evil, balked at the church using its political influence for the saving of souls, and was concerned that the king protected ancient liberties.[8] Care must be taken, however, not to blur the boundaries between Hooker's substantive, doctrinal convictions and incidental overlap with liberal thinkers with respect to possible political implications. As Stout observes, the search for common assumptions when they are doubtful "blurs any distinctive contributions" of a given religious tradition to public debate.[9] We are also wary of enlisting Hooker in a war between theologico-political liberalism and Radical Orthodoxy, as if he shared none of the theological commitments of the latter.

Richard Hooker on Divine Law and Human Law

Firmly set in the natural law tradition stemming from Aquinas, Hooker's theology of law presupposes that there is order and rationality embedded in creation and oriented toward Christ Jesus; human history has a teleological, forward-oriented momentum. For Aquinas, the Decalogue gives expression to the order in creation toward "the common and final good," which is God and, therefore, has relevance for everyone. The precepts of the Decalogue are not confined to Israel and the old covenant but pertain to God's care and ordering of all creation.

> Now the precepts of the decalogue contain the very intention of the lawgiver, who is God. For the precepts of the first table, which direct us to God, contain the very order to the common and final good, which is God; while the precepts of the second table contain the order of justice to be observed among men, that nothing undue be done to anyone, and that each one be given his due; for it is in this sense that we are to take the precepts of the decalogue. Consequently the precepts of the decalogue admit of no dispensation whatever.[10]

For Aquinas, the Decalogue not only directs the people of Israel toward God but expresses the will of God for all people and, therefore, has universal applicability. He makes no explicit reference to the old covenant having been extended to include those in Christ, but its precepts describe an order of justice that God intends for all people. Following Aquinas, Hooker conceives of law *not* first and foremost as rules imposed by a superior authority in terms according to which actions are determined, but as that which facilitates the ordering of created realities. The primary function of law is not to command but to direct, measure, and qualify:

> I am not ignorant that by law eternall the learned for the most part do understand the order, not which God hath eternallie purposed himselfe in all his works to observe, but rather that which with himselfe he hath set downe as expedient to be kept by all his creatures, according to the severall condition wherwith he hath indued them. They who thus are accustomed to speake apply the name of *Lawe* unto that only rule of working which superior authority imposeth; whereas we somewhat more enlarging the sense thereof the terme any kind of rule or canon, whereby actions are framed, a law.[11]

"The essential point," as A. S. McGrade notes, "is that Hooker's concept of law was non-authoritative, a peculiarity to which he himself drew discreet attention."[12] Law is not to be conceived of only as something "which superior authority imposeth" but "any kind of rule or canon, whereby actions are framed." The "first eternal law" in accordance with which God himself acts comprises those rules of working that he has purposed to keep. The law of nature comprises the laws that God instituted to be observed in creation: the laws of physics, chemistry, and so on. The laws of the angels are those by which their several functions may be performed with joy. The laws of reason as accessible to humans facilitate the attaining of knowledge and wisdom by means of education, instruction, discourse, and exercise of the faculty by which judgments are made between good and evil, truth and error; "goodnesse is seene with the eye of the understanding. And the light of that eye, is reason."[13] The laws of well-doing are the dictates of right reason, even though individual wills might incline persons to misapprehension and insensitivity to the true value of things. Consistently, Hooker recasts his understanding of law from what "the learned for the most part" think of as a rule conferred simply by authoritative command, an event or performance of judgment, the execution of a right on the basis of supremacy gained by a victory of some kind, to that which God has purposed as a set of living conditions to protect life and direct people to their true end in himself. The gifts of law and gospel both derive from God, and their unity in duality is found in him.

The extent of Hooker's indebtedness to Aquinas is questioned by those who identify a break between them with respect to the relation between natural law and human law. Joan Lockwood O'Donovan speaks of a separation in Hooker's work between the law of nature and the law of reason: "Hooker's non-Thomistic separation between nature's law and the law of reason flows from his sharp division of natural from voluntary agents, according as God is the efficient cause or the final cause of their motion."[14] Her claim is that Hooker distinguishes sharply between God's dealings with natural and rational agents. With the former, God directs their appetites toward appropriate ends. With the latter, God directs voluntary agents toward appropriate ends by means of scripture and natural reason. God's dealings with rational agents include his provision of universal axioms or principles of natural justice. Lockwood O'Donovan's comments concern inter alia the nature of the distinction between nature's law and the law of reason, and the implications of this distinction for the relation of human law to each. She accepts that Hooker adopts the traditional identification of the law of reason with the law of nature: "Hooker concedes to the traditional usage that the law of reason is, indeed, the law of nature: 'the Law which human Nature knoweth itself in reason universally bound unto . . .' (1:223)."[15] Her claim, however, is that Hooker regards human law as having its origin in the law of reason rather than divine law or natural law, and that the need for human law originates in the sinful depravity of individuals. This meshes with Insole's emphasis on Hooker's insistence on the corruption and frailty of human nature[16] and, arguably, with the fact of Hooker's writing of the *Laws* to effect a consolidation of the English church with systems of constitutional law in subordination to the law of reason.

There is little doubt that Hooker insisted on the eschatological distance between divine and human law, and the need for a clear distinction between the visible and invisible church. He saw the need to distinguish between secular government and the law of the Spirit of Christ proclaimed in the church, and warned against any suggestion of ontological participation between human and divine law that can be known through human means. To this end, his theology of law maintains a clear distinction between ecclesiastical and civil law. With Cranmer, however, Hooker believed that the legitimacy of rulers rests in divine providence because God has appointed them to rule and govern the people, and that to resist them is to resist a divine ordinance. This is evident in the two Collects for the Queen in the Order for the Administration of the Lord's Supper in the 1559 *Book of Common Prayer*.[17] Dissatisfaction with a ruler is more likely to stem from ignorance of the theological truth that "*by me Kinges raigne, and by me Princes decree justice*" (Prov 8:15) than from the ruler's declarations being inherently unjust.[18] Earthly law and governance are gracious gifts of God, who ordains laws, courts, and officers to defend good and punish evil.

The monarch is the spiritual or ecclesiastical governor to whom deference is due. Thus, Hooker denies explicitly that synodical powers of making ecclesiastical laws should be annexed to the clergy alone.[19] Monarchs are "princes under Christ" and, while the kind of dominion exercised by both cannot be compared, the monarch has power in making ecclesiastical laws. Even so, the distinction between ecclesiastical and civil law is sharp.

Clarification of the theological as well as cultural import of this distinction is offered by Jeremy Taylor. Witness his comment on two types of obedience:

> Our superiors are set over us in affairs of the world, or the affairs of the soul and things pertaining to religion, and are called accordingly ecclesiastical or civil. Towards whom our duty is thus generally described in the New Testament. For temporal or civil governors the commands are these: "Render to Caesar the things that are Caesar's;" and, "Let every soul be subject to the higher powers: for there is no power but of God, the powers that be are ordained of God; whosoever, therefore, resisteth the power resisteth the ordinance of God; and they that resist shall receive to themselves damnation:" (Rom. 13:1) and, "Put them in mind to be subject to principalities and powers, and to obey magistrates:" (Tit. 3:1). . . .
>
> For spiritual or ecclesiastical governors, thus we are commanded: "Obey them that have the rule over you, and submit yourselves; for they watch for your souls, as they that must give an account." (Heb. 13:17)[20]

Obedience in temporal matters is owed to civil governors and obedience in spiritual matters is owed to ecclesiastical governors. Taylor is convinced nevertheless that all authority descends from God and that those in authority bear the image of the divine power. Any person defacing the king's image should be regarded by Christians as despising the divine authority that imprinted it. He is also clear that human law should be obeyed for the sake of conscience because public order, charity, and benefit are concerned, and because good governance by those in authority "are actions of religion, as they relate to God."[21] "We must not," says Taylor, "be too forward in procuring dispensations . . . it signifies an undisciplined and unmortified spirit."[22] Cranmer assumes a similar distinction to that maintained by Taylor with respect to two types of obedience. His *Catechism* makes plain that kings of the world rule by force whereas God rules in his kingdom like a gentle father by the word of his gospel and the Holy Spirit. Emperors and kings in this world have realms and kingdoms, and people in their realms obey their laws; whereas God has on earth his church, a heavenly kingdom where faithful people keep his commandments, pertaining to his kingdom.[23]

None of this detracts from the yearning in Hooker's work that human laws—in both church and state—be godly in character and subject to the Ten Commandments. He believed that the grace of God can be mediated through human authorities and that the church has a duty to bear witness to this. At a time when Anabaptists and some Puritans were talking about freedom from positive law on the grounds of antinomian notions of Christian liberty, Hooker and his fellow Anglicans argued that Christians should presuppose an obligation in favor of obedience for the sake of conscience and because human law was ratified ultimately by God, who provides for human governance.[24] This is because a good law, whether divine or human, is "that which doth appoint the forme and measure of working" according to a particular end.[25] A good law commands and also directs, measures, and qualifies. It is not a demand for obedience made by a superior upon an inferior, nor first and foremost a limitation of liberty, but a rule that directs an action toward its appropriate end. There are plenty of examples in the political sections of his work in which Hooker treats law as a necessarily constraining force and accepts that law authorizes coercion. Fundamentally, however, his concept of law does not derive from sin and the need for correction but from the voluntary purpose that assigns a thing to its end. Law is not something that belongs exclusively to the fallen world but to the operations of goodness, especially the will of God in directing all things for his pleasure and their fit purpose (Prov 16:4) and perfection.[26] Because of the nature of divine law, human law is properly conceived as noncoercive, and in terms that relate actions to their appropriate ends. Thus, in seeking to discern the practical meaning of goodness in difficult situations, Hooker understood himself to be straining to hear the voice of God and to glorify him: "In reasonable and morall actions another law taketh place, (Rom 1:21) a law by the observation whereof we glorifie God in such sort, as no creature els under man is able to doe; because other creatures have not judgement to examine the quality of that which is done by them."[27]

Our claim in what follows is that this theological heart of Hooker's work provides good reasons for retrieval of his insights today. His fundamentally noncoercive definition of law is a significant factor in our reclaiming of his insights. It cannot be denied that the patterns of social relation of which he approved were asymmetric and far removed from the democratic processes that characterize modern, liberal democracies. Nor should we downplay the distinction in his work between the law of nature and the law of reason, and between ecclesiastical and civil law. Nevertheless, he casts the theological question of the nature of God's law, and the relation between divine and human law, in terms of the will of God in directing all creation toward its perfection. Hence we may return to his work with questions about what characterizes good human law and the characteristics of Christian engagement with lawmaking. With Hooker, "the point about which wee strive is the qualitie of our lawes."[28]

Reasons for Caution When Reading Hooker

There are, of course, further reasons for caution when reading Hooker. He was accused in his own day of promoting "Romische doctrine" and "the darknesses of school learning" as his Puritan contemporaries sought to assail his theology as incompatible with the doctrine of the Thirty-nine Articles.[29] An anonymous letter published during his lifetime challenged the doctrine contained in the first five books of *On the Laws of Ecclesiastical Polity*, for overthrowing the foundation of Christian religion professed by Queen Elizabeth I and the whole of the kingdom.[30] With Thomas Cranmer, Robert Sanderson, Jeremy Taylor, Richard Baxter, and others, Hooker assumed that reason is a preparation for faith; axioms given by God to Moses and the Gentiles are so manifest to all right-thinking persons that they need no further proof:

> We see, therefore, that our sovereign good is desired naturally; that God the author of that natural desire had appointed natural means whereby to fulfil it; that man having utterly disabled his nature unto those means hath had other revealed from God, and hath received from heaven a law to teach him how that which is desired naturally must now be supernaturally attained.[31]

The laws of reason, or what he calls "the light of reason whereby good may be known from evil,"[32] are fallible guides but vitally important human capacities that can be employed to distinguish between better rather than worse courses of action.

Caution is further required because of dispute regarding the extent to which Hooker's account of law is compatible with the assumptions of Augustinian and Reformation theology. Hooker's appeals to reason have been denounced as incompatible with the core assumptions of Reformation theology—and for good reason. It is an error, he says, to think that scripture is the only guide that God has given to humans with respect to moral reasoning. In addition to revelation, there is a "universall law of mankind, the law of reason" written in human hearts that can direct people toward glorifying God, even if they did not recognize and magnify his holy name.[33] In Hooker's defense, it must be said that he never once suggested that natural reason could stand on its own or make sense of itself. He never wavered from the belief that the divine law, revealed in scripture and preeminently in Christ, is needed to guide people in the task of making and obeying good law: "In morall actions, divine lawe helpeth exceedingly the law of reason to guide man's life."[34] His comments on the proper ends of positive law are part of a Trinitarian ontology and epistemology in which he maintains a clear distinction between spiritual and rational truths: "The mind conceiveth Christ by hearing the doctrine of Christianity. As the light of nature doth cause the mind to apprehend those truths which are merely rational, so that saving truth, which is far above the reach of human reason, cannot otherwise than by the Spirit of the Almighty be conceived."[35] Nevertheless, the attention that he gives to natural reason, and the fact that John Locke's citations of his work associate him with moves to recognize reason and discourse as binding sources of morality, render him vulnerable to this kind of criticism.

The Ten Commandments in the Anglican Tradition, 1530–1650

Like many patristic thinkers, sixteenth- and seventeenth-century Anglican divines identified the natural moral law with prohibitions contained in the Decalogue. Axioms given by God to Moses and the Gentiles were so manifest to all right-thinking persons that they need no further proof. The Ten Commandments are not exclusive to the spiritual realm but inform temporal and ecclesiastical law. The laws of reason, or what Hooker calls "the light of reason whereby good may be known from evil," are fallible guides in both church and state but enable humans, nevertheless, to exercise moral reason.

It is difficult to overestimate the significance attached by Cranmer, Hooker, and their fellow Anglicans to the Ten Commandments as guides to Christian moral standards in harmony with God's will. In 1548 Cranmer instructed catechumens that "the beginning of wisdom is to say the ten commandments."[36] In 1635 William Laud gave instructions to churches and chapels about their ornaments and possessions. Each place of worship was to have a large volume of the whole Bible and the *Book of Common Prayer* "both fairly and substantially bound," a font of stone, set up in the ancient usual place; a convenient and decent Communion Table, with a carpet of silk or some other decent stuff, continually laid upon the same at time of the Divine Service, and a fair linen cloth thereon at the time of the receiving of Holy Communion. Each was also to have "the Ten Commandments set upon the East End of your Church or Chapel where the people may best see and read them."[37] This high regard for the role of the Ten Commandments in Christian life is especially evident in the 1559 edition of the *Book of Common Prayer* in which the Collect for the monarch is preceded by a rehearsal of the Ten Commandments and prayers seeking mercy for their transgression.

Hooker often approaches the Decalogue through Christ's summary of the law (Matt 22:36-40). Yet, he and other sixteenth- and seventeenth-century Anglicans regard the Ten Commandments as guides to *universal* moral standards in harmony with God's will, and congruent with the law of reason. Anthony Sparrow expresses this nicely in his 1676 *Rationale upon the Book of Common-Prayer of the Church of England* when discussing how some laws of God cannot actually bind until mediated through human laws:

> We must know that some laws of God suppose some human acts to pass and intervene before they actually bind: which act of man being once passed, they bind immediately. For example, "You shall not steal" is God's law which cannot bind actually until humans are possessed of some goods and property; although property is not usually determined by God himself immediately but by the laws of those to whom God has given authority to determine it. God has given the earth to the children of men, so, [for example,] he gave Canaan to the Israelites in general; but men cannot say "this is mine" until human laws or acts determine the property of the Israelites . . . [they] could not claim a property on this side of the Jordan until Moses had assigned them their several portions. But when the portions were so assigned, they could say, "This is mine, by God's as well as human law; and whoever took away their rights sinned not only against man's but against God's law too that says "You shall not steal."[38]

All judgment belongs to God, and his gift of the law was to all people. A clear distinction must be drawn between what Luther called a legal knowing (*cognitio legalis*) as opposed to a saving knowledge of the gospel that is inaccessible to reason. Nevertheless, the human law is needed to give socially binding expression to the natural law as summarized in the Ten Commandments. Consider Cranmer's exposition on the eighth commandment in his *Catechism*:

> For God himself has ordained laws, courts and officers to defend the good and to punish the evil, without which, there can be no peace or quietness in this world. They are the succour and sanctuary of fatherless and motherless children, of widows and of all oppressed persons. And he that should go about to overturn this common refuge of all persons that suffer wrong, it can not otherwise be, but he must needs sin against the ordinance of God, and grievously hurt his neighbour. . . .
>
> But no man doth pervert and overturn justice, courtesy and judgement more than a false witness, wherefore this is a very heinous sin before God. For a false witness doth foreswear himself against the second

commandment, he doth as much as lieth in him to overturn and destroy courts and judgements, founded and established by God, he despiseth and deceiveth the judge, he hurts his neighbour, but in name and good, he stops peace and friendship and agreement between the parties.[39]

God is obeyed in loving his ordinances, obeying the monarch, doing good to all people, and hurting none. To this end, human laws should teach what love of God's ordinances requires and the church should pray that kings, princes, and governors should minister justice for the punishment of wickedness and vice and the maintenance of true religion and virtue. No divide exists between God's law as mediated by secular government and the law that Christ fulfilled on the cross, that law which believers are called to fulfill after their justification by the sanctifying Spirit of Christ.[40]

These Anglican divines were under no doubt that the law of God condemns whereas the gospel offers the free gift of life to all. John Bradford, the Manchester-born accountant and preacher martyred under Queen Mary in 1555, put this most clearly when he wrote:

> The law is a doctrine which commands and forbids, requiring doing and avoiding. Under it therefore are contained all precepts, threatenings, promises upon conditions of doing and avoiding, &c. The gospel is a doctrine which always offers and gives; requiring nothing on our behalf, as of worthiness, or as a cause, but as a certificate unto us, and therefore under it are contained all the free and sweet promises of God; as, "I am the Lord thy God, &c."[41]

Christians do not come to justification by performance of the law, by their own deeds and merits, or by any other means than Christ himself, but may trust instead that whatever they have not fulfilled of the law because they were sinners, Christ himself has fulfilled for them.[42] These Anglican divines were not idealistic or naive with respect to Jesus' own relation to the law as interpreted by the religious leaders of his day. Hugh Latimer (1485–1555) distinguished between Jesus' flouting of the outward demands of the law and his faithful fulfillment of its spiritual requirements:

> It is also to be considered what our Savior did against the law outwardly, for there was a law that no man should touch a leprous man, yet Christ touched this man. Here you must consider that civil laws and statutes must be ordered by charity; for this act of Christ was against the words of the law, but not against the law itself. This law was made to that end that no man should be hurt or defiled by a leper; but Christ touched this man, and was not hurt Himself, but cleansed him that was hurt already. Here we may learn rather to follow the mind of the law than the rigor of the words; and to bring charity with us, which is an interpreter of the law for else we may miss by extremity.[43]

Jesus Christ accepted being "born under the law" (Gal 4:4), having been circumcised thereby becoming a debtor to the whole law, and submitting to the worst death that the law had to inflict. In his death he paid its penalty so that no part of its penalty might light upon us. In his life he fulfilled the directive part of the law by meeting its requirements in love. Of interest for our purposes is the emphasis on how the impress of the divine nature and personhood extends to human law in the streams of both secular government and the law of the Spirit of Christ proclaimed in the church.

The Ten Commandments and Three "Writings" of the Law

Hooker is thus convinced that God's law is "the patterne to make" and "the card to guide the world by."[44] He is also persuaded that human law is a gracious gift of God that has, since Old Testament times, "constrained evil and supported the forces of government for the common good."[45] The more difficult questions concern the relation between the two. In what follows, we see that Hooker does not succumb to a form of theological positivism in which law is laid down or written by a sovereign lawgiver to be obeyed unquestioningly by minions. Instead, he wants to "enlarge" our understanding of the kind of responsibilities exercised by Christians involved with human law and jurisprudence. To understand Hooker's meaning we turn to his treatment of the Ten Commandments in relation to human law. Consider the following passage:

> In the first age of the world God gave lawes unto our fathers, and by reason of the number of their dais their memories served in steed of bookes; whereof the manyfolde imperfections and defects being known to God, hee mercifully relieved the same by often putting them in minde of that whereof it behoved them to be specially mindefull. . . . After that the lives of men were shortned, meanes more durable to preserve the lawes of God from oblivion and corruption grewe in use, not without precise direction from God himselfe. First therefore of Moyses it is said, that he wrote all the wordes of God (Ex. 24:4); not by his owne privat motion and devise: for God taketh this act to him selfe, I have written (Hos. 8:12). Further more, were not the Prophets following commanded to do the like? Unto the holy Evangelist Saint John how often expresse charge is given, Scribe, Write these things? (Rev. 1:11; 14:13)[46]

Hooker speaks of God's gift of the law and conceives of at least three (of what are herein designated as) "writings"—God's own writing of the law at creation; Moses' writing as recorded in Exodus; and later writings by the prophets. Further "later writings" are implied shortly afterward as Hooker proceeds to speak both about the sufficiency of scripture for knowledge of God and the need to comprehend by reason "all things which are necessary" where the laws of the church and positive laws are concerned. For example, he mentions how the apostles and leaders of the early church instituted laws and customs, not all of which were committed to writing but which are "knowne to be Apostolicall."[47] He also mentions other laws, including the laws of heraldry, civil constitutions, and all positive laws, that are also "written" and that reflect and/or concern people's duties before God in varying degrees. In other words, Hooker's theology of law has a threefold pattern: God's own writing of the law eternally; Moses' writing in obedience to divine command; and later writings by the prophets, apostles, leaders of the church, and also governors in the temporal realm. God's giving of the law is not tyrannical or authoritarian but anticipatory of further "writings" by human collaborators.

Let us look more closely at each "writing." The first is God's "writing" of the "first eternal law" and also the universe and its laws of nature, including humankind according to their perfections not least the use of natural reason: "He *made a law for the raine*; He gave his *decree unto the sea, that the waters should not passe his commandment*" (Jer 5:22).[43] We saw above that law is defined by Hooker as a rule that relates an action to its appropriate end—"that which doth appoint the forme and measure of working, the same we tearme a *Lawe*"—and we are familiar already with the teleological framing of his ethic.[49] Here we see how Hooker construes this teleology in relation to God's creation of the natural order, including the gift to humankind of reason. It is by reason that humans attain to knowledge of things that facilitate their flourishing and thereby honor or dishonor their maker; "the laws of well-doing are the dictates of right reason that teach a person to live rightly and discern the will of God."[50] "Goodnesse," says Hooker, "is seene with the eye of the understanding. And the light of that eye, is reason."[51] The first "writing" is thus God's eternal law that incorporates all laws of nature and the gift of reason to humankind.

The second "writing" is God's giving of explicit direction to the eye of reason in scripture, including the gift of the law to Moses:

> Whereby it appeareth how much we are bound to yeelde unto our creator the father of all mercy, eternall thankes, for that he hath delivered his lawe unto the world, a lawe wherin so many thinges are laid open, cleere and manyfest; as a light which otherwise would have bene buried in darknes. . . .[52]

God's first writing of the law should have been enough to teach and enjoin humankind what natural reason requires, namely the principles of reason that are (or should be) self-evident: "The maine principles of reason are in themselves apparent," meaning that God illumines everyone with the ability to distinguish truth from falsehood, good from evil, and thereby to learn the will of God and frame laws accordingly.[53] However, sin has clouded humans' judgment and misdirected their endeavors. Alluding to Augustine's teaching, Hooker talks elsewhere of those "halfwaking" persons who are insensitive to the light of true understanding.[54] Hence God's second writing of the law in his epiphany to Moses and other writings of sacred Scripture. The Bible is said to be "fraught even with lawes of nature" in an allusion to the compatibility of the laws written by Moses and those given previously by God to the first humans.[55] Significantly, however, Hooker's recounting of God's gift of the law to the first humans and to Moses are affirmations to the effect that God has not written or spoken the law as a sovereign prince or king might do. God's gift of the law is not pharaonic in character but relational, collaborative, and open to the future. The Ten Commandments, part of the second "writing" of the law, are a revelation of the divine law but are not finished or complete in the sense that they do not require further writing or interpretation.

The third writing is what Hooker calls "the substance of the service of God" or the daily struggle to discern appropriate applications of God's laws, to make or alter positive laws, and to live dutifully in political societies wherefore positive laws are justly constituted:

> [S]eeing that God hath indued us with sense to the end that we might perceive such things as this present life doth neede, and with reason, lest that which sense can not reach unto, being both now and also in regard of a future estate hereafter necessary to be knowne, should lye obscure; . . . use we the pretious giftes of God unto his glory and honour that gave them, seeking by all meanes to know what the will of our God is, what is righteous before him, in his sight what holy, perfect and good, that we may truely and faithfully doe it.[56]

Hooker is fully aware that human law might often entail the authoritative imposition of a rule by force. He recognizes this necessity and speaks of obedience to humanly imposed laws while discussing the legitimacy of coercive power.[57] Yet, he does not treat humanly imposed laws as worthy of obedience for either positivistic or naturalistic reasons but speaks both of the power of lawmaking as a gift from God and of the availability of laws to consent.[58] Any positivistic or naturalistic assumptions to the contrary would, to borrow Arthur J. Jacobson's words, be "our own pharonic temptations."[59] The writing of law does not happen only once or twice, as in positivism and some forms of natural law; there are many more writings. Indeed, this third writing of law is regarded by Hooker as an ongoing process that involves struggle and dialogue with one's fellows, as well as collaboration with God.[60] Hooker's emphasis on the responsibilities of natural reason does not allow the third "writing" of the law to harden into positivism or naturalism. Lawmaking is always a fallible process, the benefits of which are likely to be increased if an informed consensus is reached. Law, like reason, should direct the human will to discover and embrace the good in particular actions, and should be evident to those who rejoice in God and/or avail themselves of the light of reason: "God illuminateth every one which cometh into the world, men being enabled to know truth from falsehood, and good from evil."[61]

Lawmaking as a Fallible and Discursive Process

For Hooker, human jurisprudence and execution of the law is a fallible and discursive process that involves communication and the search for consensus. God could command all humankind as a sovereign prince or king might do, but Hooker seems reluctant to concede that God ever does act arbitrarily or not for humankind's best interests. Instead, humankind must undertake the difficult processes of moral reasoning that move between justice and "right," defined objectively with reference to God, and the needs of given societies for good law. For this, he regards general consent as one of the most accurate and certain means of testing a hypothesis. He even goes so far as to say that "the generall and perpetuall voyce of men is as the sentence of God him selfe."[62] Because of God's gift of reason to all, the power of lawmaking belongs to the whole of a given society and not only to an individual prince or ruler. All reasonable members of a society are expected to consider the laws that bind its members and to give reasoned consent to those that have public approbation. "The chiefest instrument of human communion," writes Hooker, "is speech (Arist. *Pol.* I. *c.* 2), because thereby we impart mutuallie one to another the conceiptes of our reasonable understanding. . . . Civill society doth more content the nature of man than any private kind of solitarie living, because in societie this good of mutuall participation is so much larger then otherwise."[63]

Like some liberal discourse theorists, Hooker holds that consensus is hugely important even to the extent that laws that lack public approbation are not deemed binding.[64] Consensus is, however, never more than a sign of a God-given good. Significantly, Hooker holds that consensus is the sign or token of the goodness of an action rather than being constitutive of it:

> Signes and tokens to know good by are of sundry kinds: some more cer-
> taine and some lesse. The most certaine token of evident goodnes is, if the
> generall perswasion of all men do so account it. . . . the universal consent
> of men is the perfectest and strongest in this kind, which comprehendeth
> onely the signes and tokens of goodnesse.[65]

His idea of law as a "directive rule unto goodness of operation," or
a regulating principle that points toward or determines human action
in accordance with the good, makes it impossible that consensus should
constitute the good. Because of the destructive effects of sin, Hooker still
maintains that all persons actively ignore or pervert the main principles
of natural reason, notably "that the greater good is to be chosen before
the less," "parents are to be honoured," and "others to be used by us as we
ourselves would by them." Such principles are, he says, given by the light
of reason (Rom 2:14), which illumines all persons and guides them toward
what is good. Even so, Hooker believes that God, as the author of law,
makes the main principles of reason apparent to all. A weakness of Hooker's
work is his failure to examine many of the practical implications of his
convictions, though he recognized the need to do this—"It resteth ther-
fore that we consider how nature findeth out such lawes of government as
serve to direct even nature deprived to a right end"—and speaks of the primary responsibilities of rulers to remove penury or "want of things without
which we cannot live."[66] Despite problems in this respect, his work offers
encouragement to policymakers, lawyers, and politicians today to subject
all positive law to the precepts of the Decalogue and to acknowledge that
"right" is defined objectively with reference to God and denotes that "due"
to a person or thing within divine providence.

Unlike liberal discourse theorists, Hooker sees the relation between discourse and good law as mediated through the prism of dutiful living before
God. Hooker's theology of law is characterized neither by positivism, which
insists that law achieves order only by force, nor by "naturalism" (a perversion of natural law), which looks for norms "written" or "engraved" in
nature. Instead, there is considerably more emphasis on duty as a response
to God's revelation of himself as Redeemer and Lord, and to the needs of
one's neighbor. As a constitutive factor in the third "writing" of the law,
duty is guided and directed by the first and second "writings" of the Ten
Commandments and by other revelations of divine law. For Hooker, the
force of all ethical and moral obligation is traced back to God as the author
of nature and maker of the laws of the universe. God himself is the last and
best end of the human mind, and knowledge of this end can be sought by
reason and is perfected by love.[67] As Aquinas writes, "[T]he supreme good,
namely God, is the common good, since the good of all things depends

on God."[68] In all creation, says Hooker, "that and nothing else is done by God, which to leave undone were not so good."[69] The goodness of the divine being informs and structures the whole created order, directing all created things for goodness and their proper ends. All things were created "to shew beneficence and grace in them."[70] Consequently, duty is not simply an expression of submission, deference, or respect but a way of living as properly human before God and one's neighbor. Duty is the positive content of human freedom in relationship, that which makes possible a full sharing in life within the boundaries of God's command. A superficial similarity exists between Hooker's treatment of duty and that of later liberals to the extent that duties are not imposed by a ruler or even by God but "by the understanding of the faculty of the mind."[71] A sense of obligation follows from recognition of those things that should be done "necessarily and naturally," and this gives rise to duty. But this account of the faculty of the mind and laws of reason should not be abstracted from the broader theological considerations that determine it.

For Hooker, the duties of humans are primarily a response to God-given signs of goodness (e.g., beauty, a discernible rectitude about a course of action, consensus). Duties are expected of all persons, regardless of whether they have the light of scripture and revelation. "Infinite duties there are, the goodnes wherof is by this rule sufficiently manifested, although we had no other warrant besides to approve them."[72] Duty is a response to a particular kind of claim that arises in the course of seeking goodness and those things that are "fittest for our use." Some such duties are, says Hooker, so obvious that they require no further proof, for example, "God to be worshipped," "parents to be honored," "others to be used by us as we ourselves would by them." These are integral to the structure of creation, belonging to the bowels of the earth, and are summarized by Jesus in Matthew 22:36-40.[73] These fundamental duties are not prescribed by God in a way that bypasses the human activity of reason or violates free will, but may be found out by discourse, because it is natural for humans to recognize their duty toward God and other humans: "naturall inducement hath brought men to knowe, that it is their dutie no lesse to love others than themselves."[74] For example, "Thefte is naturallye punishable, but the kinde of punishment is positive, and such lawful as men shall thinke with discretion convenient by lawe to appointe."[75] Where the relationship between natural and human law is less direct, Hooker speaks of laws as either "mixedly" or "meerly humane," and urges obedience to them provided that they do not require a law of reason to be breached.[76] Hence the importance of consensus: "Lawes they are not therefore which publique approbation hath not made so."[77] Widespread agreement that a law is just and right is a sign that the law prescribes something that reason requires, even if it bears little relation to the main axioms of the law of nature (e.g., the peculiarities of inheritance law or laws concerning embassage between nations). In other words, a law might be declared positivistically by an unelected ruler but unless the people consent to it as a rule or measure that directs action toward an appropriate end, it should not have the status of law—the implication being that it need not be obeyed. Regardless of its status as posited or prescribed, the real duty to obey or disobey arises from an underlying fact of some kind and the claim that it evinces. Evaluation of these claims has to be guided by natural reason and discourse, as well as (for believers) scripture, tradition, and conscience.

Hooker's concepts of right and duty thus bear little comparison with later liberal theories, for instance, the neo-Kantian Hohfeldian analysis of claim-rights and liberty-rights in which rights are correlative with duties on the part of others: "To assert a right to freedom of expression is to claim that others have a duty to refrain from preventing my expression; to assert a property right in some object is to claim that others must not trespass upon, or interfere with my use or enjoyment of that thing."[78] For Hooker, a "right" is a principle discovered by reason and discourse that facilitates the flourishing of all living creatures. "This did the very Heathens themselves obscurely insinuate, by making *Themis* which we call *Jus* or Right to be the daughter of heaven and earth."[79] Ancient peoples could discern the meaning of "right" because it reflects an objective state of affairs existing in the mind or reason of God (*ratio Dei*). "Right" is not, at least primarily, a subjective property residing in individuals. Hooker's notion of duty is also different from later liberal thinkers because, for him, duty to God is the duty of duties. This is where ethical responsiveness begins and ends, and the pattern established in faith is repeated in the duty of humans to each other. Duty precedes human lawmaking and is not first and foremost the correlate of subjective rights. Duty is not primarily prescriptive or imperative, but a particular kind of response to theological claims (that we later term rights) that reflect that x and y are claim-possessing facts or circumstances.

God's Eternal Law and the Church's Witness in Liberal Democracies

To summarize, Hooker's difficulty, and ours, is the disjunction between the objective rightness of God's law as revealed to us and the subjective impossibility of humankind attaining to knowledge of it. Hooker does not compromise the objective truth of God's law as that which teaches all humankind how to desire and reach for him as our "soveraigne good," but knows that the human exercise of authority, even when it seeks what God wills, is corrupt due to the intervention of sin. His usefulness to us today lies in negotiation of this tension—that we should work and pray for human law to resonate harmoniously with God's eternal law even while sin obscures and prevents this possibility. Hooker neither downplays the effects of sin nor delimits Christian engagement with God's law to within the walls of the church. It is a tension that takes different form today than in sixteenth-century England but still requires us neither to compromise witness to the eternal law of God nor to delimit its relevance.

Beyond Sect and Compromise

Today, the most familiar conceptual frame for addressing such issues is showing signs of strain. Any bridge between church and state is often caricatured as positions on a scale between "bad" forms of Constantinianism and the extremes of modern liberalism, ranging between perceptions of the church as the spiritual organ of the state, functioning to sacralize the laws of an institution that exists by force, and the church as totally disconnected from the state because religion is a private affair that rarely impinges on public life. These caricatures or "types" were popularized by Ernst Troeltsch, who has been described by some as the single most influential voice in twentieth-century Protestant thought as it bears on religion in the public square.[80] Whatever we think of Troeltsch's work, the categories and questions left by him are never far from the surface in such debates. They are attacked by inter alia Stanley Hauerwas, who questions the objectiveness of the sociology involved—at least as utilized by H. Richard Niebuhr in mid-twentieth-century studies of religion, the church, and American life, the problem being that Troeltsch's categories had forced the church into an all-or-nothing relationship to the secular culture of the day, so "that we must choose to be 'all,' or irresponsibly choose to be sectarian nothing."[81] Nonetheless, much energy has been expended in exploring why Christian involvement in lawmaking has been often conceived either in terms of problematic compromise or sect-like nonengagement with social issues.

Reading Aquinas and his Protestant interpreters suggests to us, however, that Christian involvement in lawmaking *need not* be conceived either in terms of problematic compromise or nonengagement, antagonism or indifference. These are not the only options available to the church, and, we may infer, Troeltsch's "types" must not be allowed to become self-fulfilling prophecies that constrain the theological imagination.[82] Nor, of course, is it the task of Christian ethics to sort out the problems of modern and/or postmodern liberalism. The challenge for Christian theologians and moralists is to develop an ethic of law *beyond sect and compromise*—neither retreating from the responsibilities of Christian witness and mission with respect to the human activity of lawmaking nor allowing the insidious temptations of our own age so to impair our judgment that, to cite Ernst Bloch's observations on Reformation theologies of natural law, we ally ourselves with the Neros, having "too little of anything, of Christ and of his community."[83]

With Hooker, then, we proceed on the basis of three observations. First, human law exists within divine providence despite the effects of sin, and struggles both with and against the consequences of the Adamic fall. Second, knowledge of God's law was bestowed innately at the creation of humankind but does not survive in our experience as a universally held system of beliefs or practices. Third, the witness of the church must be to God's revelation, but this does not, indeed should not, denigrate moral reasoning about the quality of human laws. Human moral reasoning is still capable of identifying some of the worst effects of sin and of framing laws that curtail the worst excesses of our post-fall state and point toward how humans ought to behave toward one another. Together, these observations mean that Christian engagement with public policy and jurisprudence will never be satisfied with definitions of justice that bear no relation to God's goodness and righteousness, and the risk of compromise is always present. There is work to do, however, in investigating and promoting (what Hooker recognizes as) the relevance of God's law for the whole world.

Witness in Secularist Liberal Democracies

Hooker's challenge, then, is that we consider how the *character of witness in public arenas* might best reflect God's own noncoercive and discursive engagement with his world. "A law," writes Hooker, "be it civil or ecclesiastical, is as a public obligation . . ."[84] A subject who follows his conscience in obeying the just, equitable, and useful laws of governors, writes Sanderson, "is so far from *serving men* by his submission that two of the greatest Apostles expressly declare that *he serves the Lord God and not men.* . . . He is a servant of men indeed, as he obeys the laws of men, but he is the servant of God by paying his obedience from a principle and consciousness of duty to God."[85] Of course, the massive constitutional and social changes in England between the times when these thinkers lived and our own make it impossible to draw close analogies between their times and ours. As noted above, Hooker et al. assumed that monarchs would be Christians and would, therefore, acknowledge the supreme Lordship of Christ. Consequently, for him, Christians should presuppose an obligation in favor of obedience to earthly authorities. Read unfavorably, this might be said to imply a servile acceptance of bad human laws—something of which many in the UK are especially wary as security threats coincide with a retreat from civil liberties. Read more critically, the theologico-ethical principle that human laws do not oblige the Christian directly and of themselves, but only as a consequence of divine law that requires all persons to seek justice and promote peace, should still encourage humane and passionate questioning of such matters as how law promotes human dignity and preserves civil liberties, treats persons with equity, does not disadvantage the poor, and facilitates critical assessment.

In our own day, the democratic processes that we enjoy are vastly different from the quasi-feudal patterns of social hierarchy and intrinsic authoritarianism with which Hooker et al. were familiar. The heir to the role of Defender of the Faith and Supreme Governor of the Church of England has said that he would personally rather see his future role as "Defender of Faith, not the Faith."[86] We cannot disregard the fact that Hooker's theology of law has served for many years as an apology for the divine ordination of monarchs and royal supremacy. Nonetheless, it is still because of divine law and the gospel of grace that Christian people are urged to seek justice and promote peace. All ethical and moral obligation is still traceable back to God as the author of nature and maker of the laws of the universe. God himself is the last and best end of the human mind, and knowledge of this end can be sought by reason and is perfected by love.[87]

This places a heavy responsibility on Christian people, especially those involved in the spheres of legal and public policy, because most alternative viewpoints in the "marketplace of ideas" favor the separation of religious convictions and policy making. So, for instance, the kind of neutrality exemplified by Rawls's now-familiar notion of justice as fairness that asks us deliberately to omit religious ideas of the good life, moral precepts, or beliefs from our considerations. "The veil of ignorance secures equality by allowing strangers to ascend to a high level of abstraction."[88] Stripping persons culturally naked, so to speak, risks reducing us all to abstract (albeit reasoning) egos that, precisely because we become abstract, are interchangeable. Consequently, the society in which this kind of "public reason" dominates is unable to engage practically with significant cultural differences.[89] In the minds of many, the risk associated with this worldview—namely, that democracy serves the interests of the majority and not that of the people as a whole, including minority groups, is potentially less noxious than faith-based arguments in public spheres and/or public servants motivated by religion. The challenge is to demonstrate at least a weak version of Hooker's claim that "So naturall is the union of Religion with Justice, that wee may boldlie denie there is either, where both are not."[90] Even if modern liberal democracies will not stomach a strong version of this claim, the church and its members might show that the public administration of justice for the common good is consistent with its beliefs and practices.

Beyond this, the church and its members might also warn against the failure of wisdom in attributing ultimacy to the procedures of discourse. Jürgen Habermas represents this kind of extension of the modern project of communicative and purposive rationality, critical theory, and the embodiment of reason in social action:

> Discourse theory explains the legitimacy of law by means of procedures and communicative presuppositions that, once they are legally institutionalized, ground the supposition that the processes of making and applying law lead to rational outcomes. The norms passed by the political legislature and the rights recognized by the judiciary prove their "rationality" by the fact that addressees are treated as free and equal members of an association of legal subjects.[91]

Habermas's reconstructive approach to law through discourse and procedural reason urges that the participation of all private legal subjects in the common exercise of political autonomy should be oriented toward agreement about justified interests and standards of behavior.[92] Hope is located in discursive resolution of the tension between law as something exhibiting moral value or integrity and as an inherently value-free social phenomenon; that is, as something morally neutral and sociologically descriptive rather than morally substantive in nature because of an association with metaphysics. Citizens are the authors of the legal order and *legitimacy is a project or fallible process* in which the only dogmatic core is the idea of individuals as autonomous agents who must obey the laws they make for themselves through democratic structures of recognition and accountability at every level of society as a whole.

Hooker, as we have seen, urges the Christian faithful toward a more positive appreciation of the search for consensus and the work of demonstrating practical reasonableness than might have been expected. This does not mean, however, that a Christian ethic of rights should accept the absolutism of Habermas's claims or what Agnes Heller calls his vision of "an all-encompassing liberal universe."[93] Habermas's theory of communicative action is unnecessarily comprehensive, offering an all-encompassing account of truth, practical reason, meaning, and ethics. His version of liberalism borders on becoming a quasi-religious belief in human rights and individual freedoms by claiming to be "*the* rational language of the human race beyond space, time and history," thereby making "a (fraudulent) plea for total impartiality."[94] John Rawls makes a similar observation:

Habermas's own doctrine, I believe, is one of logic in the broad Hegelian sense: a philosophical analysis of the presuppositions of rational discourse (of theoretical and practical reason) which includes within itself all the allegedly substantial elements of religious and metaphysical doctrines. His logic is metaphysical in the following sense: it presents an account of what there is—human beings engaged in communicative action in their lifeworld.'[95]

(Rawls's own weaker and more acceptable position is that legitimate law requires persons of different religions and none to accept the idea of public reason as the reason of free and equal citizens required to satisfy the criterion of reciprocity and morally obliged to regard as binding laws that have been enacted by the opinion of the majority. Habermas's assertion is that the conditions of communicative reason require liberal thinkers to undertake their reconstruction of law and lawmaking "without the support of a higher or prior law enjoying moral dignity" because this at least seeks to leave "comprehensive doctrines" untouched.)[96] This unashamedly absolutist claim that democratic procedures are the only postmetaphysical source of legitimacy cannot be accepted by a Christian ethic of rights. Nor is it, we suggest, the kind of ethic best suited to present-day needs of dialogic pluralism and the need to take account of the kinds of commitment operative in religious perspectives.[97] Against this backdrop, Hooker invites Christian people not only to a ministry of critical engagement but to hard thinking about the practical reasonableness required to support Christian practitioners working within legal contexts.

Our final point in this chapter concerns Hooker's challenge to consider *reasons for Christian engagement with lawmaking*. We mention this because of the particular need in our churches today to help discern and nurture vocations among persons of all ages. Like the varying intensities of the reds, blues, and yellows in thermal imaging or infrared camera images, members vary in giftedness for given roles and responsibilities. Unfortunately, churches are often ill equipped to help their members understand their "workplace" calling as discipleship. The discerning, affirming, and supporting of lay vocations, according to God's gifts of grace (Rom 12:6), needs far more sophistication and astuteness than is often managed. Firmly convinced that human law has a place within divine providence, Hooker might yet help the church better to support those called to work in establishing and maintaining legal frameworks in societies around the world. Subsequent chapters attempt to unpack how the *measure* and *content* of Christian engagement with human rights, as well as the warrant for Christian engagement in public policy with respect to human rights, is given in God's command.

❧ 3 ☙

Revelation and Christ the Measure
of "Natural" Rights

*When man is summoned to do the right, primarily and decisively he is summoned
only to adhere to the fact that the gracious God does the right. . . .
"To accept as right" means to lay aside hostility to God's action . . .
to love Him with all our heart, and soul, and strength.*

—Karl Barth[1]

*Christ has entered into natural life. . . . Only though Christ's becoming human do we
have the right to call people to natural life and to live it ourselves.*

—Dietrich Bonhoeffer[2]

Disciples of Christ are called on to attest God's law and to seek to understand the gospel politically. This challenge was put to us in chapter 3 by
Hooker and his fellow sixteenth- and seventeenth-century Anglicans. They
reminded us that human laws should teach what the love of God's ordinances requires, and that the church should pray for kings, princes, and
governors to minister justice for the punishment of wickedness and vice,
and for the maintenance both of true religion and of virtue. Hooker in
particular challenged us to take seriously the role of human law within
divine providence and also the importance of consensus building when
issues of ecclesial and social polity are at stake. There are no easy comparisons between his day and our own. Massive shifts have occurred, not least
with respect to conceptions of law.[3] Today, democratic legitimacy demands
that governments make possible a discursively structured legislature within
which none has special privileges for seemingly arcane historical and/or
theological reasons. Nonetheless, Hooker challenges us to consider how

Christian witness in public arenas might best reflect God's own noncoercive and discursive engagement with his world. In this chapter we attempt to take up this challenge, in a more explicitly Trinitarian manner than Hooker sometimes managed, by asking how biblical teaching about God's self-revelation in Christ might bear on Christian engagement with human rights. The claim is that a Christian ethic of rights must proceed from and through an account of Christ himself and of the meaning of the Incarnation for Christian social and political engagement.

Toward a Command-Rights Dynamic

Neither antagonism nor indifference are the only options available to Christian people in dialogue with, or working with, secularist approaches to human rights. Alternative ways of thinking and acting are possible. In this chapter we draw especially on Karl Barth's *Church Dogmatics* II.2 and IV.1, Dietrich Bonhoeffer's *Ethics*, and the English Reformed theologian Colin E. Gunton's development of Barth's theology of "the natural." The central claim is that the gospel of judgment and reconciliation does not separate believers from the commands of God the Creator but restores these commands to believers in Christ. Believers, says Barth, hear God's command given to all humanity from their position both under judgment and reconciled to God in Christ. They cannot do other than enjoy a twofold status as creature and adopted heir: "Only as God's command comes to us as Christians does it also come to us as God's creatures. If it really comes to us as God's creatures, it also comes to us as Christians."[4] Every human subject is addressed by the Creator of all but only believers recognize as much. Only those who trust themselves to be reconciled to God in Christ can probe the meaning of God the Creator's commands for contexts outside the church. Even when working in contexts hostile to faith, persons of faith may strive to understand and act on the obligations that arise with creaturely, as well as ecclesial, existence.

Within this theological conceptuality, the question facing us is whether, and if so how, to move between theological affirmations of "right" and recognition of subjective rights, that is, claims or entitlements attaching to persons (and potentially other living beings). This is the problem of the gap between "right" as judged by God and rights residing in creatures existing before God and one another. In response, we draw initally on Bonhoeffer's christological and eschatological account of natural rights especially in determining the meaning of "right" with respect to Christ. Christ is the eschatologically new human being whose humanity is definitive for our own and whose personhood bridges the gap between objective, theologically referenced definitions of "right" and subjective natural rights. Herein is the answer to the question about bridging the gap between "right" and rights. Here we may begin to address how subjective natural rights correspond, or should correspond, to what we know in Christ of true humanity and its flourishing. Bonhoeffer's eschatologically framed account of "the natural" in Christ helps us toward a positive rather than predominantly problematic account of "the natural" and "natural rights." His christological and eschatological treatment of "the natural" challenges us with respect to the specification of natural rights even though, as we see below, Barth holds back from this. Bonhoeffer's work, and that of Gunton, helps us to see that occupation with natural teleology does not necessarily equate to a logic of individual and social self-sustaining, self-regulation, and self-sufficiency.[5] Teleology in Christian ethics cannot be exclusively a debate about the norms of natural human flourishing, or what is good in itself, because it is preeminently about human rescue and fulfillment in God, and ultimately supernatural communion with him. Consequently, Christian ethics must include questions of natural teleology and the norms of natural human flourishing because all human ontology is ordered by grace. To the extent that Christian ethics treats natural teleology—that is, normative capabilities and the maximum flourishing of created beings—under the aegis of grace, our topic is concerned deeply with natural ends. A Christian ethic of rights cannot but be occupied passionately with the natural ends of human beings, especially when these ends are frustrated. On this basis of a Christologically revised natural law, part of this chapter thus examines the implications for how Christian ethics will talk about natural teleology (e.g., of the kind propounded by John Finnis) and concomitantly about natural and human rights. (Part of chapter 6 below considers the capabilities approach to moral reasoning as developed by Amartya Sen and Martha Nussbaum.)

In unpacking the question of whether, and if so how, to move between theological affirmations of "right" and recognition of subjective rights we are interested in how human moral action and recognition of subjective natural rights and/or human rights may correspond (or correspond better) to what we know in Christ of true humanity and its flourishing, and to divine command. The nub of our answer is contained in the claim that the law is restored to believers as a form of the gospel. God's law is restored in Christ, thereby gifting believers with guidance in matters of human being and action. As Barth states: "[W]e have to do with the Gospel in so far as it has always the form of the Law."[6] John Webster summarizes nicely: "Barth's insistence that the law is the form of the gospel is rooted in a conviction about God which is inseparable from a conviction about humanity."[7] God's election of all humanity in Christ establishes a claim to all humanity; consequently, discourse about humanity, including its natural ends, is an integral part of theology. God's law is a gift to all humanity, but we need an account of how the gospel enables us to hear afresh the law of God that speaks love to all creation, not least how "good human action is action set free by the command of God."[8] Chapter 5's reading of Genesis 9:1-17 pursues this claim in a more exegetically focused manner. Christ's saving work restores to believers the content of divine command given in the law, including the requirements to all *humanity* given through Noah.[9] The covenant between God and all humanity is treated in chapter 5 as a basis on which to move between theological reflection on the mysteries of grace and practically oriented deliberation without falling into ethical occasionalism susceptible to arbitrariness,[10] and without pretending that biblical teaching translates directly into present-day rights discourse in a literal-factual way. In this chapter we prepare for this work by attempting to clarify aspects of the "grammar of doing" that follow from a firmly Christocentric theology of "the natural" informed by an ethic of divine command.[11]

This is not to suggest that Barth himself develops a Christian ethic of rights. To the contrary, he delimits the language of rights to human polity and the secular vocation of the state, and draws back from the language and conceptuality of subjective and/or natural rights for fear that human concepts substitute for divine revelation, thereby rendering theology captive to ideology. He tends not to speak of subjective rights but of "right" as an objective reality (whether theological or political) with its source outside of human selves. The struggle against fascism made him intensely alert to how "bad" forms of natural theology put illusory ideas about human beings in place of the objective, liberating God of biblical witness. But this is not the end of the story. The stereotype that Barth emphasizes the objective givenness of the meaning of "right" in Christ so rigorously that he leaves absolutely no room for talk of subjective rights must be dismantled. An ethic of divine command does not exclude the suggestion that human rights can be "aids to hearing" or useful practical tools in the heeding of God's word.[12] Barth's focus on the practical demands of faith supplies at least some of the resources that we need for a biblically informed, christologically centered political ethic of critical engagement with secularist approaches to human rights today. Talk of God and God's actions is determinative of the scope and environment of Christian moral reasoning. As Webster put it: "[T]he moral field is thus defined as the arena of God's activity as creator, reconciler and perfecter, the one who brings all things into being, upholds them against all threats and enables them to attain their proper end."[13] True witness to Christ demands "concrete decisions in relation to the world in which we live."[14]

Ecce Homo!

Ecce Homo! "Behold the man!" (John 19:5) is Dietrich Bonhoeffer's starting point for his discussion of natural rights.[15] As Pilate directed the gaze of the crowd toward Jesus and declared him innocent, says Bonhoeffer, so disciples of Jesus Christ must do the same today. It is in the person and body of Jesus Christ that human beings are reconciled to God. Here God took upon himself the sin of the world, accepted the world as it is in sinfulness, and renewed its life. Because of the Incarnation, believers have neither an idealized picture of humanity nor a hatred of it, but a victim of Roman injustice is for us the very possibility of human justice and neighborliness. More than this: because of the resurrection, Jesus Christ is the mediator in whom humanity is reconciled to God. In him we meet all for whom God's justice is true although for whom human justice is probably wanting. "In Christ the form of humanity was created anew. What was at stake was not a matter of place, time, climate, race, individual, society, religion or taste, but nothing less than the life of humanity, which recognized here its image and its hope."[16] All humanity is gathered up and affirmed in Christ. Not merely the exemplar for our actions—though he is this—Christ is the reality of God's saving love toward us. In Christ, and by the power of the Holy Spirit, we both know of God and meet our neighbor: "The person who loves God must, by God's will, really love the neighbor. But love is nothing other than realizing the purpose of establishing God's rule over humanity."[17]

In other words, the meaning of the objective reality of "right" is found in Jesus Christ. Everything in Christian ethics and political action centers around his person. His incarnation is the ground on which to affirm human worth. The ontological reality of humanity renewed in him constitutes the gospel imperative to pray for the coming of God's kingdom and to fight against all that defies and dishonors God. "There is no way from us to others than the path through Christ, his word, and our following him. Immediacy is a delusion."[18] In Christ we know how much the world is loved by God. In him the true meaning of "right" is revealed. His crucifixion reveals to us God's judgment upon sin, and his resurrection carries the hope that God will establish justice throughout the earth (Isa 42:4; Rev 18:10). This hope is definitive of our conception of "right" and also generative of ethical activity because Jesus Christ is the mediator in whom the universal meaning of "right" is both established and revealed (1 Tim

2:5; Heb 9:15; 12:24). The very possibility of a Christian ethic of rights is that the word of God breaks into secular life and calls all humanity back to its origin in God and forward in hope. Until Christ's kingdom comes, God's command, or—to use Bonhoeffer's phrase, the "concrete" claim laid to humanity by the merciful and holy God in Jesus Christ—stands between every person and the other.[19]

The way forward for Bonhoeffer is thus an eschatological focus that supplies a definition of "the natural" as the form of life preserved for Christ by God the Father after the fall and directed toward redemption and the coming of Christ. Bonhoeffer defines "the natural"—and we adopt this definition – with reference to God's providential preservation of the fallen created order until his kingdom comes on earth. Natural life has been formed and given by God, and it is to be preserved and protected for his sake. The word "natural" implies an element of the independence of a being's status as creature.y. "The natural" is the form of life that embraces the entire human race and may be understood as both an end in itself and the means to an end.[20] "Natural rights" may therefore be affirmed as inherent in the nature of human beings. It is for the sake of Christ's coming again, and because of the work of the Holy Spirit in enabling the world to become itself, that natural life must be lived within a framework of respect for one another as creatures before God and may be expressed in terms of rights and, consequently, of duties. For the sake of Christ and the coming kingdom, the human body has a claim to food and shelter. The human body has a claim to joy because God created and wills it for joy.[21] The claim to joy, or to food and shelter, is not grounded in mutual obligation but in God's will and purpose: "It is in the first place God who stands up for these rights."[22] For Bonhoeffer, the content of natural rights is a proper topic for Christian ethics and reason for action: "[T]he urgent question of what guarantees these rights will arise again and again."[23] Similarly, we may affirm on this basis that natural rights are God-given.

Of himself or herself the individual can claim no rights before God, but rights may and should be recognized in relation to other individuals and in society because "the natural" preserved for Christ yields an understanding of "natural rights" as an expression of the respect due to God the Creator: "There are no rights before God, but the natural, understood as a pure gift of God, becomes rights with respect to human beings. The rights of natural life are the reflection of the glory of God the Creator in the m.dst of the fallen world. They are not in the first place what human beings can lay claim to for their own interest, but what God guarantees."[24] Natural rights are not guaranteed by human law nor by consensus but by God who orders what is required to protect, preserve, and enhance natural life until Christ comes again. Thus, for instance, we may say that bodily life contains within itself the right to its own preservation because God has willed the continuation of life: "Since it is God's will that there should be human life on earth only in the form of bodily life . . . it is for the sake of the whole man that the body possesses the right to be preserved." Similarly, subjective rights attach to human life because it is God's will that human life exists on earth as bodily life: "It follows from the will of God, who creates individuals to give them eternal life, that there is a natural right of the individual."[25] In other words, a Christian ethic of rights does not rely on a general notion of universal humanity or shared human experience for its rationales, coherence, and norms. Humanity per se is not the measure of human rights. Rather, as mediator between God and humankind, and between one individual and another, Christ's humanity is the reason and the measure for a theological account of natural, subjective rights. This is the ground on which, we may extrapolate, Christian people can engage in human rights advocacy in workplaces *etsi deus non daretur* (even if, or as if, there were no God).[26]

True Right in Christ

Barth affirmed something similar, though not identical, in his 1928/1929 lectures at Münster and Bonn when stating that my neighbor's right is found in Christ and that I must submit to it because he or she is the bearer of God's command to me. Like Bonhoeffer, Barth's account of ethical responsibility is Christologically and soteriologically structured.[27] This theological focus is not optional or secondary but irreducibly part of Christian ethics. Whatever can, and should, be said about ethical responsibility begins with the encounter between God and humanity that we know preeminently in Christ. One cannot break free of one's neighbor because Christ is present for me in him or her. Consequently, says Barth, "right" is not only a means of setting limits between people and regulating potential conflicts but a way of expressing the truth that Christ lives in my neighbor.[28]

> Right seeks our acknowledgement, not as the right which has fallen from heaven, but truly and honestly as human right, as what it undoubtedly is in its whole content, namely, codified prudence of all others in opposition to me, and the organized defense of all others against my possible encroachments, a defence and prudence in face of which I cannot possibly forget that I, for my part, have to rely on them too in relation to all these others.[29]

It is important to note that the language here is not of "rights" but of "right." Whereas Bonhoeffer speaks freely not only of right (*G Recht*) and

God's right (*Gottes Recht*) but of "natural right" (*natürliche Recht*), "natural rights" (*natürlichen Rechtes*), "rights" (*Rechte*), "the rights of natural life" (*die Rechte des natürlichen Lebens*), human rights (*Menschenrechte*), "the right to bodily life" (*das Recht auf das leibliche Leben*), "the right to life" (*das Recht auf das Leben*), and so on, Barth's language is more constrained. He speaks of "right" more than "rights," "human right" (*in seinem Wesen menschen-recht*[30]) more than "human rights" (*menschliche Rechte*), the neighbor as "the bearer of right" (*Rechtsträger*) rather than as subject of natural rights. In other words, Barth's language reflects his emphasis on subjective "rights" as belonging to human law and public polity (*öffentliches Recht*[31]) and "right" as having an objective meaning because of God's self-revelation in Christ. Whereas Bonhoeffer is relatively comfortable with the transition from this affirmation to recognition of subjective rights, Barth holds back—apparently because of the ambiguity of meaning that such language contains.

For Barth, theological discussion centers around "true right" as revealed by God in Christ and understood under the concept of reconciliation. To speak of "true right" is to say that God has revealed himself to us in Christ. Talk about "right" is a doctrinal undertaking that calls into question all other approaches. Any attempt to do so outside of God's reconciliation in Christ is misguided: "We have to see that our life is apostasy from God."[32] This leads to wariness about investing too heavily in any secularist account of human rights, or worldly right, that "is not in us but comes to us."[33] The implication is that acknowledgment of worldly right(s) might have more to do with bourgeois ideology, class warfare, the perverted desires of a governor, and such, rather than with witness to Christ. Hence his strong language to distinguish between true right (*wirkliche Recht*) and profane right (*weltliches Recht*). True right is revealed in Christ in whom we are reconciled to God. Our neighbors can be the bearers of true right by virtue of divine grace—though, he warns, neighbors can also be messengers of the tempter! "It is not self-evident that those who come to us are indeed the children of God whose right is the true right to which we must submit, just as it is not self-evident that we ourselves are such."[34] Claims for true right honor God's name: "True right is that which is made over and loaned to me, loaned directly from the source of all right."[35] Profane right belongs among sin as part of the social order that begets conflict and perpetuates collisions of interests and indifference to the needs of others. The problem of profane or worldly right(s) begins where one person's right comes up against that of another: "The problem of right begins where the collision of my activity with the social order begins."[36] Profane right might be devilish and wrong. It begins at the point of conflict between public order and private life, social disorder and personal aggrandizement, self-interest and the common good, and its enactment is characterized too often by selfishly motivated coercion.

So far, then, we have seen that Bonhoeffer's theological account of subjective, natural rights has three parts: first, "the natural" is that preserved by God until Christ's coming; second, any action to undermine "the natural" denies that it is preserved by God and dishonors him;[37] third, natural rights may serve as a way of expressing the gifts of biblical revelation with respect to "the natural" and of responding to them. Bonhoeffer's account of God's providential preservation of all creation oriented toward Christ is the axiom between the objective reality of God's right and its subjective import. By contrast, Barth avoids the language of subjective, natural rights and, to the best of my knowledge, offers no such account on theological grounds. He fears that a faulty synthesis between natural and/or human rights and general revelation outside of Christ seems to entail resistance to the question of natural rights. For our purposes, the problem raised here is a matter not so much of what is affirmed but of what is denied. The problem is not the affirmation that Jesus Christ is the measure and uncontainable content of "right," but the hesitancy to consider how natural, subjective rights might be recognized as imputed to humanity by God. It is Barth's hesitancy, rather than any questions with respect to the affirmations that he does make, that is the reason for this chapter. Jesus Christ is the measure and content of "true right," but how does this truth take shape in our lives? What trail does it leave for Christian people engaged in human rights advocacy to follow? Barth's emphasis on the objective side of true right in Christ reminds us of the basis for all meaningful speaking about "right." But where does this leave us with respect to the kinds of moves made by Bonhoeffer regarding subjective rights?

We ask these questions with caution because it would be wrong to suggest that Barth is unconcerned about the role that the modern concept of human rights has to play in earthly governance. To the contrary, that Barth maintains a positive stance is evident at several points in his career, especially toward the end. Under the general heading "The Struggle for Human Righteousness," Barth writes in *Church Dogmatics* IV.4, *Lecture Fragments* about the "divinely ordained" role that human rights can play in seeking after and inquiring into the practical import of God's kingdom (Matt 6:33; Luke 12:31), in revolting against unrighteousness, in taking a stand against the wiles of the devil (Eph 6:11), and in shouldering one's share of the sufferings of Christ (2 Tim 2:3):

> Christians pray to God that he will cause his righteousness to appear and dwell on a new earth under a new heaven. Meanwhile they act in accor-

dance with their prayer as people who are responsible for the rule of human righteousness, that is, for the preservation and renewal, the deepen-
ing and extending, of the divinely ordained human safeguards of human
rights (*menschlichen Rechtes*), human freedom, and peace on earth.[38]

The language of human rights is not absent from his writings even
though, as noted above, he appears typically more comfortable with that of
"human right" and "human righteousness" than that of subjective rights,
or human rights. Rights belong to human law. "Theologically the concept
of right (or law), like that of education, falls under the concept of reconciliation, of the kingdom of Christ among sinners. It does not fall under the
concept of creation."[39] Nevertheless, the implication is that human rights
can perform a useful function in the fight against disorder or what Barth
refers to as "the lordless powers."[40] Rights are part of the secular vocation
of the state to administer human justice in contexts where politics is often
conflictual and poisoned with sinful desires. Rights belong to the reality in
which we now live and that is distorted radically by sin. Rights as we know
them today do not drop from heaven, as it were, but are acknowledged in
societies where people try to protect themselves against others in a variety
of ways. Even so, Barth holds back from an account of subjective, natural
rights of the kind that Bonhoeffer develops.

Resisting Trojan Horses

Barth's resistance to the language and conceptuality of subjective, natural
rights is an important and vitally necessary safeguard against compromise
with respect to the theological beginning point of all Christian ethics and
anthropology in God. He opposes with every ounce of his being the kind of
natural law thinking that allows persons and events other than the revelation attested in Holy Scripture (notably Nazi ideology) to become binding
and obligatory, and we must do the same. Any such notion demands the
response "No!" (*Nein*). "The logic of the matter demands," writes Barth,
"that even if we only lend our little finger to natural theology, there necessarily follows the denial of the revelation of God in Jesus Christ."[41] He and
others affirmed that theology should make no appeal to the knowability of
God other than through Christ and Holy Scripture. Otherwise a Trojan
horse would be present in the city; the standard and content of church
proclamation would be in danger. The same point is expounded in *Church
Dogmatics* II.2 where Barth states clearly that unless ethical reflection takes
its starting point in the command of God, then it has nothing to do with
the truth of God:

The problem of ethics generally—the law or good or value which it seeks as a standard by which human action and modes of action are to be measured, and according to which they are to be performed, the problem of the truth and knowledge of the good—is no problem at all in the ethics immanent in the Christian conception of God, in the doctrine of the command of God. For in virtue of the fact that the command of God is the form of His electing grace, it is the starting-point of every ethical question and answer. It is the starting-point which is already given and to that extent presupposed and certain in itself, so that it can never be surpassed or compromised from any quarter.[42]

Too often, ethics that appeals to natural law imply a general revelation outside of Christ. Like the Israelites entering the land of Canaan, the temptation for Christian ethics is to worship the gods of the original inhabitants of the land. This temptation must be recognized for what it is and avoided.[43]

We still need to say "No!" to all free-standing conceptions of natural law independent of God and his will. A Christian ethic of human rights cannot head off down a route of natural theology that would in effect amount to an attempt at self-justification before God, seeking knowledge of good and evil like Adam and Eve behind God's command. Western societies today are in situations similar to Nazi Germany, albeit in the limited sense that widely recognized standards of right and wrong are not God's standards; the aggressive militarism and unbridled capitalism of our own day must, like the atrocities of previous generations, be confronted with God's gracious, reconciling, and redeeming action, and the hope of his kingdom to come. It is not the 1930s and 1940s all over again, yet there is no innocence outside of Christ. The human condition is no less sinful now than when Barth and Bonhoeffer wrote. All human rights discourses are subject to perversion and fall short of the glory of God. In the relatively affluent West, human rights are readily associated with a "me culture" in which the protection of individual liberty takes priority over redistributive or attributive justice, or collective rights. Some construals of basic human rights, such as a supposed right to self-ownership give rise to supposedly unrestricted rights to noninterference that run counter to Christian convictions.[44] A human rights culture can easily generate conflictual modes of settling disputes. The history of human rights is so closely allied to Western liberalism that aspects of its global expansion can be construed as yet another form of Western imperialism.[45] Postmodern notions of deconstructed legal subjects offer a ceaseless welter of new meanings of rights but with little recognition of "group rights,"—for example, for workers, refugees, groups of displaced persons, and so forth.[46] This list of deep-rooted problems in human rights cultures could go on. But can we, must we, say more?

The flip side of the risk of compromise is that we isolate all talk of creation from Christology, thereby plunging Christian ethics into an unnecessary dualism between creation and redemption that weakens the mission of the church. Christian ethics becomes dysfunctional when it forgets any of the commands of God, who is both Creator and Reconciler, and if the bonds between creaturehood and discipleship disintegrate. Why? Because this turns redemption into something unconnected to the created order and bearing no real relation to it; this denies, or at least neglects to affirm, the fully Trinitarian nature of God's action toward the world. Bonhoeffer was aware of this danger. Hence his emphasis on recognizing the truth of the entire world in Christ. "Things work out quite differently," as Bonhoeffer says, "when the reality of God and the reality of the world are recognized in Christ. In that way, the world, the natural, the profane, and reason are seen as included in God from the beginning."[47] "God accompanies *the creature*," Barth writes. "This means that He affirms and approves and recognizes and respects the autonomous actuality and therefore the autonomous activity of the creature as such."[48] The question is what it means to enact faith in Christ as it concerns our interactions with fellow human beings. When we say "I believe in God . . . ," what is implied about our fellow human beings as creatures of the living God? Faith has an objective side but is not detached from implications for our attitudes and actions toward others. Our question is whether confession of these doctrinal truths is compatible today with the affirmation of subjective rights. In other words, we want to explore the implications that might at least follow from confession of true right in Christ for all human subjects.

Revisiting the Problem of "the Natural" in Protestant Ethics

We take up these questions initially against the backdrop of the so-called problem of "the natural" in mid-twentieth-century Protestant ethics because it is important to ensure that appropriate distinctions are drawn between Trojan horses of the kind discussed above and accounts of "the natural" informed by the Christian doctrine of the Holy Trinity. Bonhoeffer's perception of the problem is summarized in the section of his *Ethics* entitled "The Natural," in his observation that the concept of the natural has fallen into disrepute in Protestant ethics.[49] Strands of Protestant theology had allowed the natural or penultimate to be diminished in significance for the sake of the ultimate. This one-sidedness was manifest in a "two spheres" kind of thinking that kept the realm of the natural subordinate to that of grace, the spiritual separate from the secular, and in its most extreme form, the world apart from Christ: "The monk and the cultural Protestant of the nineteenth century represent these two possibilities."[50] This kind of divided worldview opposes the rational and the revelational, the sacred and the profane, the natural and the supernatural, and severs "the natural" and "natural right" from the operation of God's grace. Bonhoeffer's attack is not against Barth. Both are clear that an outlook that divides or opposes the two is profoundly unbiblical and neglects to affirm the truth of the world as reconciled to God in Christ: "The New Testament is concerned only with the realization [*Wirklichwerden*] of the Christ-reality in the contemporary world that it already embraces."[51] Yet, as Bonhoeffer anticipated, it has been difficult to break the spell of this kind of thinking.[52]

More than fifty years since Bonhoeffer made his observations, the problem persists in remarkably similar form. Witness Colin E. Gunton's *Brief Theology of Revelation—The 1993 Warfield Lectures* in which, like Bonhoeffer, he is concerned at how the problem of "the natural" in twentieth-century Protestant theology had constrained adequate engagement with the world. Like Bonhoeffer, Gunton is aware of the divorce in Protestant theology of creation from redemption and of the grave consequences for a Christian outlook on the world. His diagnosis entails exposure of a fundamental weakness in modern theologies, notably the tendency to overemphasise the immediacy of revelation rather than its mediacy in nature, scripture, and tradition. This weakness he blames, at least in part, on Barth's hesitancy to develop a theology of the natural in fully Trinitarian terms:

> The overemployment of the category [of revelation] arose in the course of a proper reaction to the neglect, particularly in Barth's attempts to overcome the epistemological challenges presented to him by his predecessors and to allow the God of Jesus Christ to come to rational expression on his own terms. But it was, I believe, an overemployment, and resulted in an imbalance in the systematic structure of Barth's theology, as well as in those that were influenced by him.[53]

Gunton presents his analysis with reference to G. W. F. Hegel's phenomenology of consciousness where "immediacy" requires "mediation" for its growth or development. For Hegel, there is a deep connection between this conceptuality and his idealist notions of history as the process whereby humans become ever more rational. Modern theologies countered this, says Gunton, by emphasizing the immediacy of revelation. Similarly, Gunton observes that twentieth-century Protestant theology tended to frame its response to Kant by elevating revelation to a first-order doctrine, thereby repeating "the Kantian and foundationalist error that epistemology is prior to the practice of a discipline."[54] Barth, says Gunton, demonstrated effectively that the doctrine of creation is as much a product of revelation as other doctrines of faith but failed to develop an adequate account of the Holy Spirit as mediator of the knowledge of creation: "Although he [Barth] has a doctrine of creation, there is reason to suppose that he scarcely begins to do justice to the ontological question of the kind of reality that the world is."[55] Barth, he says, held back from seeking revelation in the structures of the created world, thereby producing a stunted and inadequately biblical theology of revelation.

The effect was to leave Christian people without the means of expressing the logical link between a theology of nature and an account of the human capacity to appropriate the commands of God the Creator. What is needed, says Gunton, is a fuller account of the world's worldliness that allows "God to be God" and "the world to be the world." We need to see again that "a theology of nature is the gift of biblical revelation."[56] Working with the grain of Barth's theological convictions, Gunton suggests that we distinguish between a theology of nature (a theological account of what things are by virtue of their createdness) and a natural theology (an account of what things are based on the supposition that the world is in some way continuous with God and reveals the truth about human nature independent of revelation in Christ). Writing with concerns similar to those voiced by Bonhoeffer fifty years earlier with respect to the so-called "problem of the natural" in Protestant ethics, Gunton looks for ways to inquire into God's operations in the natural order of things without harm to a strong doctrine of revelation.

Our concerns are similar but are focused on the implications for Christian engagement with teleological ethics of natural and human rights. The suggestion in what follows is that the conceptual framework that Gunton develops bears directly on an ethic of human rights and, in particular, on Christian engagement with teleological approaches to the ethics of natural and human rights. The issue may be construed as follows: What is the relation between a self-standing conception of natural law that is independent of God and one that is derivative of the revealed will of God and an account of divine providence? Alternatively stated: What are the differences between teleological and eschatological reasoning with respect to natural rights, and are these differences important for Christian ethics and engagement with public policy in this field? Following Gunton's moves to develop a fully Trinitarian theology of "the natural," we argue that it is not simply a matter of natural theology over against a theology of revelation, or of teleology over against eschatology. We need instead a theology of the natural world, and its revelation to us of both itself and God.[57] It is not simply a matter of positing a Christological and Trinitarian theology of nature over against a natural theology, the command of God as Creator over against the command of God as Reconciler, but of perceiving and giving expression to the role of Holy Spirit in the natural order.

Mediation and the Role of the Holy Spirit

Consider, in particular, Gunton's account of the Holy Spirit's mediation throughout creation of the saving presence of Christ. In an attempt to develop an adequate theology of nature and of general revelation, he draws heavily on the Johannine account of God's giving of the Spirit to the church. He writes:

> without the revealing action of the Spirit, we shall not know Jesus as the way of God. But because the Spirit is not the Son, and the Son is not the Father, there are differences of function and action, and therefore differences of mediation. The clue to the doctrine of revelation is accordingly to be found in unravelling the different patterns of mediation with which we are concerned.[58]

"Mediation" is an important word in this quotation. A fuller recognition of the distinctive role of the Spirit in revealing the mysteries of God to us will, says Gunton, allow the possibility of mediation through otherness: "The Father is indeed made known by Jesus, but as one who is greater than he (John 14:28), and so beyond all we can say and think: one revealed by humiliation and cross, but revealed none the less as other."[59] Knowledge of God is mediated preeminently through Christ but also, by virtue of the power of the Holy Spirit, through the "otherness" of, for example, music or the findings of modern science. If the Holy Spirit is the presence of God in many and diverse human attestations to God's creation, then each of these realities can potentially mediate the presence of God to us. God himself mediates his revelation to us.

For radical Protestant ethics, faith in reason of the kind expounded by secularist ethics usurps faith in Christ and must be replaced by the evangelical and eschatological hope of new being in Christ. Eschatology eliminates or significantly downgrades teleology. But is this theologically adequate? The implication of Gunton's position is that we may not simply reject as comparatively inferior a teleological ethic when set over against an eschatological ethic. Radical Protestant ethics is often antiteleological and suspicious of eudaemonistically construed ethical thinking because the latter claims to take humans on what Socrates called "the upward journey of the soul to the intelligible realm."[60] Teleological ethics with roots in Plato and Aristotle tends to hold that moral conversion and progression is possible through reason, the identification and acceptance of basic and shared truths, the shunning of ignorance and striving for knowledge, and the fully perfected soul. For Gunton, however, mere dismissal of all such ethics fails to give an adequate pneumatological account of the kind of reality that the world is, even in its fallen state, within divine providence. Merely to reject a teleological ethic that expresses the fundamental human desire to flourish and attain well-being on the basis that such an ethic has not died with Christ hinders a full theological conceptuality of the relation between creation and revelation. A more adequately Trinitarian construal of "the natural" is needed to determine systematically the relation between God and the world; "distinct beings and yet personally related by personal mediation as creator and creation."[61] By implication, it is not enough merely to reject teleological notions of natural rights as inadequate because they are not conceived as rooted in and moving toward God. Trinitarian theology offers other possibilities for an understanding of creation informed by revelation: "The fact that the world is rational at all is a mark of its coming from its creator, but even that is an insight that has been attained only in cultures where the Bible has been a determinative influence, suggesting that it is the fruit of divine revelation."[62] Rather than rejecting a teleological ethic merely because it is not a revelation ethic, Gunton's challenge is that we think theologically about the truth and untruth of reason. Rather than simplistically opposing the rational and the revelational, or setting natural theology over against a theology of revelation, he wants us to consider the mediated reality of God's Spirit in the world. Whatever else it is, says Gunton, revelation in Christian theology is mediated; the truth of the gospel is realized for us, or mediated to us, by the Spirit of truth.[63]

For our purposes this means, on the one hand, that a Christian theology of revelation and/or ethic of rights *does not* expect human reason to ground itself or to seek an understanding of human existence, including natural rights, apart from revelation. John Finnis, as we see below, roots natural rights and human rights (which are, for him, synonymous) in universal and teleological truths about human nature and the rationality of human persons. The obvious theological problem is that this nullifies the relation of natural rights to divine providence in a manner that potentially cuts practical reason off from the source of human life and the possibility of renewal. On the other hand, Christian eschatology directs us not only toward the end times but also to responsibilities in the present day to work for God's praise and glory. We must seek the Holy Spirit's mediation of God's glory in the things that have been made (Ps 19:1). Gunton puts the matter in terms of a ladder between the created and uncreated: "Revelation—God's personal interaction with the world through his Son and Spirit—suggests ways of seeing parallels between uncreated and created rationality, but we need not be too anxious about finding a ladder between them. God has let that down already in the incarnation of his eternal Son within the structures of worldly being."[64] My preferred image is that of a dual focus lens that allows us to "see" or to think both eschatologically and teleologically, to see both the forest and the trees, to confess the truth of Christ risen and ascended while working in secularist contexts with teleological frameworks of ethics. Dual focus lenses have two points through which light passes. Their various applications in, for example, laser technology offer processing advantages because either or both focal points may be used at any given time. The "focal points" in question for our purpose are eschatological and teleological ways of conceiving of natural rights.

Consequently, we may neither leap to condemnation because an ethic is teleological rather than eschatological nor accept a teleology in which we reach God rather than God reaches us. Neither of these options is adequate. The former is unlikely to be sensitive enough to the work of the Holy Spirit in the world. The latter founds an ethic of natural rights on universal truths about human nature rather than with reference to the triune being of God. Instead, says Gunton, we need a desire to learn from the economic activity of the Spirit of God—which is oriented toward particularity. A central argument in *The One, the Three and the Many* is that the economic activity of the Holy Spirit brings to completion that for which each person and thing has been created: "[T]he Spirit's peculiar office is to realize the true being of each created thing by bringing it, through Christ, into saving relation with God the Father."[65] By extension, the way forward in developing a Christian ethic of natural rights must be based on the operation of the Holy Spirit in bringing to perfection the work of Christ and God's saving purposes. We need a pneumatologically and eschatologically informed conception of human reason in order better to discern God's indwelling of the world and, on the basis of theological confession, to explore the implications that follow for Christian moral reasoning and engagement in politics.

This strongly Christological and eschatological focus on natural rights is a necessary prerequisite for the dual focus mentioned above. Only if we believe that God's Spirit mediates to us the hope of the gospel and its demands is there any reason to employ the dual focus of historico-teleological and eschatological ways of looking at natural rights. Only if we believe that natural rights should be respected *for God's sake* is there reason enough to engage in human rights advocacy. If we act for God's sake, however, the high-energy density of God's presence promises what Michael Welker calls "a charged field of experiences."[66] In this "field" Gunton's question about

how the "secular features of the world's being" are relevant for an understanding of its capacity to be the vehicle of revelation becomes intensely
pertinent.[67] Gunton's tentative answer, namely that we pray in faith for
God's assistance to see "what is there before our eyes," is answered only
as the Spirit enables believers to bring prayers of intercession before God,
and as the eschatological hope sends us back in faith to the historical to
seek God's presence in the everyday work of identifying and protecting
natural rights.[68] An ahistorical eschatology would amount to a flight from
the created order. As Bonhoeffer wrote: "Christ died for the world, and it
is only in the midst of the world that Christ is Christ."[69] Only unbelief can
wish for something less than Christ or shun involvement in the world. It
is only in the world that we may let the reality of the Holy Spirit come to
us in ever-new ways, not least as we seek both to support and to learn from
practitioners in various fields of human rights (many of them disciples of
Jesus Christ) who work daily to identify and lobby for the protection of
human rights.

"The Natural" and the Economic Activity of God's Spirit

To illustrate the issues involved we turn to the teleological account of natural rights offered by John Finnis, the neo-Thomist and philosopher of jurisprudence. Briefly, Finnis's work is arguably the most substantial attempt in
recent years to develop a natural law-based conception of human rights.
Indeed, his restatement of natural law is one of the few to warrant serious
interdisciplinary attention by thinkers outside Christian theology and ethics. He claims that human rights as we know them today are close enough
to theological (notably Aquinas's) treatment of *ius* for theorists not to
worry much about the differences between them.[70] Despite the fact that
the expression "human rights" is relatively new, having entered everyday
parlance only since the founding of the United Nations in 1945, he claims
that "human rights" talk is compatible, if not more or less synonymous,
with premodern theological concepts of "natural right(s)." Both discourses
emphasize "the truth that every human being is a locus of human flourishing."[71] When the idioms and cultural differences of Aquinas's day and our
own are taken into account, he says, any outstanding issues are more like
differences of dialect than of moral language. Modern rights discourse tends
to focus on the beneficiary of a just relationship, above all on the individual's
doing and having.[72] Yet, the modern grammar of rights provides a way of
expressing virtually all the requirements of practical reasonableness—which
is precisely what Aquinas wanted to do. We consider briefly Finnis's claim
that natural law is, in effect, something freestanding and independent of

the knowledge of God. There will be implications for Christians working in secular contexts where God's existence makes no apparent difference to an ethic of rights or to moral reasoning about rights.

Four points about Finnis's work are relevant. First, he argues that medieval and modern writers express the same demands of justice, albeit in different contexts and using different terminology. Hence his claim of synonymity (or "as near as damn it," as he says, when one has taken into account the differences of context and idiom) between human natural rights and human rights.[73] This claim probably fails on strictly historical grounds, but the debate is related only tangentially to our argument here.[74] Second, he holds that modern rights-talk amplifies "undifferentiated reference to 'the common good' by providing a usefully detailed listing of the various aspects of human flourishing."[75] The manner in which he does this is different from that employed by Aquinas but, again, this issue is not centrally relevant to our purposes. Third, he believes that all persons are capable of discerning basic human goods because of the universal nature of human experience. There is no need to ground ethical obligation in God's will because the reasonableness of self-evident human requirements carries its own force. A philosopher of jurisprudence in the Aristotelian tradition of natural law, Finnis treats ethics as practical because it is "questioning and reflection *in order to be able to act.*"[76] Ethics, he says, is about practical knowledge or knowledge that seeks the realization in practice of real and true goods attainable by human persons. Basic human goods (bodily life, knowledge and aesthetic experience, harmony between individuals and groups, harmony between the different dimensions within the self)[77] can be grasped prereflectively and immediately by practical reason. Fourth, like Aquinas, Finnis demands acceptance of the basic value of truth in order for the basic requirements of reasoning to be grasped, and he assumes the existence of a comprehensible reality independent of human minds. He recognizes an essential directiveness in human reason.[78] This directiveness was recognized, he says, by Plato and Aristotle, and supplies the essential content of reasons for actions.[79] It is premoral and transcultural because the basic requirements for flourishing pertain to all humans; basic human goods are the fundamental requirements of practical reasonableness for all societies. Points three and four are of most interest to us here.

For Finnis, a good explanation can be made of the reasonableness of particular acts without reference to the existence or will of God. Some people, he says, allow belief in "God" to provide them with an added dimension of reasoning for pursuit of the common good. For them, God functions as the basis of their obligation, and their explication of the requirements of practical reasonableness is a direct expression of their religious concern.

Others think that "God" is a term burdened with widely varying associations. Peculiarly theological investigation of the requirements of practical reason is unnecessary for the moral life. God might be the conclusion to moral reasoning but is not necessarily the premise. In any case, little is to be gained by positing the existence of God because human goods are grasped prereflectively and immediately by practical reason; basic human goods provide all the objective knowledge needed for human flourishing. His claim is thus of functional synonymity between Aquinas's theological understanding of natural right(s) and present-day human rights. Aquinas's notion of right as the object of justice may be understood, he notes, as referring to "the other person's right(s) [*ius*]."[80] This is, he implies, close enough to the present-day function of human rights to warrant their being treated as more or less synonymous.

There are a variety of problems with Finnis's position, many of which have been noted elsewhere. Jean Porter is unconvinced that the principles of practical reason adequately express the way that reason functions.[81] Anthony J. Lisska demonstrates that Finnis omits from his account of Aristotle and Aquinas an adequate theory of human essence, thereby severing his treatment of practical reasonableness from Aquinas's metaphysics of finality: "Finnis uses only a method and rejects the core."[82] Ralph McInerny argues that Germain Grisez's treatment of basic human goods (on which Finnis draws) does not equate to Aquinas's teaching about the good.[83] Historical critics challenge the extent to which modern concepts of subjective rights had conceptual equivalents in the medieval and ancient world, and whether Aquinas and his fellow Scholastics recognized a subjective sense of "right."[84] Secularist critics have complained that Finnis gives little indication of how to get from prereflective intuitions about basic human goods to human rights law that could protect these goods.[85] We may agree with Porter and McInerny about the exaggerated role given to the principles of practical reason in comparison with Aquinas's own definition of *jus* as "the fair" or "what's fair" within a theology of the *ratio Dei*. We may also agree with historical critics that Finnis goes a step too far in claiming that human rights as we know them today are close enough to Aquinas's treatment of *ius* for theorists not to worry much about the differences between them. He goes too far in minimizing differences between Aquinas's concept of right as "the just thing" within a theology of the *ratio Dei* and *ordo* and modern analyses of claim- and liberty-rights.[86] Self-evidently, however, Finnis's rehabilitation of Aquinas's theory of natural law is developed without reference to God and/or metaphysics. He offers "a rather deliberate sketch of a theory of natural law without needing to advert to the question of God's existence or nature or will,"[87] holding that the existence of God should not be used to justify claims about objective norms of human flourishing. The challenge is to account for this kind of natural law thinking, or teleological humanism, evangelically, and to work with the resources that it offers.

Gospel and Law

So far, then, we have seen that in Christian ethics there is no meaningful human telos apart from the grace of God in Christ; any other end that we might set for ourselves is invalid or, at the very least, incomplete when not subordinated to God's word: "The concrete form of this teleological power of grace is the person of Jesus Christ himself."[88] Natural teleology (of the kind propounded by Finnis) is not a foundational concept for Christian practice but a derivative practice that, for the believer, depends on talk about God—Father, Son, and Holy Spirit. Christian humanism has reference beyond the merely human—though this reference might not always be explicit. If, however, the truth of nature's telos is found in Christ, then Christian moral reasoning has work to do if Christian people are to speak about the practical meaning of this truth in present-day contexts. Repair work is needed in Protestant ethics if talk about teleology, the natural, and natural rights is to be pursued without sinking into either antagonism or indifference. Both Bonhoeffer and Barth contributed considerably to this repair work. Even so, a challenge remains for our own day with respect to how believers may push toward ethical concreteness in their everyday lives and moral reasoning, not least in a human rights culture. If "right" is not a matter of subjective taste or human decision but an attribute of God, a power concealed in the crucified Christ and an aspect of the triune God's revealed glory, then we might expect revealed knowledge and the vision of God to inspire more than vagueness and generalizations in both prayer and moral reasoning. If Christian people are called to be "doers of the word" (Jas 1:22 AV), then questions about how believers make moral choices in ways that seek the kingdom of God before all else are both appropriate to and necessary for the life of faith.

At its broadest, this challenge may be construed as questioning how believers make moral choices about human ends and flourishing that implement their commitment of faith. As Webster puts it: "How does the Christian agent's reading of the way the world is (a reading which is articulated through the language of justification, faith and so on) actually translate into moral policy?"[89] General answers may be offered as, for instance, in Rowan Williams's essay "Making Moral Decisions" in *Cambridge Companion to Christian Ethics*: "[E]thics is not a matter of the individual's likes or dislikes but . . . a difficult discovering of something about yourself, a discovering of what has already shaped the person you are and is moulding you in this or that direction . . . discovering what is most 'natural' to you."[90] Qualifications might be added about how the lives of believers are shaped by membership in the church, partaking of the sacraments, participation in worship, and so on. The problems of formalism, rigorism, and codification in Christian moral reasoning might be denounced routinely, and one might guard habitually against implying that Christianity is a rules-based religion that binds its followers into particular patterns of conduct and thought. Even so, the operations (or intuitions) of the Christian moral agent often remain somewhat vague and mysterious. Our question is whether Barth's account of how the law is contained in the gospel can help us to analyze better which moral choices correspond to what we know in Christ of true humanity and its flourishing.

Contrary to many interpretations of his work that center around the ecclesiastical almost exclusively, Barth's writings are packed with considerations for the believer at work in diverse secular contexts. In seeming anticipation of Gunton's insights, he writes: "Knowing that the world outside is not just darkness without light, Christians have the freedom—and in obedience are to a large extent under the obligation—to take seriously their solidarity with those outside and to take their place alongside them without making any claims."[91] Reference to Bonhoeffer's *Letters and Papers from Prison* follows immediately after this statement. So, too, does an account of the nature of witness at times and in places where spoken proclamation is not possible. Do not, he urges believers, underrate the objective knowledge of God that is at work in the world outside the church. To be a witness might mean making one's whole life a text that is accessible to non-Christians as well as fellow believers: "In the way that Christians shape their lives as people of the world confronting the same problems as others, their life's task in the midst of others documents the Word, brings it to notice, and draws attention to it."[92] As people of the world, they owe their fellows reasoned participation in its affairs. "Their affair is to be unassuming and resolute doers of the Word and in this way to be witnesses to it in the non-Christian world."[93] Their witness might often have the character of resistance and will seek an end to vacillation in the face of evil. The "good fight of the faith" (1 Tim 6:12) will necessarily entail battles and a share of suffering as a soldier of Christ (2 Tim 2:3). It relies on the unity of the commanding God in all times, places, and situations, and on unity between God and man in the living Mediator.[94] In him, God the Creator is God the Reconciler. Christ Jesus does not cancel but fulfills the law of the Old Covenant (Matt 5:17-19; 1 Cor 9:21; Gal 6:2). The requirements of the law are not abrogated or overturned but fulfilled: "For freedom Christ has set us free" (Gal 5:1).

> Do not think that I have come to abolish the law or the prophets; I have come not to abolish but to fulfill. For truly I tell you, until heaven and earth pass away, not one letter, not one stroke of a letter, will pass from the law until all is accomplished. Therefore, whoever breaks one of the least of these commandments, and teaches others to do the same, will be called least in the kingdom of heaven; but whoever does them and teaches them will be called great in the kingdom of heaven. (Matt 5:17-19)

The gospel cannot be separated from law because the latter exposes the true nature of sin, leads to knowledge of sin, and answers the question: "What should we do?" The gospel contains the form of the law (as the tablets from Sinai were in the Ark of the Covenant).[95] How we formulate the relation between the two has a crucial bearing on the practicalities of moral reasoning, not least for believers in workplace scenarios.

A warning is necessary at this point, because attention to the precepts of the law is vulnerable always to the charge of self-righteousness on the part of believers, and rightly so. "For I tell you, unless your righteousness exceeds that of the scribes and Pharisees, you will never enter the kingdom of heaven" (Matt 5:20). Thus, Christopher Insole decries Barth's condemnation of the hubris of post-Enlightenment modernity as "a judgment sometimes characterized by the very self-righteousness that is being so effectively resisted."[96] Despite Barth's awareness of the problem, Insole smells a whiff of judgment over others in any claim that ethico-political actions are justified by distinctively and irreducibly religious reasons. He is concerned that attempts to use irreducibly religious or theological reasons when discussing the use of public power trample on "the frailty and vulnerability of our shared human condition."[97] Witness, he says, the heady political activism of late sixteenth- and early seventeenth-century English Puritans or the crusading certainty of George W. Bush's division of the world into "good" and "evil" following the terrorist attacks of September 11, 2001.[98] The visible and invisible church are too often conflated by those who think they know God's will for society. And we must agree to a considerable extent that this problematic conflation occurs. Any supposed duty to create a heaven on earth, a "city on a hill," is likely to slip into civil religion mingled with patriotism or other terrestrial loyalties. Samuel P. Huntington makes a similar point when describing America's civil religion as "the belief that Americans are God's 'chosen,' or, in Lincoln's phrase, 'almost chosen' people, that America is the 'new Israel,' with a divinely sanctioned mission to do good in the world."[99] Self-righteousness on the part of believers who march into

the public square with convictions that conflate religion and politics allows
George Washington to become Moses, and Lincoln to become Christ.[100]

Charges of self-righteousness and the potential abuse of religious power
cannot be dismissed lightly by a Christian ethic of rights that wants to push
toward ethical concreteness. Overzealous theological affirmations of "right"
action are potentially far more alarming than a defense of political liberalism
as compatible with Christian teaching about our fragile status as creatures
whose solidarity in sin requires frameworks of governance that respect the
dignity and freedom of individuals. Equally, however, indifference to the
political among churchgoers whose faith affects only their private morality
is a heartbreaking betrayal of both gospel and society. "Neither isolation
from the world nor a militant approach to it can be a consistent law of his
[the Christian's] action in the world."[101] "Hearers of the word, therefore,
who are not at the same time also doers, necessarily deceive themselves
(Jas 1:22). Believing that by knowing they possess the word of God, they
have already lost it again, because they assume that it is possible, even for a
moment, to have the word of God other than by doing it."[102] Worries about
pharisaic self-righteousness must not be allowed to diminish. If, however,
theological depiction of natural teleology is about giving expression to the
conviction that divine providence orders creaturely realities toward their
true natural and supernatural ends, Christian people cannot but risk rebel-
lion against that which threatens and imperils them. That nature's telos is
in Christ means that the true character of "right" is found in God and that
the shift to recognizing subjective rights is part of an essentially theological task of moral reasoning. As Eberhard Jüngel says of Barth's approach
to Christian moral reasoning: "[A] theory of praxis stands in need of dogmatics, not ethics."[103] Matters do not end with this affirmation, however.
We must ask what these truths look like practically and politically, and
what bearing they have on the Christian's role in society. Hence our push
toward ethical concreteness in the next chapter, where the claim is that the
requirements placed on Noah, in the covenant made between God and all
humanity, provide a basis for critical interaction with the reasonableness of
God's revealed moral law.

℘4℃

Human Rights and a Tropological Reading of Genesis 9:1-17

"Human rights" are a fine thing, but [the difficult question] is how can we ourselves make sure that our rights do not expand at the expense of the rights of others.

—Aleksandr Solzhenitsyn[1]

[Scripture] ought to be constantly poured into our ears or should ever proceed from our lips . . . And so it will come to pass that not only every purpose and thought of your heart, but also the wanderings and rovings of your imagination will become to you a holy and unceasing pondering of the Divine law.

—John Cassian[2]

The modern idea of subjective human rights is foreign to the Bible. This is not to say that the Bible and Christian tradition do not share many of the values for which the human rights movement has campaigned, but a Christian ethical perspective on rights is very different from that bound up with the revolutionary movements of the late eighteenth century, most notably in America and France, and the liberal philosophy of that era. "We hold these truths to be self-evident, that all men are created equal, that they are endowed by their Creator with certain inalienable Rights, that among these are Life, Liberty, and the pursuit of Happiness."[3] So begins the Declaration of Independence of the Thirteen Colonies, adopted by Congress, July 4, 1776—the quintessential example of natural law conceived as a free-standing entity, conceptually separate from God's will for humankind, and thus very different from an account of rights developed on the basis of a specifically Christian doctrine of God, Creator and Reconciler.

91

For Christian people engaged in human rights advocacy, however, merely to assert this difference is potentially harmful to the establishing of justice, reduction of poverty, protection of the environment, and other worthy goals, for which many strive day by day. Most practitioners seem to get on fairly well without the ministrations of theologians and moralists! Even so, Holy Scripture and theological perspectives on rights might yet yield insight and criteria for practical decision making. We argued in the previous chapter that this kind of investigation is both justifiable and necessary because the gospel of judgment and reconciliation does not separate us from the commands of God the Creator but restores them to us in Christ. Consequently, we turn to scripture to hear afresh the commands of God the Creator—with all that this teaches humankind about the call to life, respect for the life of others, the gifts of marriage, friendship, kinship, work, and so on. This is not to suggest that the Bible functions like an ethical textbook. To the contrary: "One simply cannot read the Bible the way one reads other books."[4] God's self-revelation in Holy Scripture invites readers whose exegetical reason is caught up in faith's abandonment of itself to divine grace. Nor is it to suggest that the Spirit of God does not speak from the experiences of human rights practitioners and those with whom, and for whom, they work. The theological framework outlined above resists resolutely what Bonhoeffer called a "two realms" kind of thinking; we need not think of worldly-Christian, natural-supernatural, profane-sacred, rational-revelational as static opposites that designate mutually exclusive spheres of operation.[5] Instead we press toward ways of thinking and acting that recognize the togetherness in Christ of the reality of God and the reality of the world, and thus seek to frame an ethic of natural rights as a way of talking about the proper dignity and worth of the creatures of God. This chapter moves toward a tropological reading of Genesis 9:1-17 for precisely such guidance.

So far, we have seen that human rights as we know them today are for many the culmination of morality in the modern period as a self-standing reality independent of God. For some, human rights are the best available political means of advancing peace and justice around the globe. For others, they are ideologically imbued political "fictions" that unite "the rights of man" in the liberal tradition with French Revolution-type conceptions of social justice.[6] There is no single understanding of human rights, and the rhetoric can be used for both good and ill. As Noam Chomsky pointed out in 1979, powerful governments have used human rights rhetoric to justify the supply of armaments to selected regimes that might be repressing the rights of their own people.[7] Yet, the witness of many faithful Christian people—lawyers, labor leaders, politicians, and the like—is that human rights can be a form of testimony to the righteousness of God. Practicing Christians, theologians, and moralists can say only a qualified "yes" to human rights as we know them today. Our interest in human rights is *indirect rather than direct*. Arguably, however, there are strong theological reasons for human rights advocacy, and this mode of struggle for human righteousness can be a powerful witness to the saving love of God. This chapter is thus a response to the disjunction that practitioners have to negotiate every day between theologically conceived notions of "right" and natural right on the one hand and present-day human rights on the other—without either pretending that there is unbroken continuity between the two or perceiving their difference in terms of unbridgeable strangeness.

Seeking Ethical and Moral Guidance from Scripture

Mindful of these considerations, our question is whether we may seek further ethical and moral guidance from Holy Scripture about the identification and significance of some rights as compared to others. So far, our observations have been broad based and general. Our pressing concern, however, is that human rights practitioners face specific questions about such matters as categories of rights; minimum ethical standards; relations between absolute, limited, and qualified rights; margins of appreciation in different countries; procedures and remedies; legal precedent; and proportionality. Holy Scripture does not provide direct answers to these kinds of questions yet remains "a lamp to my feet and a light to my path" (Ps 119:105). "All scripture is inspired by God and is useful for teaching, for reproof, for correction, and for training in righteousness, so that everyone who belongs to God may be proficient, equipped for every good work" (2 Tim 3:16-17). Traditional Christian witness is that scripture is in some sense normative. Faithful disciples have found guidance from Jesus Christ in its pages more than anywhere else. Consequently, we return again and again to exegesis and biblically informed questioning: "God must teach us if we are to become wise."[8]

Three "Short-Circuit" Options

Our problem, of course, is that it is not enough for a Christian ethic of rights to make easy allusions or uncritical jumps between biblical teaching and secularist notions of human rights. So, for instance, witness to Jesus as healer and teacher might be said to translate into rights to health care and education, but as J. Robert Nelson writes in "Human Rights in Creation and Redemption: A Protestant View"—a contribution to a volume of the

Journal of Ecumenical Studies devoted to human rights in religious traditions—issues arise quickly for those pursuing such a literal-factual approach to both biblical exegesis and human rights. What can be said, asks Nelson, about the supposedly self-evident right of freedom from slavery (UNDHR, Article 1) when the New Testament admonishes slaves to "be submissive to your masters" (1 Pet 2:18 *NASB*), or to the right to daily food (UNDHR, Article 25) when Paul says, "Anyone unwilling to work should not eat" (2 Thess 3:10)?[9] Human rights cannot simply be adopted unquestioningly by the church as their own because what is found in the Bible is nothing like an account or catalog of rights. There might be no incompatibility between the divine command "do not murder" and the human right to life. Similarly, the command "do not steal" might be said to support the human right to hold property. The command "do not commit adultery" might translate into the human right to marry and found a family, and so on. But a Christian ethic of human rights must do more than search for superficial resemblances.

Nor is it enough to suggest some kind of ontological participation between human and divine law that can be known, or even guaranteed, through human means. This was the theological risk incurred by Alabama Supreme Court Chief Justice Roy Moore when he placed two and a half tons of granite displaying the Ten Commandments in the rotunda of the Supreme Court building. A federal court later ruled that the monument violated the separation of church and state, but Moore refused to remove it, saying that Christianity forms the bedrock of the U. S. Constitution and of his conscience. As the deadline for the removal of the stone passed, Christian activists kept a 24-hour vigil to ensure that the monument was not moved.[10] The monument was, however, eventually removed, as some protesters shouted, "It is a lamentable day in Alabama and the United States."[11] Other justices on the Alabama Supreme Court voted to remove the monument, and the chief justice was suspended on charges of violating canons of judicial ethics. Justice Moore rejected the accusation, saying the Ten Commandments are featured in the seals of many states, as well as on the wall of the Supreme Court Building in Washington, D.C. *The Times* of London reported that Moore had become a folk hero among conservative Christians for insisting that God was the basis of all law.[12] Younge concluded his article in *The Guardian*, "[T]here is no arguing with faith. Fundamentalists deal with absolutes. Their eternal certainties make them formidable campaigners and awful negotiators—it is difficult to cut a bargain with divine truth."

The Alabama case represented an inappropriate merging of the authority *of* God and human authority *from* God. Displaying a granite monument of the Ten Commandments in the courthouse is at least vulnerable to the false suggestion that the affairs of the court parallel God's gift of the law to Moses, thereby positing a suspect analogy between creaturely, human law and God's law. The presence of the monument could have been interpreted to signify some kind of continuity between the affairs of the court and God's judgment, the judgment and sentence passed by the court and God's specific will. This is not to say that Christian judges should refrain from seeking after God's justice. Nor is it to divide the whole of reality into the two spheres of the sacred and the profane. Nothing of our world is outside of Christ. Rather, it is to guard against false claims about the reconciliation of the world to God, an analogy of being (*analogia entis*) that suggests that something created (human law) could of itself express or apprehend the uncreated law of God. It is also to guard against the heretical potential of the analogy of faith (*analogia fidei*). This problem is relatively little discussed in Barth-influenced Western theology but has been noted by some Orthodox theologians, notably John Romanides. He identifies the problem as the confusion of Holy Scripture or the Ten Commandments with divine revelation itself, claiming that unjustified assumptions are made about the supposed similarity between God and his self-disclosure in scripture.[13] There is nothing in the pages of the text, or the engraving of a stone, he suggests, that has real similarity with the uncreated God. Any suggestion that faith (albeit enabled by grace) can see the essence of God in the pages of the Bible has to be denied if bibliolatry is to be avoided.

Nor can we be satisfied with emptying Christian ethics into historical considerations, or what Sheila Greeve Davaney calls pragmatic historicism. For Davaney, theology for the twenty-first century must become more obviously a mode of cultural analysis whose task is critical, constructive, pragmatic, and normative.[14] Christian ethics must evaluate its options for action according to likely consequences. Only by following this kind of approach, she says, will theology enter the public arena once more. Davaney's determining question is how to attain the historical knowledge and insight necessary for good judgments, as she relinquishes claims about eternal truth because all such claims are temporary and fallible. Theology is thus reduced to "a practice of critical analysis and of construction whose norms and criteria are pragmatic in character."[15] It "isn't true; it's just something we do," to paraphrase a recent pop song. Davaney is surely correct to remind us of Jesus' words "each tree is known by its own fruit" (Luke 6:44); Christian ethicists are prone to maddeningly vague assertions when tough decisions are required. For Davaney, however, there is only the hard task of addressing concrete problems and real dilemmas in the hope of new possibility. For the Christian ethicist there is always more because decision making never stands independently and autonomously apart from faith. Davaney reminds us, however, that no one can ever escape from "the historical task of asking what it means to believe this or that, to live in this manner or that one."[16]

Tropological Readings

These "short-circuit" options do not exhaust the resources available to us. In early Christian tradition, scholars drew variously on hermeneutic techniques from Jewish and Greek circles to develop tropological or moral readings that aim at both obedience to God's law and the conformation of lives to Christ. Forms of midrash as well as allegorical interpretations were common in the first and second centuries.[17] Later, the so-called Alexandrian school was critically open to Greek influences, and Origen's threefold division of the sense of scripture (literal, spiritual, and moral) is now well known. Differences, albeit overexaggerated, characterized the Antiochene school. The model from which we draw most assistance is that suggested by John Cassian, the fifth-century monk sometimes described as a "bridge between the East and West." In *Collations* 14:8 he proposes a variant on Origen's approach in which the literal or historical sense of scripture is supplemented with three types of spiritual interpretation: the allegorical or typological (which reads passages for what they tell us of Christ and the church); the tropological or moral (which reads passages for what they tell us of the soul and its virtues, and for guidance about how to act); and the anagogical (which reads passages for their spiritual, mystical sense—especially concerning the eschatological hope and heavenly realities).[18]

Briefly stated, the *literal sense* of Holy Scripture is not a form of "wretched slavery," as Augustine so aptly said, or a being bound to the letter of the text rather than its spirit, but a seeking after its direct communication of the word of God.[19] (Stephen C. Barton made a similar point recently when drawing a distinction between what the Bible "says" and how the Bible "speaks." These are not necessarily the same, says Barton.)[20] *Typological readings* assume that all Old Testament history moves forward toward Christ. Sometimes included under the heading "figural" reading, typology "is not an exegetical technique but an effort to hear the two-testament witness to God in Christ, taking seriously its plain sense in conjunction with apostolic teaching."[21] A "type" has its own independent and historical existence but at the same time can be understood as prefiguring a future person, thing, or action. The antitype, or that which is shadowed forth or represented by the "type" or symbol, is not merely an allegory but a shadow or impress of what is to come (Col 2:17), the substance of which belongs to Christ. Thus Adam "is a type of the one who was to come" (Rom 5:14). Joseph is a type of Christ and Rahab a type of the church. Noah's ark prefigures salvation through the waters of baptism (1 Pet 3:20-22). The *tropological or moral sense* of Holy Scripture, says John Cassian, is "the moral explanation which has to do with improvement of life and practical teaching."[22] *Anagogical readings* lead us toward the world to come and relate to eternal glory and the heavenly Jerusalem. Anagoge, from the Greek *anagōgē* meaning "leading up" as of the soul being drawn to the things above, is oriented to the future glory promised in Christ, the heavenly city of Jerusalem, and the hope of a new creation.

Thus, typological readings relate Old Testament events to salvation in Christ. Tropological or moral readings relate salvation in Christ to everyday life and practical decision making. They concern the human soul as subject to praise or blame from God and demand discernment of whether actions are useful and good. Tropological readings are closely related to anagogical readings, which bear in mind the eschatological hope and what we know of heaven. The remainder of this book is an extended tropological engagement with Genesis 9:1-17 in the hope that it will yield moral insight into God's commands for a world in which all humankind shares a disposition to wickedness and violence.

Jewish exegetes have traditionally identified seven Noachian laws (symbolized by the seven colors of the rainbow and reaffirmed in the law given to the Israelites at Sinai) as a clear expression of God's plan for humankind. According to Maimonides, "Anyone who accepts upon himself the fulfillment of these Seven Mitzvos [commandments] and is precise in their observance is considered one of the *chassidei umos ha'olam* ["Hasidim of the nations of the world"]—the righteous among the nations—and will merit a share in the World to Come."[23] According to Jewish traditions, these laws of Noah are the sevenfold prohibitions of idolatry, blasphemy, murder, theft, illicit sexual relations, eating meat taken from an animal while still alive, and failing to establish courts of justice. These are the minimal requirements for righteous Gentiles and compare with the 613 commandments that God gave to the Israelites to keep for righteousness, but they apply to all the descendants of Noah—that is, to everyone. The Noachian laws represent God's sovereign will for the whole earth.[24] In some continuity with Jewish tradition, the challenge for our purposes is to consider human rights with reference to absolute divine sovereignty and God's promise in the rainbow to remember every living creature of all flesh.

Similar moves have often been made in Christian tradition with respect to the Decalogue. For Aquinas, the precepts of the Decalogue were the primary scriptural resource for guidance about God's will for all humanity. The commandments are not confined to Israel and the Old Covenant but pertain to God's care and ordering of all creation:

> Now the precepts of the decalogue contain the very intention of the law-giver, who is God. For the precepts of the first table, which direct us to God, contain the very order to the common and final good, which is God; while the precepts of the second table contain the order of justice to be observed among men, that nothing undue be done to anyone, and that each one be given his due; for it is in this sense that we are to take the precepts of the decalogue. Consequently the precepts of the decalogue admit of no dispensation whatever.[25]

The Decalogue expresses not only God's will for the people of Israel but an order of justice that God intends for all people. As noted in chapter 3, this same witness is found among early Anglican divines who, like many patristic thinkers, identify the natural moral law with prohibitions contained in the Decalogue. More recently, Clifford Green's introduction to *Ethics* states: "For Bonhoeffer, thinking about law begins not with interest-group politics but with God and the Decalogue—positive civil law is to reflect in some way or to be an analogy of the law of God."[26] Curiously, the Noachian covenant has been somewhat neglected. This is surprising, given that the covenant entails no calling of an individual or nation into a relation of particular fellowship with God, but is made between God and all flesh on the earth (Gen 9:17); the covenant, "high above man," is made visible in the rainbow, which touches heaven and earth.[27] This covenant is made with all people.

God's Covenant with Noah

In what follows, we do not adhere to the seven laws of Noah identified in Jewish traditions but delimit ourselves to the tropological sense of Gen 9:1-17 as it concerns the value of life as given by God, humanity's dominion over living things, the command not to kill, and God's requiring of justice. Made uncultically on the basis of God's right of dominion over all life, this covenant contains ordinances for all humankind. Given to a world in which sin, especially violence, has become a defining feature, this unilateral covenant specifies God's renewed demands on humanity if life is to continue. The conceptuality and language of the passage is not that of human rights but of divine sovereignty and all life belonging to God; this is the sole explanation of the commands given to all humanity. The covenant is theonomous not anthroponomous. As Peter Harland observes, God's command not to kill is radically different from the right to life.[28] Human rights presuppose freedoms intrinsic to the human person as such. In Gen 9:1-17 all rights belong to God and his authority over all life is unquestioned. The laws given to the world via Noah are valid for all and obligatory upon everyone because they issue from God. Hence the suggestion in what follows that guidance or directions from this passage might yet inform a present-day ethic of human rights.

The Wickedness of Humankind

The backdrop of Genesis 9:1-17 is the great wickedness of humankind in all the earth. The literary context reminds us of tales about humans attempting to grasp power to themselves and to go beyond the bounds allotted by God. Adam and Eve had progressive aspirations; Cain and Lamech killed (Gen 4:8; 4:23). Those at Babel tried later to build a tower to the heavens to make a name for themselves (Gen 11:1-9). All coveted their own excellence and fell victim to pride. [29] God saw this wickedness, and that every inclination of human hearts was evil, and repented that he had made humankind on the earth. "[I]t grieved him to his heart" (Gen 6:6), but God announced his judgment to Noah: "I have determined to make an end of all flesh . . . along with the earth" (Gen 6:13). The whole earth shares the effects of human sin and all its species will be engulfed in waters of judgment. The Flood, or what Gerhard von Rad describes as "God's deadly anger over sin," brings judgment that hangs like an iron curtain between our present world age and the first splendor of creation.[30] Yet, paradoxically, the story of the Flood (Gen 6–9) speaks of the value of created life before God. Only Noah receives a command to build an ark in which God will save some from judgment. Noah—a type of Christ through whom God will take steps to restrain the destructive effects of sin and give to humanity a new future (Matt 3:17; John 17:4; Heb 7:26)—thus begins the largest building project in human history to date through which God will restrain the destructive effects of sin and give humanity a new future: "God could see and reconcile the whole of humanity in one man."[31]

Frustratingly, perhaps, the universality of sin and corruption in Genesis 6 overwhelms any specification of particular sins and makes it difficult to detail moral limits suggested by God's covenant with Noah. Indeed, the terms of the covenant appear to be so broadly drawn that it would be impossible for humankind to break it.[32] Similarly, the command to "be fruitful and multiply" is, as we shall see in chapter 6, open to a range of morally lax, as well as overly restrained, interpretations. Nor is it immediately obvious how to respond to the prohibition against eating blood (Gen

9:4), or the seeming demand for capital punishment (Gen 9:6). These are problems for subsequent chapters. For the moment, we recall Bonhoeffer's emphasis on how the sinful acts of individuals affect the guiltiness of all humanity, and vice versa.[33] He calls for an ethic of the species that begins in the concept of sin and with experience of wickedness and notes that there is a sense in which human solidarity in wickedness *is* the relationship between Christian and non-Christian ethics. All the descendants of Adam and Eve, that is, all of humanity since them, are coessential or consubstantial (Gr *homoousiotitos*) with their humanity.[34]

In our own day, the inseparability of the individual culpable act and the culpability of the human race is frighteningly complex. Global markets mean that individuals are frequently indirectly (and often directly) implicated in trade injustices. Cheaper products in our shops probably mean that workers in another country are being exploited with low wages and few benefits such as maternity leave or pensions. Yet, when international trade unions protest against International Labor Organization conventions, we fear the protectionism that allows developed countries to bar products from countries that do not meet international labor standards.[35] Journalistic advocates of evolutionary sociobiology tell us that the human capacity for guilt is an evolutionary version of a thirst for social approval; a developmental evolutionary program supposedly calibrates guilt and "turns the knobs" of the human conscience.[36] "Natural selection does the 'thinking'; we do the doing."[37] So, for instance, it is supposedly because of the benefits of skillful lying that natural selection has made experimental lying exciting. Historians tell us that the moral history of the twentieth century was the worst of all time.[38] Environmental scientists predict our mutually assured destruction if we continue to pump "greenhouse gases" into the earth's atmosphere at current rates. We can barely begin to comprehend the complex ways in which the sinful acts of individuals affect the guiltiness of all humanity, and vice versa. The challenge is to conceive theologically of how all humanity is included in both Adam and Christ. Far from being a hindrance to Christian ethics today, a doctrine of sin—which takes account of the interconnectedness of individual culpable acts and the corruption of the human race—is needed to help us face problems of pride and violence today.

Pride and Violence

According to Harland, the priestly source behind Genesis 6–9 focuses on one sin in particular—violence (Heb *smh chamas*).[39] There is disagreement about how best to translate the term. Some scholars suggest that it is used as a general, comprehensive term for sin. Others translate as lawlessness or violence. Harland considers that H. Haag comes closest to the essence of the meaning: "Thus *smh* is cold-blooded and unscrupulous infringement of the personal rights of others, motivated by greed and hate and often making use of physical violence and brutality."[40]

While the modern notion of rights is alien to the Old Testament, Haag encapsulates the sense of *chamas* as "an attack on people which leads to an infringement of their dignity."[41] *Chamas* is used especially in connection with harm against people, though also against property (Ps 55:9; Prov 10:6; Isa 59:6; Joel 3:19). It has connotations of oppression and lawlessness (Ezra 7:23; Amos 3:10; Hab 1:1-4). It threatens life (Judg 9:24; Job 19:7) and is associated particularly with bloodshed (Ezek 7:23; Hab 2:8). It is also used of unfair dealings, such as unfair judgments issued by corrupted judges that deal out violence (Ps 58:2). Violence, says Harland, as a translation of *chamas*, implies a deliberate breach of the way ordained by God in Genesis 1:26-31 since God did not permit the oppression of one's fellows. "The function of the *imago Dei* is corrupted, because instead of faithfully exercising his role as God's representative (*mlx*) and vice-regent, man grasps at powers which are not rightfully his."[42] Instead of using the dignity and power given by God for the benefit of the world, humanity assumes a false and arbitrary authority, corrupted by violence. Humanity is destroying itself and all living creatures.

The Value of Life and Lawfulness

With this in mind, we move to preliminary suggestions about how Genesis 9:1-17 might bear on Christian engagement with human rights. These comments cannot be taken "literally" because the differences between the worldview of the text and a modern human rights culture are huge. Tropologically, however, Holy Scripture witnesses to the sovereignty of God in whom all life and justice originate. Biblically informed ethics is about obedience to God's command before it is about the value of freedom to which every human has an innate right.

Three broad considerations or axioms present themselves to us. First, God deems human life worthy of preservation. Humanity's wickedness and violence has corrupted the original ordinances of creation, yet God renews the command to be fruitful and multiply (Gen 1:28) and sets limits to ensure that violence can be contained. God pledges that the waters shall never again destroy all flesh. Humanity is expected to observe God's laws—though not in such a way that a universal flood will result if it fails; the covenant is unilateral in this sense. Life is to be respected because God commands it. Life is not to be respected for its own sake but because God is sovereign. The theological dynamic between God's command and appropriate human response is thus central to our work. In broad terms, our claim is that recognition of natural rights is an appropriate response to God's command; this is what I call the command-rights dynamic. Thus, for instance, God's command is "Be fruitful and multiply" (Gen 9:1). One way of heeding this command might be recognition of the right to reproduce. Similarly, God says: "For your own life blood I will surely require a reckoning" (Gen 9:5). One way of heeding this command might be recognition of the right to a fair trial within a functioning and just legal system. Divine commands, as witnessed in Holy Scripture, do not translate directly into natural rights, nor is the recognition of natural rights necessary to the heeding of God's command. Our claim is weaker because the language of rights is context determined, contingent, and provisional. Nonetheless, within the theological framework of "the natural" as that preserved by God and oriented toward "the ultimate" in Christ, the recognition of natural rights and/or human rights may be deemed an appropriate response to God's promises and commands—what Bonhoeffer might describe as a "nonreligious" or "worldly" response in a world come of age.

Second, the command to be fruitful and multiply is linked to dominion over other living creatures. That the animal order will fear and dread humanity as "into your hand they are delivered" (Gen 9:2) contrasts with the harmonious and responsible care of nonhuman animals in Genesis 1:26. Human dominion now includes the consumption of flesh for food; the vegetarian state of the garden of Eden is ended, though the eating of blood is prohibited. This reminder that life belongs to God, and that his sovereignty extends to all things, sets limits to human dominion and warns that "killing carries with it the danger of blood lust."[43] It places restrictions on humanity's overweening power high up the list of ethical priorities. At a time when most of us turn a blind eye to animal suffering and the environmental costs of our lifestyles, or even collude with violations of the world's natural habitats, God's covenant recalls us to the central place of respect for living creatures within divine providence. At the very least, a tropological reading of this passage might suggest a heightened priority or status for animal and/or environmental rights in Christian ethics.

Third, the human community has responsibility before God for the exercise of justice. This is because God will require a reckoning for all human life. "Know that all lives are mine" (Ezek 18:4), says the Lord. The taking of human life is primarily an affront to God, who made humanity in his own image (Gen 9:6). Only subsequently is it a crime against one's fellows. Yet, humanity is charged with the solemn responsibility of preserving community life by exacting punishment for murder—indeed, humanity is entrusted with the ultimate sanction of the death penalty. The *imago Dei* in all humanity is the reason for this responsibility as the passage grounds the claims of justice in the express command of God and his providential purpose.

A Methodological Observation

These three broad considerations or axioms get us started. They far from exhaust the guidance that Holy Scripture supplies. Nor do they translate directly into today's political and rhetoric of human rights. Rather, they shape the ethico-theological backdrop of the selected case studies treated in the following chapters—(1) the value of life because of humanity's position before God; (2) humanity's proper exercise of dominion over other living creatures; and (3) human responsibility before God for the exercise of justice. Something like Ronald Preston's "middle axioms" or Bonhoeffer's "mandates," these axioms enable movement between exegesis of the text and present-day decision making. Despite the relative unfashionability of this methodology today—supposedly because our fragmented cultures deprive us of the consensus required for "middle axioms" to be effective—such conceptual tools remain one way of moving between general scriptural affirmations and practical decision making.[44] Such axioms are, as William Storrar has said, attempts to define the directions in which the Christian faith might express itself ethically and morally in particular historico-social contexts.[45]

The Genesis texts alone do not provide a sufficient basis for a theological anthropology or ethic of right(s), and there can be no question of cutting lose our discussion of right(s) from a typological consideration of the New Covenant fulfilled in Christ Jesus, in whom we find true humanity and with reference to whom God tells us who we are. Christ Jesus, God's Son, is the "image of the invisible God, the firstborn of all creation" (Col 1:15). If he were not the image of God, the light of the glory of the gospel of God (2 Cor 4:4), we should have no ground upon which to speak about what it is to be truly human.[46] We are *not* treating an ethic of human rights as part of what Gunton calls a natural theology (see chapter 4) but as part of a fully Trinitarian theology of nature in which the commands of God, Creator and Reconciler, are not divorced. As Francis Watson says: "To claim, with Paul, that Jesus is the image of God is by no means to forget Genesis."[47] Noah's descendants—that is, human persons, all of whom are created in the image of God, are prophetic of, or anticipatory of, the human Jesus, the Son of man. God's covenant activity invites and evokes human responses that correspond to his initiative. God's commands as Creator and

Reconciler remain the very condition of human existence. If, in our own day, the social import of these passages is cast in the language of rights, then so be it.[48] The task for Christian practitioners remains that of witness, albeit hidden, to God's commands and reconciling grace.

The Command-Rights Dynamic

To summarize, no *analogia entis* or false correlation has been claimed between the righteousness of God, "right" defined with reference to God, and natural and/or human rights. We have claimed, however, that natural and/or human rights may be understood as (at least potentially) appropriate expressions of the claims that the human body has—and perhaps all living beings have—to life, shelter, food, appropriate liberties and/or immunities, and so on. Natural rights may be understood as the claims necessary to express the dignity that God bestows on creation by making it subject to his commands; they are not guaranteed primarily by human law nor by consensus but by God, although, to the eyes of faith, human law has a role to play in protecting these rights as an expression of the respect due to God, the Creator. For believers, natural and/or human rights may be understood as contingent responses to the revealed commands of God as Creator.

Second, the two parts of the command-response dynamic of Christian ethics (divine and creaturely) should not be allowed to divide into two separate themes. Barth insisted on this in the opening chapters of his 1928–1929 and 1930 lectures in ethics at Münster and Bonn, respectively. His major concern with eighteenth- and nineteenth-century Protestant ethics (F. D. E. Schleiermacher, G. Wünsch, C. Palmer, A. Ritschl, T. Haering, W. Herrmann, I. A. Dorner) was on precisely this point. Dogmatics and ethics had been allowed to fall apart into the former, showing what Christians believe, and the latter showing how we should act on the basis of the holy. Eternal truths were thought to illuminate human consciousness and to set goals for human action. For Barth, however, this had reduced both dogmatics and ethics to "an idle intellectual game."[49] The difference between dogmatics and ethics had become analogous to that between the divine and the human. Dogmatics set before us what God has done and achieved for our salvation. Ethics had to do with the human side of practical affairs, mediated through human free will and action. Either this, or dogmatics became swallowed up in ethics (W. Herrmann, E. Troeltsch, H. Wendt, R. Rothe) such that ethics became the superior discipline that pronounces upon the acceptability of God's word. By contrast, for Barth, the unfolding task of Christian ethics is inseparable from dogmatics. Only as the hearer of God's word does humanity come under the divine command and live by grace. Distinct moments of the dynamic are distinguishable but not separable. God's word comes to humanity and claims us: "The task of theological ethics is that of presenting the claiming of man by the Word of God."[50]

To this end, we have reminded ourselves of ancient Christian teaching about the interaction of literal, typological, tropological, and anagogical readings of Holy Scripture. At least in the writings of John Cassian, the ethical contours of the Bible's teaching are treated in an essentially Christological manner. Tropological readings, which aim at obedience to God's law and the conformation of lives to Christ, presuppose typological questioning concerning what a passage says about Christ. Tropological readings concern practical discernment about whether certain actions are useful and good, as, for instance, when early church members had to judge whether it is fitting for a woman to pray to God with her head uncovered.[51] Such judgments are impossible to undertake if severed from their root. Thus, Cassian writes in the same passage as that mentioned above:

> The tropological sense is the moral explanation which has to do with improvement of life and practical teaching, as if we were to understand by these two covenants practical and theoretical instruction, or at any rate as if we were to want to take Jerusalem or Sion as the soul of man, according to this: "Praise the Lord, O Jerusalem: praise thy God, O Sion." (Ps 147:12).

The covenants to which he refers are those between God and Abraham and between God and the people of Israel at Sinai. God's covenant with Noah is not complete in itself but anticipates greater realization in Christ. We cannot think about human rights as though God had not made a covenant with all humanity through Noah nor renewed it in Christ. We can ask, however, how God the Creator's command to all humanity meets believers in the midst of our present-day reality of a human rights culture, what is commanded, and how we might guard against caprice in addressing these questions.

❧ 5 ❧

God's Command to "Multiply" and the Right to Reproduce

In spite of profound disturbance, mankind may know in the continuance of its reproducing generations that God has not withdrawn himself, but that it has a right, which is not theologically self-evident, even in this condition to continue to multiply.

—Gerhard von Rad[1]

Men and women of full age, without any limitation due to race, nationality or religion, have the right to marry and to found a family. They are entitled to equal rights as to marriage, during marriage and at its dissolution. . . .

The family is the natural and fundamental group unit of society and is entitled to protection by society and the State.

—UNDHR, Article 16

God's command to "be fruitful and multiply" is given to all humanity (Gen 9:1; 9:7). It is not the unconditional command of Genesis 1:28 given before humans fell into sin and disobedience. Unlike the same words spoken to Adam and Eve in paradise, this command is given to humanity in a situation of dire need and subject to conditions affected by sin. "[P]*ost Christum natum* the propagation of the race ('Be fruitful and multiply,' Gen 1:28) has ceased to be an unconditional command. It happens under God's long-suffering and patience, and is due to His mercy, that in these last days it may still take place."[2] So, too, after the Fall. Nonetheless, the covenant with Noah is noncultic and inclusive. God's dealings with Noah extend to the whole human race and his blessing "is effective in the begetting, conception, birth and the succession of generations."[3] Despite the failure of humanity to live up to the aims of creation, the command to "be fruitful and multiply" still has a place of priority. Our question is what sense we are to make today of this command and whether recognition of a universal right to reproduce and/or to found a family is an appropriate, present-day response to it. Should a Christian ethic of rights promote the successful application of reproductive rights? If so, on what grounds? within what interpretive framework? with what, if any, qualifications?

God's Command: "Be Fruitful and Multiply"

We begin, then, with God's command to "be fruitful and multiply" as given to all humanity (Gen 9:1; 9:7). Subsequent biblical texts pursue the theme of being fruitful and multiplying (Gen 17:2; 17:6-7; 28:3-4; 35:11-12; Exod 1:7; Lev 26:9), often in situations of uncertainty or threat for the people of Israel. Here, in a context of blessing, God promises freedom from further all-destructive deluges and gives humanity a new start. The very same command given in Genesis 1:28, 31 is repeated in Genesis 9 as God's "yes" to life in the face of near annihilation, and takes the form of an encouragement to the well-being and growth of the species. As Calvin notes in his commentary on Genesis 9, the voice of God is actually heard by Noah. This particular honor is an encouragement in the face of tribulations endured and as assurance of the benediction declared. Noah's progeny will contribute to the restitution of the world. Indeed, says Calvin, God turns his discourse again to Noah and his sons, exhorting them to the propagation of offspring "as if he would say, 'You see that I am intent upon cherishing and preserving mankind, do you therefore also attend to it.'"[4] The covenant raises humankind from death to life, but humankind has its role to play—a role that, as Calvin insists, includes lawful intercourse and the procreation of children. In blessing Noah and his sons, God blesses the entire human race, which is expected to respond in ways that reflect the dominion given to it to share in the renewal of the earth. This is not to suppose that everyone working today for the protection of reproductive liberties will understand their work as a response to divine command. The issue for Christian ethics, however, is the relation of human rights to God's command or, more specifically, how obedience to the universal divine command to "be fruitful and multiply" bears on the recognition and construal of a right to reproduce and/or found a family.

The broad claim in what follows is that recognition of a right to reproduce and/or found a family is a potentially appropriate response today to the divine command to "be fruitful and multiply." Dietrich Bonhoeffer came close to claiming as much. The will to have one's own child, and to choose the mother or father of this child, is, he said, like the claim to life itself, one of the oldest orders of creation that may be expressed as a universal human right. The right is not earned by, or awarded to, human beings but follows from God's command to "be fruitful and multiply" and is born with every one of us. It rests in what actually exists (*im Seienden*) and dies with us.[5] Our own response is more cautious, initially at least, for reasons that will become apparent. The global and transgenerational perspectives entailed in the covenant do not allow us to approach the topic of reproduction via the door of individual choice and reproductive autonomy that so often characterizes rights discourse today, but require us to think inter alia about how deficiencies in many contemporary approaches to human rights play a role in sustaining global inequity or, at the least, not correcting it. We cannot be satisfied with interpretations of reproductive rights that focus on the extension of individual choice at the expense of global and transgenerational concerns. Arguably, however, there is sufficient analogical continuity between the obedience invited by God's word and present-day human rights standards relating to reproduction for Christian people to take this work seriously and engage critically with it.

Article 16 of the UNDHR and Issues of Interpretation

Our practical focus is Article 16 of the United Nations Declaration of Human Rights, which states:

(1) Men and women of full age, without any limitation due to race, nationality or religion, have the right to marry and to found a family. They are entitled to equal rights as to marriage, during marriage and at its dissolution. . . .

(3) The family is the natural and fundamental group unit of society and is entitled to protection by society and the State.

Article 16 does not recognize the right to reproduce as explicitly as, for instance, the right to life, the right to equal protection by the law, or the right to own property, though many regard the right to reproduce and/or found a family, and typically, the right to avoid doing so, as fundamental liberties that should not be dependent on any given state's moral rules and that should be protected at law.[6] This said, whatever is implied by Article 16 cannot be deemed absolute in the sense that it may never be curtailed or delimited in any way. Some people are infertile and cannot reproduce. Others do not marry. Yet others—for example, a justly convicted life-prisoner—might be deemed to have forfeited the right to reproduce. It might even be defensible for a state to limit reproduction if unlimited reproduction threatens the very survival of the group—though this is not the place to test this claim further. Moreover, the article speaks of the right to found a family rather than to reproduce. This suggests that the biological processes of reproduction do not exhaust the special nature of this right. What matters is not merely population growth or the transmission of genetic material to offspring but the rearing of children in families. Some interpret the right to found a family within the constraints set by moral obligations to provide adequate and lasting care for the hoped-for child. Onora O'Neill, for instance, casts the debate with this test in mind.[7] Article 16 should not be used, she says, to defend a woman who discards her babies at birth because she likes being pregnant and giving birth but finds child rearing tiresome. For these reasons, the remainder of this chapter deals with the right to found a family rather than merely the right to reproduce.[8]

Beyond this, it quickly becomes apparent how hotly contested the interpretation of this article is in diverse contexts, and for widely variant reasons. *De simplicitur* appeals to the article are vulnerable to the same philosophical weaknesses as appeals to any textual authority without explanation of the grounds and methods of interpretation. Too often, its interpretation is torn between cultural relativism and unrestrained individualism. This is not to deny that talk about human rights looks and sounds different from different cultural and political perspectives. The promotion of human rights standards and policies is widely recognized as globally uneven: "Global discourse is gripped by the sounds of voices expressing diverse perspectives about the promotion, application and evolution of human rights norms."[9] Diversity is inevitable as different cultures and traditions interpret human rights standards in light of their own traditions and norms. Hence the growing importance of academic journals such as *Muslim World Journal of Human Rights*, which offers a medium for scholarly debate on various aspects of human rights as they relate to the Islamic world.[10] The UNDHR is less a document frozen in time than a set of standards that require application among and within diverse cultures. However, as we see below, there is a difference between recognizing that a strategy of decentralization is required for the successful application of human rights standards in differing situations and denying that certain universal norms should be central for political purposes in all nations.

The matter is complex and multilayered. Few agree, for instance, about what it means to say that the rights affirmed by Article 16 of the UNDHR are universal. In affluent contexts, debate about the meaning of the right to reproduce often centers around the extent and the proper limits of reproductive autonomy defined in terms of individual choice. Elsewhere, the disadvantaged status of women means that their basic reproductive rights are often severely compromised. So, for instance, when *cast negatively*, Article 16 can be interpreted merely to infer a right not to be prevented from procreating by, for example, the imposition of sterilization or contraception on individuals. Violations have included Nazi forced sterilizations and abortions, and forced childbearing, all of which brutal crimes grossly violated women's and men's reproductive rights as part of eugenic attempts at ethnic and racial extinction. And such violations persist. Coerced or enforced sterilizations are still reported by human rights watch groups. Today, abysmal poverty is perhaps the most significant circumstance that violates the right to reproduce. Since one-fifth of the world's population lives in absolute poverty, we might also wonder what it means to assert international standards that are not backed up by resources to combat severe need. Gross violations of rights occur in various ways. The dire poverty that, in effect, violates women's and men's right to found a family leads us to ask if a meaningful right to reproduce belongs only to people in the developed world.[11] (See further the discussion below of "threshold capabilities.")

When *cast positively*, the right to marry and found a family can be interpreted to include far more than the prohibition of violations. Claims for reproductive liberty are such that some Western theorists now more or less dismiss as nonsense worries about the opportunity to choose one's children's phenotypic traits. John Harris, for instance, wants the kind of bioethical thinking that would facilitate the best kind of choice and wonders why the phrase "designer children" is used pejoratively to conjure up images of instrumentalization when most would-be parents value their future offspring for the children's own sake, and seek only the best for them.[12] He argues that reproductive rights should be respected as an expression of reproductive autonomy, including the genetic choices that they make for their future offspring. In other words, in affluent societies, assertion of reproductive rights is increasingly a matter of extending autonomy to those otherwise unable to have children—to those with inheritable genetic disorders who do not want to pass on affected genes to their offspring, to those who wish to use their partner's postmortem sperm or eggs, to postmenopausal women, to those who wish to select the sex of their child or to clone cadaveric eggs to replace a lost daughter, and more besides.

Some deny altogether any ethical warrant for recognizing universal reproductive rights. Witness Garrett Hardin's now infamous argument to the effect that population control requires that individual rights asserted by the descendants of John Locke and Adam Smith be significantly curtailed where population growth threatens the well-being of society.[13] Hardin discourages loose talk of universal rights and, instead, promotes population control as a philanthropic goal and personal objective. In a democracy, he argues, population control should be by means of laws that are agreed to by the majority, though coercion may be necessary under all forms of governance. Dreams of universal rights are not acceptable substitutes, he says, for hard-headed and well-researched assessments of the carrying capacity of nations. A poor person's need creates neither obligations on others nor rights that warrant protection. The long-term interest of the nation and its need to ensure the survival of future generations trump individual rights and warrant authoritarian coercion to manage population growth. Reproductive rights should not be promoted, especially in nations suffering from poverty and overpopulation.

Counterarguments are often mounted to the effect that excessive focus on population growth distracts attention from related problems, such as resource abuse by richer nations.[14] It is said that Hardin risks confusion between the justified interpretation of facts and unwarranted prejudice based on use of the "lifeboat" metaphor. Incentive- and education-based management of population is more effective than coercion in the long-term.[15] The split is, as Bonnie Steinbock notes, between those who see overpopulation as the primary problem that leads to famine, disease, environmental catastrophe, and social unrest and those who argue that the problem of overpopulation will correct itself if the quality of life for people in poor countries improves. Debate centers around whether overpopulation itself is the main problem or a symptom of deeper problems, such as political instability. Even so, the unambiguous assertion of reproductive rights is contentious. Both sides of the argument can be presented in equally dogmatic, ideological, and unscientific ways. "But the question about the intrinsic value of procreative rights, independent of their effectiveness in controlling population, is crucial."[16]

The Myth of Universality?

Such diverse interpretations of Convention rights have led some to describe the universality presupposed by the UNDHR, including Article 16, as fantasy. Antonio Cassese, a professor of international law at the University of Florence, observes: "[U]niversality is, at least for the present, a myth. Not only are human rights observed differently—certainly to differing degrees—in different countries; they are also *conceived of* differently."[17] This may, or may not, be true to the extent that Cassese claims, but *de simplicitur* appeals to the UNDHR are self-evidently inadequate as grounds for political action. Similarly, the mere fact that the UNDHR has attracted political consensus does not make appeals to human rights morally right.

Nor does consensus infer ethical justification. Merely to appeal to a Convention right as a basis for action does little more than make a procedural point.[18] The meaning, scope, and application of articles can vary considerably depending on the interpretive framework chosen. Hence a growing sense that human rights discourse will either collapse into myriad, relativist visions of the good or drift further into the kind of moral individualism that is unconcerned about human action as a mode of sociality and the structures that express this sociality in cultural and tradition-specific ways.

Michael Ignatieff describes this concern as the cultural side of the human rights dilemma, where competing conceptions of the good can make the objective of promoting unity and cohesiveness difficult to handle such that fear of Western, cultural imperialism and the tyranny of even well-intentioned linguistic or national groups leads politicians and practitioners to back off from the enforcement of uniform minimum standards. We look below at differences between secularist and theological construals of the universality of rights claims. For the moment, we note that a so-called postmodern focus on the local risks surrendering universal values to parochialism and arbitrariness, and that the flip side of this concern is another—what Ignatieff dubs a "spiritual crisis"—pertaining to the ultimate metaphysical grounds for these norms.[19] Foundational claims that appeal to religion and metaphysics are seen to divide, "and these divisions cannot be resolved in the way humans usually resolve their arguments, by means of discussion and compromise."[20] That human rights do help to improve the lives of individuals is basis enough, says Ignatieff, for juridical and other forms of advocacy. Human rights are practical tools for the protection of human agency, and this is all that we need to know to defend them. Drafters of the UNDHR were silent on matters of faith, and, says Ignatieff, we should adopt their deliberate silence with respect to substantive beliefs—especially if human rights instruments are to be kept out of political debates about sources of rights in traditional, religious, and authoritarian sources of power.[21]

Taking Ignatieff's work as indicative of much recent secularist debate, we note his assertion that the myth of universality has already collapsed. There can be no doubt about his personal commitment to the promotion of human rights for the sake of human flourishing. He judges the success of human rights advocacy, however, by practical and measurable results. Universal claims cannot be built, he says, on religious beliefs or metaphysical systems without either stripping human rights of their inherently individualistic bias or becoming embroiled in debates that have no resolution and are more likely to impose restrictions on human rights agendas designed to protect and enhance individual agency. Far better, he says, to opt for theoretical minimalism than to promote plural foundations for human rights in a plural world. Beware even an elevation of "the human" to a quasi-transcendence.[22] Human rights are not a secular religion that should facilitate humanity worshiping itself. Persons of diverse faiths and none might find affinity around fundamental human rights, and it is enough to recognize and promote this. We can, and should, forgo the kinds of foundational arguments that try to root human rights norms in metaphysical or transcendental rationalist ground. It does not matter, he says, that disputants are often unclear about what underpins faith in the assertion that "[a]ll human beings are born free and equal in dignity and rights . . . and should act towards one another in a spirit of brotherhood" (UNDHR, Article 1). Human rights protection ought to be compatible with moral pluralism but ought not to seek more than "thin" theories of what is right.

Contra Ignatieff and others, this book urges the examination of human rights instruments from religious and theological perspectives. Secularists such as Ignatieff refuse exposition of plural foundations for human rights in favor of theoretical minimalism. Yet, religion is having an increasing impact on international politics, and cooperation between the religions with respect to human rights advocacy requires solid theoretical foundations. As Charles Taylor writes: "Contrary to what many people think, world convergence will not come through a loss or denial of traditions all around, but rather by creative re-immersions of different groups, each in their own spiritual heritage, travelling different routes to the same goal."[23] We need to recognize, examine, and question plural foundations for human rights in a plural world. Similarly, as Philip Alston argues, we need imaginative initiatives for the promotion and implementation of human rights that are "less Western, more diverse, and more closely tailored to meet local cultures and traditions."[24] Secularist debate about reproductive rights can, as Lisa Sowle Cahill notes, divide easily into a laissez-faire combination of "trendy postmodern philosophical deconstruction" on the one hand and "old-fashioned political liberalism" on the other.[25] Either this, or metaphors such as the carrying capacity of a "lifeboat" are used in highly problematic ways to justify the neglect of fundamental reproductive rights. The effect is that too often the rights of the world's poorest women are undermined while the rights of the richest morph into myriad claims for minimally restrained reproductive autonomy. Against this background, explicit engagement is needed with and between the religions to engender meaningful debate about the specifics of rights claims. Serious engagement within and between the religions is necessary if the work of forming and promoting global norms is to continue.

God's Command and the Universality of Human Rights

What, then, of the supposedly universal right to "found a family" from a Christian perspective? Should a Christian ethic of rights promote this universal reproductive right as a basis for policy decisions? So far, we have argued in general terms that human rights can serve as contingent, provisional means by which believers may heed God's commands. But more needs to be said about the gap between the theological imperative to live in obedience to divine command and recognition of particular moral and legal rights. So far, we have seen that Bonhoeffer's broad-based recognition of the natural right to reproduce allows us to negotiate the difference between theologically grounded notions of objective "right" and subjective "rights." Human life should be preserved, protected, and transmitted in the penultimate because everything penultimate is directed toward the ultimate, and one way of doing this is through appeal to human rights. This is still a long way, however, from Article 16 of the UNDHR. More is required if we are really to examine what difference, if any, theological construal of concepts such as universality, equality, and capability make to practically oriented engagement with reproductive rights.

Universality and Equality

In a Christian ethic of rights, the concept of human universality originates in God; that is to say, God's eternal being and self-communicating word is the source of claims about human universality. Contrary to diverse secularist approaches to human rights, the very concept of universality in Christian ethics is a gift from God. Received from somewhere higher than thought and/or human volition, the concept of universality is sustained by an appeal to transcendence not to human nature or reason. The people of Israel proclaimed this universality and the absolutely universal claims to which it gives rise. The Flood and covenant with Noah are accounts, albeit mythic, of early universal events—the core message of which elicits universal recognition today. Universality is a gift established in particularity. Not an ideal or aspiration, a theologically derived notion of universality is an overarching concept that derives from revealed truth, knowledge of which springs from particular events. The global and transgenerational reach of God's command is the ground on which faith asserts that human rights have universal application. Divine authority is the origin of what John Milbank calls "the first irruption of an absolutely universal claim."[26]

Paradoxically, this theological construal of universality is realized in the lives of individual persons. In blessing Noah and his sons God also blesses the entire human race. Conversely, in blessing the entire human race he commands individual persons. The universal and the particular, or what Bonhoeffer calls the "concrete" nature of the divine command, are inseparable.[27] Like the "mandates" (church, family, culture, and government), the command is given to all humanity but encountered by individual persons in the form of an historical occurrence: "it [the divine commandment] encounters us in historical form."[28] Bonhoeffer elaborates on this by noting that God's command is never given in abstract terms as if without relevance to the lives that people actually lead. The divine word is not given as a self-contained task that can be obeyed and completed, such as Orpheus's descent into Hades in order to recover his dead wife, Eurydice, or the test that Portia's father set for her suitors in *The Merchant of Venice*.[29] Divine command is less an ought to be obeyed or performed than a freedom given to each person for their enjoyment. God's command, which is supreme and total, neither annihilates human freedom nor makes individuals judges or critics of themselves and their own deeds. So, in Genesis 9, the command to "be fruitful and multiply" sets the horizon of possibility for new human life in ways mediated through vocations given to particular individuals.

In other words, Christian moral reasoning does not begin from a general, universalizable norm that we should treat all persons at all times equally, according to their infinite and equal worth, as if the principle of equality demands a form of literalism. Rather, every person is equally subject to divine command because everyone is addressed personally by God's word. Like the logic of universality, the logic of equality entailed in Christian faith does not depend first and foremost on the abstract principle of "to each the same," which, says Bonhoeffer, turns a concern for universal or natural rights into "an abstract law [*Gesetz*]."[30] It is not idealistic in the sense that the equal and infinite worth of every human being requires identical recognition at all times and places, or, at least, the hope of such. Rather, "[t]he equality of human beings is an aspect of the doctrine of creation. It locates every human being equally to every other as one summoned out of nothing by the creator's will, whose life is a contingent gift, created for fellowship with others and answerable to judgment."[31] This equality is also an aspect of the doctrine of redemption because all are included in the covenant with Noah and because Christ died for all in the new covenant of his blood (Isa 53:6; 1 Tim 2:6; Heb 2:9). To slip, therefore, between a theological construal of equality and loose talk of universal rights is likely to be irresponsible and problem-ridden. Practical moral reasoning informed by consideration of human universality is required to discern both what is at stake and where equal treatment for the sake of equal worth is morally desirable, or potentially harmful, in given circumstances.

It is important to be clear that equality before God does not translate necessarily into identical moral or political programs to treat all the same in every respect, that is, to equalize without difference. None of the above necessarily means equal treatment without regard to circumstance or predicament.[32] Nor, of course, does it mean that vast disparities between rich and poor, advantaged and disadvantaged, are justifiable—though demonstration of this must wait for another day. Our central point here is that the "out-narration" of secularist accounts of universality by appeal to universal truth beyond human thought, reason, contract, volition, consensus, and so on, releases Christian ethics from various forms of idealism and/or the dissolution of universal norms and standards into myriad forms of individualism. It might be necessary, even desirable, to take differences into account. The infinite worth of every human being is, as O'Donovan observes, "not *self-evidently* convertible into norms of social practice."[33] Moral judgment about what is really required for the sake of equal worth might be more complex. Arguably, for instance, it overspecifies the divine command to translate it into particular duties for given individuals. Such overspecification might be found in some assertions to the effect that child-rearing is basic to marriage and not optional. Bishop Nazir-Ali was reported recently by the BBC as saying: "In an age of excessive self-regard and encouragement on every side to the new religion of the 'me,' it is very important for the Church to continue saying that having children and their nurture is a basic good of marriage and not an optional extra." Children should be regarded as "part of God's will for marriage" and the planning of a family should be seen as "part of our stewardship of creation." Are those who chose not to have children being "self-indulgent"?[34] The command is given to all humanity but this interpretation leans toward construing it as an order or injunction from a commander that must be obeyed rather than a way of living in freedom. The command must surely be heeded by all but cannot be reduced to a form of vitalism that makes life itself the most highly valued goal.[35] The universality of rights (i.e., rights as derived from the global and transgenerational reach of divine command) need not be confused with the *universalism* of human rights, which denotes some kind of philosophical system or principle. Similarly, the equal and infinite worth of every human being before God does not necessarily require identical recognition and/or implementation at all times and places. We may not at any point assume to "know the divine command in itself and as such, but only in its relations."[36]

Recognizing Addressees of Divine Command

Why, then, should a Christian ethic of rights affirm a universal right "to found a family"? What might this mean with respect to promotion of the norms enshrined in Article 16 of the UNDHR? The answer lies, we suggest, in recognizing that the universality of God's command to all humanity to "be fruitful and multiply" renders every person an addressee of it. Recognition of the divine command to all humanity demands recognition of other people as addressees of that command. The operative concept here is "recognition." This integrating concept links the universality of God's word and obedience to it, thereby helping us to understand the relation between divine command and human rights as a dynamic process that comprises distinctive but related steps. Prior to the language and conceptuality of human rights is a process of recognizing that everyone is addressed by God's command and subject to its universal and noncompulsory obligation. Both self and others are participants in the covenant. The ethical task is to recognize and respond to this truth in meaningful ways.

Paul Ricoeur helps us to unpack the concept of recognition in this kind of exercise, and I am indebted to his essay "Capabilities and Rights," in which he uses the concept of recognition to bridge the logical gap between the terms "capabilities" and "rights" that his title puts side by side. Briefly, "recognition" is taken to be the "identification of any item as being itself and not anything else."[37] For Ricoeur, this deceptively simple notion leads first to the kind of recognition entailed in the assertion of selfhood at the reflexive level. In the same kind of approach as developed in *Oneself as Another*, he calls on the concept of recognition in an existential context to describe processes of self-recognition that give rise to a sense of personhood defined in terms of basic capabilities; namely, the capabilities to speak, act, and tell stories that narrate a life. Our concerns are not primarily existential, and use of Ricoeur's argumentation should not be taken to imply adoption of his neo-Hegelian phenomenology. We begin with covenantal, social, and relational concepts before treating individual processes of self-designation and interlocution. Even so, the concept of recognition as a process helps us to describe the command-rights dynamic in motion, and to bridge more securely the logical gap between the objectivity of God's word and the subjectivity of natural and/or human rights.

The universality of God's command to all humanity renders every person an addressee of that command. Everyone is addressed by the divine command to "be fruitful and multiply," and the conditions of answerability before God entail the expectation that everyone should be free to respond to it. Recognizing this is, we suggest, the reason that a Christian ethic of rights can affirm a universal right "to found a family" as enshrined in the UNDHR. Hence the affront to God and to all humanity that over 1,400 women worldwide die every day from the complications of pregnancy or unsafe abortion, or one every minute, as reported by nongovernmental agencies.[38] The World Health Organization's *World Health Report 2005: Make Every Mother and Child Count* concludes that pregnancy, childbirth, and their consequences are still the leading causes of death, disease, and disability among women of childbearing age in developing countries; 529,000 women die annually as the result of illness brought about by pregnancy, childbirth, and abortion. Maternal mortality is highest in Africa, where the risk of death in childbirth is 1 in 16. This compares with an average risk of 1 in 2,800 in rich countries. Less than 1 percent of maternal deaths occur in high-income families.[39] While equality before God does not translate as "to each the same," these women are not free to respond to divine command in even the most basic ways. At this threshold level of the protection and transmission of life, the equality of all before God means little if the conditions for response to divine command are such that poverty, deprivation, the effects of war and/or corruption, and suchlike entail death on this scale. A relatively wealthy Westerner's life is not worth more than that of one poor African, European, Latin American, or Asian. "The first threshold on which we are called to give immediate practical effect to human equality . . . is the threshold of death, when the continuance of life itself is at stake."[40]

Rights and Capabilities

The closest secularist means of discussing such matters is, we suggest, the capability approach that seeks to recognize what people are free to do or to be. We pause to consider this approach in passing because, arguably, at the threshold level, Christian ethics has much to gain from eavesdropping on debate about the relation between capabilities and rights. Briefly, the economist and Nobel Prize winner Amartya Sen and the liberal philosopher Martha Nussbaum pioneered an approach to development that characterises human beings in terms of the fundamental capacities of a human life, that is, what is required for truly human functioning. A capability, says Sen, is "a person's ability to do valuable acts or reach valuable states of being; [it] represents the alternative combinations of things a person is able to do or be."[41] Behind the defense of reproductive rights lies recognition of capabilities that are, in effect, freedoms to be healthy, to read and write, to take part in the life of a community, and so on. Recognition of these capabilities—including the freedom of bodily health, which includes reproductive health and freedom of choice—requires the removal of various types of unfreedom that leave people with little choice about whether and/or how to develop their capabilities and so to "reach valuable states of being." Nussbaum agrees with Sen about the primary notion of capability and the related need for universal norms in the development policy arena but moves beyond Sen by listing three types of capability (basic, internal, and combined) and identifying threshold levels of recognition below which truly human functioning is not possible.[42] Similarly in Christian ethics, recognizing both self and others as addressees of divine command means recognizing that all people everywhere share certain basic forms of human functioning that are essential to well-being and flourishing.

The capability approach offers a viable theoretical underpinning for fully universal descriptions of the bare minimum of what respect for human dignity requires. A just society, for Nussbaum, is one that provides its citizens with opportunities to exercise those central functional capabilities that humans both need and might choose to develop. Her claim is that the capability approach has many benefits in developing links between the basic human function of reproduction and its protection at law: "Certain universal norms of human capability should be central for political purposes in thinking about basic political principles that can provide the underpinning for a set of constitutional guarantees in all nations."[43] Moreover, its method moves between a great deal of the world's experience and human rights instruments. "Rights language indicates that we do have such an argument and that we draw strong normative conclusions from the fact of the basic capabilities."[44] Across cultures, religious and metaphysical worldviews, and political and ethical ideologies, it should be possible to reach an "overlapping consensus" about the central elements of truly human functioning.[45] The step from recognition of fundamental human capabilities—including bodily health and integrity in all matters relating to reproduction and its processes—to affirmation of Article 16 of the UNDHR should not be large in the sense that recognition of basic capabilities justifies their protection at law.[46] For Christian ethics, the approach assists in expressing at threshold level what it means to say that every person is an addressee of the divine command to "be fruitful and multiply." At least at the threshold level of rudimentary reproductive functions, recognizing these functions as basic capabilities provides a reasonable means of developing a basis of strong normative and justiciable conclusions. What Sen and Nussbaum describe as basic capabilities corresponds to our universal created nature as human beings and justifies the protection of human rights.

For all the strengths of the capabilities approach developed by Sen and Nussbaum, however, it is not clear that it provides a theoretical basis for addressing the transgenerational issues that surround interpretation of Article 16 of the UNDHR beyond the threshold level. Nussbaum's ethic is fully universal in the sense that the basic capabilities of every person form a baseline for political commitment to cross-cultural norms of reproductive rights. Together with Sen's focus on individual flourishing, her capabilities approach indicates a space within which comparisons of quality of life can be made and principles formulated for the global application of justiciable human rights norms. But its ability to cope with transgenerational capabilities in more affluent contexts is less evident. Indeed, it is at least arguable that Sen and Nussbaum treat basic human functions too much on a "liberal" model of personal choice and not enough in terms of the social roles entailed by sex and reproduction in order to meet this need. Nicholas Sagovsky puts the matter well as it concerns transgenerational issues: "To speak of a capability of handing on the future generations a world no less rich in basic 'common goods' than the one inherited from former generations is to push at the boundaries of Sen's use of the term 'capability.'"[47] While a capability approach is helpful in bridging the gap between fundamental anthropological considerations and the juridical language of rights, it does not currently take us far enough toward understanding why individual capabilities cannot be abstracted from "social capabilities" and traditions within a given culture, such as public institutions. This is especially true in democratic capitalist societies where even reproduction is subject to competitive market systems and the pursuit of self-interest by shareholders. In such contexts, discourse about both capabilities and rights can easily slip into fantasized notions of liberty with minimal constraints.

So, for instance, Lisa Sowle Cahill, Séverin Deneulin, and others have argued strongly that the capabilities approach offers many benefits but is too "thin" to offer sufficient guidelines for actions that could transform the unjust structures that impede many from exercising the capabilities they have reason to choose and value.[48] For all Sen and Nussbaum's help in considering the objective realities that lie behind justiciable human rights, we need to think more about capability building that includes the notion that development is sustainable only when grounded in "capacities in the society as a whole."[49] The goal of their approach is ultimately the ability of people to choose to function in certain ways, not simply to function minimally. This is not inherently problematic, but the concern is that they do not devote enough energy to fuller recognition of the sociality of persons; that is, the social dimensions of every aspect of embodiment, including the social nature of human freedom.[50] While their capability approach transcends the obsession among some liberal theorists with civil and political liberties, their goal remains predominantly the exercise of agency by individuals. More is needed to meet today's moral needs with respect to justiciable rights, especially in more affluent contexts where new biotechnological possibilities—such as modifying the genome of future generations through preimplantation genetic screening (PGS), and tissue typing whereby embryos are tested in order for families to have a child who could be a tissue match for a seriously ill brother or sister—are increasingly available.

PGS and Protecting Transgenerational Capabilities

Questions about the capabilities of potential offspring can be helpful in the context of the transgenerational issues raised by new biotechnologies if we allow such questions to push us toward thinking about the basic human functioning of those yet to be born, and about whether and/or how rights discourse can take account more adequately of transgenerational capabilities. Our particular focus in this closing section is preimplantation genetic screening, which currently raises significant social, political, and ethical questions about the capabilities of those yet to be born. The UK Human Fertilisation and Embryology Authority has consulted public opinion about the extension of PGS for genetic conditions that are not fully penetrant; that is, for conditions where not all the people with the gene will develop the diseases (e.g., BRCA1 and BRCA2 breast cancer genes, familial adenomatous polyposis bowel cancer, hereditary nonpolyposis colorectal cancer, neurofibromatosis type 1, and retinoblastoma cancer).[51] Debate centered around the conditions for which PGS should be available in order that children are not born with a strong likelihood of chronic sickness or severe disability. Screening of this kind is sometimes called *negative* genetics, that is, the selecting out of embryos that are likely to develop into chronically sick or severely disabled children. Some claim that eugenics of this kind may be distinguished from *positive* genetics, which is the idea that parents "might also bear responsibility for picking and choosing which 'advantages' their children shall enjoy."[52] The difficulty of distinguishing between them is just one of the issues involved when asking what sense to make of transgenerational responsibilities in the face of such possibilities. Related issues include the seriousness of the condition for which embryo screening and selection might be undertaken; whether there should be a prohibition on deliberately screening *in*, or selecting *for*, impairments and disabilities—as opposed to screening *out*; and who should decide on the particular uses of embryo screening and selection.[53]

In the United States, preimplantation genetic screening/diagnosis is an unregulated practice. The President's Council on Bioethics (PCB) has noted the relative lack of federal oversight of matters relating to assisted reproduction, including PGS; the lack of comprehensive, uniform, and enforceable mechanisms for data collection; and the lack of uniform systems for public review and deliberation.[54] Issues of family law have traditionally been left to individual states, many of which have allowed the growing reproductive industry to regulate itself. Hence the need identified by the PCB to improve the nation's capacity for future analysis of the status of this field. Its 2004 report *Reproduction and Responsibility: The Regulation of New Biotechnologies* recommended the gathering of more complete and useful information and the strengthening of existing legislation to prevent "boundary-crossing practices" unforeseen even a few years ago. In the meantime, the customization of reproduction proceeds apace. CNN International reports that wealthy couples travel to the United States for PGS services that allow them to choose a baby's sex: "The United States' lack of regulation means a growing global market for a few fertility clinics. These businesses advertise in airline magazines or post Web sites aimed at luring clients worldwide."[55] Sujatha Jesudason of the Reproductive Genetics and Public Policy Center at Johns Hopkins University is reported as saying: "Right now the market is driving practices rather than social and ethical concerns. People who have money to pay for it are getting the children of their choice."[56]

Opinion divides with respect to what the exercise of transgenerational responsibility means. For some, transgenerational responsibility is best exercised by screening out fetuses that carry identifiable but undesired genetic traits so that a pregnancy might begin with only those embryos unlikely to develop common disorders such as cystic fibrosis, Duchenne muscular dystrophy, Huntington's disease, hemophilia, fragile X syndrome, sickle-cell blood disease, and various types of cancer. For others, it means maximizing freedom of choice for potential parents so that as many screening decisions as possible are left to them. It is illogical, says the liberal philosopher and bioethicist Julian Savulescu, to prevent the use of a technology that conflicts with parents' moral duty to do the best for their children if the benefit outweighs the risk or other moral costs involved.[57] For yet others, transgenerational responsibility means that legal rights of some kind should be accorded to the developing embryo and/or fetus. If reproductive liberty is taken to mean "a right [of individuals] to control their own role in procreation unless the state has a compelling reason for denying them that control,"[58] adequate protection of future generations requires "matching" legal rights for the embryo and/or fetus. In other words, if the right "to found a family" is interpreted along liberal-individualist lines, it is necessary to recognize fetal rights as a counterbalance. In the UK, for instance, it has been suggested by some that a new kind of right should be asserted such that a person's genetic makeup may not be determined directly by the deliberate choice of another. The issue was raised, for instance, in the report of the Human Genetics Advisory Commission and the Human Fertilisation and Embryology Authority titled *Cloning Issues in Reproduction, Science, and Medicine.*[59] It arose from the fact that several respondents to the consultation document had wanted to assert "a new kind of right" to protect future persons' genetic identity from abuse. Hilary Putnam has made a similar suggestion to the effect that every child might be given the right "to be a complete surprise to its parents."[60]

Against this complex backdrop, a few comments may be offered as a contribution to the debate. First, in Christian ethics, a preliminary step toward a constructive response lies in recognizing that mere promotion of the abstract notion of reproductive autonomy is radically deficient. The transgenerational reach of the divine command to "be fruitful and multiply" means that Christian people must speak of more than individual agency and assertions of procreative liberty. A Christian ethic cannot rest content with interpretations of Article 16 of the UNDHR that treat the right to procreative liberty simply as a matter of extending autonomy. It is not enough, for instance, to treat reproductive rights as analogous to the right to freedom of religious expression, because the latter concerns an area of life in which we express our most deeply held beliefs.[61] Both religious and secularist rights discourse must evolve to take account of the transgenerational dimensions of what reproductive technology now makes possible. Unless this is grasped, the debate about reproductive liberty and interpretations of Article 16 of the UNDHR is susceptible in affluent contexts to irresolvable opposition between universal ideals versus collapse into individualist claims to the extension of reproductive choice with little reference to common humanity, narrative identity, or social structures.

Second, nothing in Christian ethics should be taken to imply that it is inherently wrong to "improve" upon nature. As John Milbank observes, "questions of right and wrong here . . . have never been decidable *merely* in terms of what has been pre-given by (as it were) initial divine design."[62] Questions about what is proper to our *humanum* cannot be decided ultimately with reference to "the natural" because its true measure is Christ, our hope of transformation. The natural order is not bestowed on us as something complete and untouchable. Humanity's responsibility before God includes decision making about how to utilize the earth's resources, which crops to till, how to increase water supplies to drought areas, whether to cross-fertilize certain plants, which technologies to develop further, and so forth. We should hesitate, therefore, before denouncing PGS as wrong because it violates the "natural" processes of reproduction or even, perhaps, because it involves the destruction of preimplantation-stage embryos.[63] The problem with PGS is not first and foremost (or, at least exclusively) that it is inherently wrong to "improve" upon nature. Rather, we have to ask complex questions about what PGS procedures do to our identities as potential parents or simply as members of society—and whether the identities that may thereby emerge "are richer or weaker identities, more viable or else more unstable and threatened."[64]

Third—and, to my mind, this point is both more contentious and less certain—PGS offers no entirely good solution to questions of identity and relations across the generations, and is incapable of making good the bad situations that gave rise to the technology in the first place. The problem is that opting for PGS is never simply a matter of seeking to have a baby unlikely to suffer during its life as loved ones have already suffered. The "screening out" of embryos with genetic defects might be less problematic than the "choosing in" of those with advantages, but both practices accustom us to treating procreation more like the making of a product to a specified standard than the accepting of a gift.[65] In both, admission to life has become conditional on meeting a certain standard of "fitness." This could lead to diminished tolerance for the imperfect, increased burdens on children to live up to expectations, false ideals about parental responsibility not to have disabled children, and so on. The victims may be indeterminate but the potential harms are significant as pursuit of a child "better" than the child born by chance becomes commonplace. As a "gradualist" who holds that meaningful individual human life begins at implantation, or even later, and that a human embryo before implantation is not the ethical equivalent of a human person, I confess to much personal sympathy for potential parents who opt for PGS. Given that we have the knowledge to prevent the transmission of these conditions in families affected by the disorder, it is painfully understandable that potential parents want to "improve" upon nature by avoiding the birth of a child with a gene that they know to be faulty. Our concern, however, is that the status of the preimplantation human embryo is not all that is at stake. PGS requires prospective parents to choose between good and evil, between embryos with and without a faulty gene, setting them up as judges over the quality of human life in ways that, arguably, exceed our creaturely limits before God.[66]

Fourth, this requires us to ask whether the kind of theological arguments developed above translate into the recognition, or extension of the recognition, of legal rights for the fetus to include some kind of right for the earliest embryo to protect future persons' genetic identity from abuse. Several factors point in the general direction of recognizing fetal rights. As Rowan Williams, archbishop of Canterbury, said recently: "Whether it is a matter of evidence about foetal sensitivity to outside stimuli (including pain), the nature of foetal consciousness, or the expanding possibilities of saving early foetal life outside the womb, the trend is inexorably towards a sharper recognition of the foetus as a natural candidate for 'rights' of some kind."[67] New technologies that display three-dimensional images of the growing fetus or record of the fetus in the womb make it easier for adults to see and thus to think about the radical particularity of these new lives. To deny the legal recognition of fetal rights risks hardening one's heart to the extreme vulnerability of the unborn. Similarly, perhaps, ignoring Putnam's plea for some kind of right to protect future persons' genetic identity from abuse risks colluding with the routinized "weeding out" of embryos carrying undesired genetic traits and/or with directed genetic change that would attempt to improve embryos in vitro by introducing "better" genes.

The urgency of the matter is drawn to our attention by Jürgen Habermas's account of the dangers entailed in the unprecedented paternalism of altering a person's genetic makeup for questionable eugenic motives. He is concerned that biotechnology now makes it possible to manipulate the genome of one's future offspring in deeply problematic ways: "It remains a horrifying prospect that a eugenic self-optimization of the species, carried out via the aggregated preferences of consumers in the genetic supermarket (and via society's capacity for forming new habits), might change the moral status of future persons."[68]

For this liberal, postmetaphysical political thinker who respects the autonomy of the individual and wants to protect the values associated with individual liberty, social fraternity, and fundamental equality, deliberate modification of the genome of a future person is potentially incompatible with morality as we know it. To divide humanity into modifiers and the modified, controllers and the controlled, would have such a negative effect on our self-understanding of what it means to be human that it would be difficult, if not impossible, to maintain existing moral notions of individual liberty, equality, and fraternity. Eugenic interventions—both possible and not yet possible—are likely to mean, says Habermas, that some members of future generations will have been programmed according to the intentions of their "controllers": "Would not the first human being to determine, *at his own discretion*, the natural essence of another human being at the same time destroy the equal freedoms that exist among persons of equal birth in order to ensure their difference?"[69] This challenges the very self-understanding that we have of the human species and the fragility of our moral communities.

Fetal Rights?

Should, then, a Christian ethics of rights take a clear stance in favor of the recognition (or extension of) legal rights for the unborn, and should this include some kind of rights-based protection against possible genetic abuse? Is it better to generate this kind of conflict than to deny a fetus or unborn child its natural right to life? This posing of the question is shocking, and I confess to finding the topic extremely difficult. Do Christian people really want to generate the kind of conflict that results in Caesarean sections being performed legally against the mother's wishes and pregnant women made liable to criminalization if their actions during pregnancy might affect the fetus detrimentally? Is it expedient to provide rights-based protection for the unborn against possible genetic abuse? Can we, on the other hand, rest content with the implications of not doing so?

The theological arguments developed so far in this book lead in the direction of supporting legal protection for the unborn—especially if we accept that legal personhood need not be a prerequisite for the recognition of justiciable rights (see chapter 7 below). Even if biblical teaching is unclear or agnostic about the moment when individual human life begins, it supports the claim that God knows, calls, and loves each person before birth just as much as after (e.g., Ps 139:13-16; Isa 49:1; Jer 1:5; Gal 1:15, etc.). Jesus and John the Baptist are introduced at the time of their conception (Matt 1:18; Luke 1:13, 31). Isaiah, Jeremiah, and Paul admit to being called to particular tasks before or during their time in the womb. The book of Hebrews refers to Levi the priest being, at one time, "still in the loins of his ancestor" (Heb 7:10). All this suggests that God's communion with people is not limited to a time slot after birth but extends back "before the foundation of the world" (Eph 1:4). Why, then, not extend human rights protection to the unborn? The claims to life enjoyed by the unborn are no less worthy of protection than those of children or adults.

Yet, the prospect of setting fetal rights against those of a pregnant woman in difficulty or against potential parents who want only to avoid inflicting suffering on their offspring is surely an unsatisfactory way of meeting whatever needs are in question. Despite urging throughout this book that Christian people have good reasons for human rights advocacy, I hesitate before the question of the legal recognition of fetal rights. A differentiated approach to fetal rights—whereby, for instance, the mother's rights are stronger at law until viability (20–22 weeks) but equal thereafter—might offer workable compromises that relieve the worst situations before us. But I doubt it. The role of litigation could easily expand around the practise of PGS, but we should, as the sages say, be careful what we wish for.[70] A mini-industry could be spawned in which battles are fought about inter alia the clinical validity of tests (e.g., the extent and limitation of association between genetic change found and the disorder, the ratios of false positive and false negative rates), clinical utility (e.g., questions about the therapeutic gap between diagnosis and treatment, whether to test for presymptomatic and/or predispositional conditions), clinical specificity (e.g., the ability or inability of a test to detect all disease-causing mutations, questions about what percentage success rate makes a good screening test—70%, 80%, or 95% sensitivity), and more besides. Legal trials could be held around the following: the nature of the "line drawing" involved in PGS is seemingly arbitrary; the meaning of such terms as "serious" and "severe" is contested; the quality of a child's life affected by a given disease or condition might vary dramatically from one family context to another; and, in some potentially serious or severe conditions, not all the persons with the gene will develop the diseases. As Alan Meisel observes with respect to litigation surrounding end-of-life issues: "[J]udicial opinions are often complex, and as the information gets passed along, it gets simplified, and sometimes oversimplified, and sometimes distorted, as in a children's game of 'telephone.'"[71] Again, however, the deeper issues of relations between the generations entailed in the kind of instrumentalization of one person's genome by another made possible by PGS and other technologies might remain largely untouched.

We live in litigious societies but lose sight sometimes of litigation's limits as an appropriate means of meeting needs. Here, perhaps, is a limit with respect to what *human* rights recognizable at law are equipped to effect. I cannot help but wonder if a human rights approach that sets mother against unborn child, and potential parents against the offspring they hope will come to birth, is the wrong solution to the problem. The Anglican moral theologian Gordon R. Dunstan was passionate in defense of personal liberties but rarely missed an opportunity to recall the language of interests, and of a duty to serve those interests, in preference to that of rights. As a pastor he knew that, "in the language of duties an answer can be framed to a real question wrongly worded."[72] This is especially true, we suggest, with respect to the ethical issues raised by PGS. Yet, it is chastening for Christian moralists that some of the most powerful writing about these transgenerational issues of how PGS and other biotechnological applications bear on creaturely limits in the context of reproductive liberty is from a philosopher who recognizes only postmetaphysical sources of morality. In concluding this chapter, we consider his broader-based approach to the difficult question of how to protect a future persons' genetic identity from abuse and offer comparisons with Bonhoeffer's observations about the nature of Christian witness.

Habermas does not, as far as I am aware, press for legal recognition of fetal rights. His response instead is to take a step behind issues regarding an immediate litigation strategy to develop a species ethic that respects the capabilities of future generations. For Habermas, a species ethic is one that respects capabilities across the generations. His baseline conviction is that being human is somehow profoundly about the capability to see ourselves as ethically free and morally equal beings. The species ethic that he propounds has roots in his discourse ethics with its tacit assumptions about the autonomy of the individual. His ethical worldview presupposes a principle of universalization that seeks the equal participation of all affected by a given decision and their freedom from constraint and centers around conditions of linguistic subjectivity. Species-ethical questions take the place of metaphysical and/or religious views of the self in relation to others. His hope is that reasonable people will perceive how morality is embedded in egalitarian universalism and that this must include future generations. This kind of domination and instrumentalization that imposes our own genetic preferences on future offspring is incompatible with our fundamental equality and fraternity. Using negative as well as positive eugenics means that we should have made such offspring, at least in part, the creature of our preferences. Liberal societies will, he trusts, become reflective enough to realize and prevent this.

The idea of a species ethic is not new to Christianity, though it looks different from that built by Habermas on the grounds of individual autonomy and mutual discourse. Like Habermas, Bonhoeffer looks for a species ethic because he grasps the transgenerational dimension of today's decision making. Unlike Habermas, Bonhoeffer's species ethic centers around human solidarity in sin and the hope of redemption in Christ rather than the conditions of linguistic subjectivity. For Bonhoeffer, everything turns on grasping how the sinful acts of individuals affect the guiltiness of all humanity, and vice versa:

> The culpability of the individual and the universality of sin should be understood together; that is, the individual culpable act and the culpability of the human race must be connected conceptually. When the human race is understood by means of the biological concept of the species, the ethical gravity of the concept of culpability is weakened. We must thus discover a Christian-ethical concept of the species. The issue is how to understand the human species in terms of the concept of sin.[73]

In a biblically informed species ethic, says Bonhoeffer, everything turns on seeing that "we are menaced by the chaos . . . crouching at the door."[74] We are coessential or cosubstantial (*homoousiotitos*) with the humanity of Adam and Eve, Cain and Lamech, those at Babel, and share their temptation to confuse supposed advancement with catastrophic error.[75] Everything turns, says Bonhoeffer, on the structure of humanity-in-Adam, which is composed of many individuals and yet one. "With sin, ethical atomism enters history."[76] Every person exists in ethical isolation, living their own moral lives, responsible for their own conscience. Everyone is both utterly alone in their sin and also deeply implicated with others.

Bonhoeffer's plea is for greater awareness of the universality of sin as "the *broadest sense of shared sinfulness*."[77] Sin committed by one individual has a significance beyond the isolation of his or her life: "Sin must be conceived as both a supra-individual deed and, of course, as an individual deed; it must be simultaneously the deed of the human race and of the individual."[78] The Christological content of the particular chapter from which this citation comes is not highly developed but it is clear nonetheless that the structure of humanity-in-Adam can be understood only when taken up into the story of Jesus Christ; "it is superseded [*aufgehoben*] only through the unity of the new humanity in Christ."[79] Where Habermas's work begins with claims about the species as a way of thinking abstractly about humanity, Bonhoeffer starts from the radical particularity of humanity in Christ, and the radical diversity of neighbors given to me in Christ, before affirming our solidarity in sin as a species before God. A species ethic for Bonhoeffer does not advocate responsibility to or for the human species *except* through the person of Jesus Christ; there is no road to the species or to universal moral concern that does not begin with Jesus Christ. "We cannot reinterpret God's incarnation in Christ as a general incarnation of God."[80] Only Christ Jesus reveals to us how the human species stands before God and restores to us the commands of God the Creator. This means that a species ethic conceived dogmatically does not start from humankind in general but from one particular human.

The witness of Christian ethics to the one particular human, Jesus Christ, finds compatible resonances (albeit limited) in the work of human rights to protect the capabilities of individuals, not least the potential capabilities of the unborn. We cannot therefore discard the possibility of recognition of legal rights for the fetus, including some kind of protection from at least the most problematic kinds of genetic manipulation—though I conclude that clear and strong regulatory frameworks set by governments and international authorities are preferable. The need to give greater ethical consideration to transgenerational issues is pressing, and discernment is required with respect to when a rights-based solution might, or might not, be the best way forward. As Bonhoeffer prompts us to see, however, the tragedy of this whole area of debate today is that original sin, death, and illness (the results of the Fall) appear to be locked in a complicity that prevents the truly good from coming to pass. No one escapes the inevitable guilt of decisions that participate in some form of corruption: "This is already the world in which we live, a modern world in which nothing shields *everyone* from tragedy or the doom of endless choice, which results in the sacrifice of some for others and irresolvable dilemmas and unhealed regret."[81] In such contexts, the Christian is not necessarily the person who finds a way to be good in any given situation. "On the contrary, the Christian can rather be seen as the person who recognizes that there is no *apparent* good to be found or performed in any given situation."[82] Neither an option for nor one against the legal recognition of fetal rights can be justified as an expression of the will of God. What Milbank calls "discerning *poesis*" remains essential at personal and political levels because violence to one party or the other cannot be eradicated, only tempered.

To conclude, recognition of legal rights for the fetus is fraught with difficulties, yet obligations rest on all humankind to protect future persons' genetic identity from abuse. In such difficult contexts, Bonhoeffer reminds us that Christian witness to divine command is not just another contribution to ethical debate but something closer to sharing in Christ's sufferings; the church's calling is to pray for God's mercy and seek new ways of witnessing that better instantiate practical service and love—perhaps through expansion in the practice of adoption and learning new ways of being family, in refraining from judgment when many demand harsh penalties (John 7:53–8:11), or recognizing unspoken complicity in social and structural sin from which only God can deliver us. Grace might yet be found "at the other side of individual and social sin."[83]

6

Animal Rights and the Responsibilities of "Dominion"

The fear and dread of you shall rest on every animal of the earth, and on every bird of the air, on everything that creeps on the ground, and on all the fish of the sea; into your hand they are delivered. Every moving thing that lives shall be food for you; and just as I gave you the green plants, I give you everything. Only, you shall not eat flesh with its life, that is, its blood. For your own lifeblood I will surely require a reckoning: from every animal I will require it. . . .

—Genesis 9:2-5

As in Genesis 1, the command "be fruitful and multiply" is linked with dominion over the animal world. Here we read, however, that the animals, birds, and fish will "fear and dread" humankind. The harmony and cooperation of Genesis 1 has been overtaken by something closer to slavery and control. As the earth was cursed because of Adam and Eve's sin (Gen 3:17), so the animals, birds, and fish have become victims in a corrupted creation. The whole of material creation, given by God as a blessing and a gift to humankind, now suffers because of sin. The vegetarian state of humankind is ended (Gen 9:2-3)—which probably explains the "fear and dread." After both Fall and Flood, the purpose of the natural order has been changed and distorted.[1] God has promised never again to destroy every living creature (Gen 9:21), but the divine will now seems to accept that "fear and dread" will characterize the relation between other creatures and humankind. The only limit placed on human actions is: "Only, you shall not eat flesh with its life, that is, its blood" (Gen 9:4).

Are there, then, theological grounds for the attribution of moral and/or legal rights to animals and even the environment? So far, we have discussed natural rights as given and guaranteed by God, arising from and belonging to the bodily existence that *human beings* enjoy. We have defined natural rights as those claims to life, liberty, and so on that arise from the bodily form of human existence and which recognize appropriately the dignity and worth bestowed by God on persons. We have seen that the topic of natural rights is not the whole of Christian ethics, and that respect for human rights is not the only way of expressing moral worth and virtue, or of struggling for justice in the twenty-first century. We have argued, however, that the social imperative that flows from the gospel finds appropriate expression in the language of rights. In what follows, we suggest that the same arguments apply to animals and plants—that is, they have claims to life and to respect by virtue of being created by God, designated by him as "good," and preserved after both Fall and Flood by his word and will. The more difficult issue concerns the relation between this theological grounding of rights and rights as legal protection against harm.

Our approach is primarily theological because everything that Christian ethics may say about respect due to the natural order follows from the creative and saving works of God in Christ. This is not to say that there is a Christian economic order as such or a peculiarly Christian mode of politics. Yet, there are distinctively theological perspectives on political matters, secularist modes of decision making, natural rights, human rights, animal rights, and so forth. Hence the obligation on Christian people to think both about how far natural rights may be conceived of theologically and about how this conceptuality relates to modern secularist notions of human rights and legal recognition of animal rights. Antagonism between Christian and secularist perspectives will sometimes overwhelm possibilities for cooperation—as, for instance, aspects of Peter Singer's account of speciesism in discussions about animal rights. Yet, cooperation for the sake of God's coming reign is also possible.

"Fear and Dread"

Genesis 9:2-4 is perhaps an unpromising starting point for such a discussion because it appears to justify consumption of animals as food and the kind of dominion that permits exploitation. The animal rights philosopher and campaigner Tom Regan notes how religious ideas based on such biblical passages are used to justify the assumption that animals are created merely to serve human needs.[2] And he has a point. Doctrine advanced by Augustine and Aquinas to the effect that God's providential ordering permits humans' approval of what they find pleasing in the animal realm, and disapproval what they find amiss, has been used to justify fur-trapping, hunting, intensive farming, and much more.[3] Hence our project might strike readers as doomed to failure before it begins. Arguably, however, Genesis 9:1-17 and Christian ethics more generally still have something important to say about respect for nonhuman life as a theological and spiritual issue.

"Food for You" or Concession to Sinfulness?

The obvious question is what sense to make of Genesis 9:2-4 and the limit that it sets on eating animals as food: "Only, you shall not eat flesh with its life, that is, its blood" is argued by some to be an interpolation.[4] The text itself flows more easily without these verses, and a dietary law is unexpected here; though, arguably, neither reason is sufficient to substantiate the claim that the verses are a later addition. The prohibition on the eating of blood meshes with later teaching (Lev 3:17; 7:26-27; 19:26; Deut 12:16-25; 1 Sam 14:32-34) and became a defining feature of Israelite life. Moreover, it would appear that Jesus ate fish and early Christians ate both meat and fish (Luke 24:42; John 21:9-14; Acts 10:9-16; 1 Cor 8). Jesus "declared all foods clean" (Mark 7:19), and Peter freed the church from kosher food laws (Acts 10:11-15; 11:5-9). The seriousness of the prohibition here rests in its being a command for the whole world and not only Israel. Life belongs to God and humankind must respect and acknowledge this. God has absolute sovereignty over all created life. Blood is equated with created life; loss of blood equates to loss of life created by God. As Harland writes: "[B]lood signified life—indeed, it was the life itself."[5] Whether or not a later addition, the prohibition emphasizes divine authority. Von Rad makes the point: "Even when man slaughters and kills, he is to know that he is touching something, which, because it is life, is in a special manner God's property; and as a sight of this he is to keep his hands off the blood."[5] In Harland's words, "[H]ere is a restriction of humanity's overweening power."[7]

According to Andrew Linzey, God's allowing of humans to eat meat is a concession to sinfulness, the implication being that the higher Christian calling is to vegetarianism.[8] One of the best-known Christian proponents of animal rights, Linzey has pioneered work that exposes questionable readings of biblical passages (e.g., Gen 1:26; 2:20; 9:2-4) that justify a devaluing of the worth of nonhuman creatures. He laments the fact that few, if any, Christian traditions have developed a satisfactory moral theology of animal treatment and argues that the anthropocentrism of Christian theology has resulted in a dulled appreciation of the beauty, creativity, and worth of creation and, worse, the abuse of those "*theos*-rights" that animals hold.[9] He is broadly critical of Aquinas's teaching that "brute animals" have no participation in understanding and are naturally subject to humankind, and that humanity's dominion over the animals includes the hunting of wild animals and the governance of others.[10] In short, biblically informed notions of justice demand that vulnerable and innocent sentient creatures are protected, and the most meaningful and effective means of doing this today is through the attribution of both moral and legal rights. Animal rights are a theological matter for Linzey, but he wants good theology and jurisprudence to keep in step. To this end, he urges Christian people to speak in stronger defense of both animal welfare and animal rights. As an ordained Anglican priest, he condemns the Church of England for allowing battery farming of chickens on some of its land and urges that the time is ripe for repentance. The only model of dominion over animals that the church should recognize is that of Christ's lordship manifest in service. [11]

Linzey's reading of Genesis 9:2-4 is of particular interest because it concentrates on the ambiguity of creation as pointing in two directions: affirming and denying God at one and the same time. Creation "affirms God because God loves and cares for it but it also necessarily denies God because it is not divine."[12] The text must be read in light of this ambiguity, Linzey argues; otherwise it will falsely justify adherence to the way things are rather than the way God wants them to be, and/or allow our fallen condition to serve as a yardstick of what is acceptable to God rather than the hope of God's new creation. The Fall and the Flood are the great symbols of why humans can no longer live at peace with either themselves or with other creatures, and must not be used to justify the killing and eating of animals. Similarly, a Christian theology of natural law must be understood *not* with reference to "*the way things are*" but "in the sense of *what should be*."[13] A similar point is made in Jürgen Moltmann's essay entitled "Human Rights—Rights of the Earth," in which the opening theological premise is that humans exist within the community of all creation. His eschatological pragmatism suggests that this ethical community has laws instilled by God at creation, including the sabbath of the earth, and that these laws equate to (or should equate to) moral if not legal rights. Living beings require the protection of law and this, suggests Moltmann, is probably best expressed in terms of rights. Moltmann represents renewed Protestant interest in natural law—facilitated, ironically, by Karl Barth's theology of the reconciliation of all things in Christ. Like Barth, both Moltmann and Linzey confront us with the reality of living *zwischen den Zeiten* (between the times). With Noah, we live under "the shadow of the divine abandonment" where a degree of enmity characterizes the relation between humankind and animals, man and beast.[14] Yet, the new order in the new Jerusalem will be vegetarian (Rev 22:2), the lion shall dwell with the lamb, the leopard with the kid, and there shall be neither hurt nor harm in all the holy mountain (Isa 11:6-9; 65:25; Hos 2:18)—the suggestion being that anticipation of this new order should entail the attribution of theological, moral, and legal rights to animals.

Karl Barth, by contrast, was not averse to meat-eating and held that the dominion of humans over the rest of the animal kingdom includes the freedom to kill and eat. Passages in *Church Dogmatics* III.4 suggest that Barth was not entirely comfortable in accepting this concession: "He must always shrink from this possibility even when he makes use of it. It always contains the sharp counter-question: Who are you, man, to claim that you must venture this to maintain, support, enrich and beautify your own life? What is there in your life that you feel compelled to take this aggressive step in its favour?"[15] Nonetheless, Barth maintained that the killing of animals is justified by divine permission—albeit only "as a deeply reverential act of repentance, gratitude and praise" and with a glance forward to the time when creation will be free of the abattoir, hunting lodge, and vivisection chamber. Barth was, perhaps, uncharacteristically slow in respect of this topic to take seriously the ethical implications of the eschatological hope. Indeed, he warns against "wanton anticipation" among vegetarians who want to behave as if the new aeon described by Isaiah 11 and Romans 8:21 is already upon us, and puts the milder question of whether the killing and eating of animals is allowed. For him, the deciding factor was the command of God, which alone draws the line between what is permitted and/or forbidden, and the eating of animals is permitted.[16] Until the new aeon, he says, God's goodness can mean both severity and kindness, slaying and nurturing. Both may occur in obedience and praise to the Creator and in respect of all life for His sake: "A good hunter, honourable butcher and conscientious vivisectionist will differ from the bad in the fact that even as they are engaged in killing animals they hear this groaning and travailing of the creature, and therefore, in comparison with all others who have to do with animals, they are summoned to an intensified, sharpened and deepened diffidence, reserve and carefulness."[17]

Ultimate and Penultimate

These differences between Barth versus Linzey and Moltmann pose for us questions about the ultimate and penultimate in Christian ethics, to use Bonhoeffer's terms. Linzey and Moltmann seek after the ultimate and want to break with the suffering and compromise associated with the penultimate. Barth, at least on this issue, is more resigned to the realities of the penultimate that for him (and I confess for me also) include meat-eating and acceptance of the use of animals by humans in regulated research contexts—albeit with heightened awareness of welfare issues. The tension between the ultimate and penultimate is, says Bonhoeffer, unavoidable, and we sometimes, almost inexplicably, opt for penultimate rather than ultimate courses of action.[18] The killing and eating of animals is one such action, and the challenge for those of us who eat meat must surely be to ask ourselves if we think the action an unworthy compromise that hinders God's work. Bonhoeffer leaves open the general question of penultimate ethics, thereby inviting readers to address it for themselves. On one point, however, he is uncompromising: arbitrary destruction of the penultimate seriously harms the ultimate. "When, for example, a human life is deprived of the conditions that are part of being human, the justification of such a life by grace and faith is at least seriously hindered, if not made impossible."[19] Wanton destruction of the penultimate is contrary to proclamation of God's word. Christian ethics is about preparing the way of the Lord (Luke 3:4-6), and careless harm can never be claimed for the ultimate. Arbitrary destruction of the penultimate is exemplified by the taking of not only human life but of animal and plant life as well.

Animal Rights as a Theological and Spiritual Issue

In Christian ethics, animal rights is a theological and spiritual issue—at least in the sense that animals have claims to respect and stewardship due to them as God's creatures. Animals have claims that we may designate as rights in order to express the kind of protection and care to which they are entitled on their own terms within divine providence. Many biblical texts suggest that the wanton destruction or abuse of life constitutes sinful disruption of our relation with God and works against the return of the world to the beauty in which it was first created (Exod 20:10; Lev 25:1-7; Deut 20:19; Ps 148: 1-12; Rev 11:18). Protection against arbitrary encroachment on the freedoms proper to the animal and plant world is essential to the exercise of dominion expected of humankind. Moreover, the church's eucharistic offering of the world to God in Christ anticipates the world to come in which the need for exploitation and experimentation is removed. Until that time, the worship and liturgy of the church is an anaphora, a lifting up, an offering and consecration to God of what he has given us. But to what extent does this theologically derived position on animal rights translate into a case for legal rights? What might legal animal rights entail, and on what grounds might Christian moralists argue in the public square?

Animal Welfare or Animal Rights?

Among secular ethicists, there are large differences between those who seek animal welfare and those who seek animal rights.[20] The latter argue typically on grounds of principle (albeit variously conceived) not pragmatism, and are not satisfied by larger cages for animals in captivity, less use of animals in science, tighter regulation of sport hunting and trapping, and so on. They want the abolition of such things because social systems that allow the infliction of pain on animals and their slaughter for meat or fur are deemed to be wrong.[21] The case for animal rights has been made variously by inter alia Peter Singer and Tom Regan—notably in the former's 1975 *Animal Liberation* (which contained graphic descriptions of factory farms, abattoirs, and laboratories across Europe and North America, plus recipes for vegetarian dishes); their 1976 coedited volume, *Animal Rights and Human Obligations*; and Regan's 1983 *Case for Animal Rights* (regarded by many as a seminal text on the topic).[22] Singer's approach is utilitarian and adapts classic modes of assessing and maximizing welfare to include animals. Animals have interests because they can suffer, and the moral principle of equal consideration of interests means that humans are not justified in disregarding the suffering of animals. R. G. Frey, also a utilitarian, is unconvinced and warns that Singer neglects to consider the consequences of vegetarianism; it is by no means clear, he argues, that either the attribution of legal rights or vegetarianism would be beneficial to long-term animal welfare.[23] Disagreements between Singer, Regan, and their critics reveal "fault lines" in the debate about what kind of moral issues are at stake and also the importance, for our purposes, of grounding animal rights in peculiarly theological grounds. Nonetheless, both urge a case for animal rights and will not settle for improved welfare; it is not merely a matter of reducing harm, or of providing good quality food, water, and air, but of enshrining at law what is properly due to animals.

Singer's argument on the grounds of supposed moral equality with humans is arguably one of the clearest and most influential arguments in favor of animal rights over against lesser measures to protect welfare based on an ethic of equal consideration to sentient beings.[24] It is deeply problematic to Christian ethics for reasons that have been well rehearsed and need not detain us here.[25] Put bluntly, his use of the concept of speciesism is unconvincing because it ignores a fundamental difference between humans and other animals, namely, that humans have moral responsibilities toward animals. The appeal to an abstract principle of equality wilts in the face of empirically demonstrable recognition that humans have responsibilities for animals of a kind that animals do not have for humans. Nor does this criticism rest solely upon biblical teaching and liturgical practice. The observation about moral responsibility, or what Christian ethics recognizes as dominion, stands on its own terms and has been defended coherently as the basis of an argument against the analogy of speciesism with racism and sexism.[26] This is not to say that animal suffering ought not to be measured in the same ways as human suffering, or that utilitarian moral theories are not properly expanded to take animal suffering into account. But the urgent need to reduce animal suffering can be addressed (and will, arguably, be addressed more effectively) if separated from weak claims about the equality of all animals and when treated in terms of how to recognize the rights of animals as animals—perhaps in ways that recognize different rights among animals.[27]

Regan's position is less problematic for Christian ethics because he argues on the grounds of the intrinsic value of animals. Indeed, it is arguable that a doctrine of creation provides a higher-order rationale that his own account lacks. His deontological approach casts the animal rights cause as a liberation movement analogous to earlier historical movements for the liberation of slaves and women. Where Singer emphasizes animal sentience and capacity for pain, Regan addresses the inherent value of animals. They should be included in our moral community as beings with rights, he says, because they are the subject of a life: "[S]ince the utilization of non-human animals for purposes of, among other things, fashion, research, entertainment, or gustatory delight harms them and treats them as (our) resources, and since such treatment violates their right to be treated with respect, it follows that such utilization is morally wrong and ought to end."[28] Human dignity, he argues, is not the only source of "right." Animals also have rights because, like us, they bring unified psychological, sensory, conative, and volitional capacities to the world. As subjects of life they are worthy not only of kindness but justice. Like most neo-Kantian theories, Regan's suffers from a gap between affirmation of inherent value and the attribution of both moral and legal rights.[29] His problem is getting people to accept the inherent value of animals and their right to be treated with respect equal to that due to humans. At the end of the day, he leaves us wondering about the reasons for granting rights to animals. Conformity to pure practical reason supplies small reason sometimes for bothering to be good; so, likewise, the mere assertion of inherent value might not be enough to raise a groundswell of support for animal rights.

It is not our role to sort out the problems of modern liberalism but to think theologically about animal rights. So far, we have argued for "theological claim-rights" that express those things due to animals as creatures of God. This is similar to Linzey's use of *theos*-rights to express something of the vital connection between *God's* rights as Creator and the protection due to his creation. For Linzey, the basic issue is that of God's rights; animal rights are recognized for God's sake and in witness to the liberatory heart of the gospel. Legal recognition should follow from this theological affirmation as the means required to effect practical recognition of the claims that animals justly have on humankind. The question is how to move beyond this to what "theological claim-rights" might entail practically; that is, how the law might reflect animal claim-rights, and the grounds on which Christians might argue to this effect in the public square.

Theological Claim-Rights and Immunity-Rights at Law

For Linzey, the *theos*-rights of animals imply vegetarianism and legal rights to effect their adequate protection against exploitation and suffering. In what follows, I cannot urge that Christians *ought* to be vegetarians, though I accept that not eating meat coincides more closely with biblical anticipations of the new aeon than does eating meat. But limited progress might be made toward the kind of dominion expected in Genesis 9:2-7 of all humankind, and the kind of human law that best reflects this. Again, Genesis 9:2-4 seems an unpromising starting point because only abstinence from blood is commanded and this could, arguably, be met by kosher or halal meat-eating practices of ritual slaughter and literal draining of blood from the meat before it is eaten. The text gives no express guidance about how the prohibition of blood should be observed. Yet, three observations might be ventured. First, we are reminded that animal life is the exclusive property of God and that wherever slaughter or other use of animals occurs this should be borne in mind. Second, lack of respect for divine sovereignty by mistreatment of an animal's life is worse than eating meat. Third, the prohibition carries a warning against blood lust and the indiscriminate killing of animal life. As Harland suggests, "[T]he prohibition then becomes a preventative measure against brutality."[30] For our purposes, this leads to the further question of whether, together, these observations might support not only generally construed moral and/or legal claim-rights but also prohibition- or immunity-rights against all that conflicts with the dignity of animals within God's sovereign providence—for example, torture or cruelty.[31] In other words, the question is whether differentiated types of rights discourse is possible and/or appropriate.

Prohibition- or immunity-rights have been suggested recently as a practicable step toward animal protection by the practicing American lawyer Steven M. Wise. Using the relatively well established Hohfeld categorization of different kinds of rights (liberty- or claim-rights, privilege- or immunity-rights), he posits that immunity rights are likely to be achieved first and thus "heads off at the pass" both those doubtful that liberty-rights are relevant to animals for the simple reason that humans might choose not to respect them and those worried that claim-rights require correlate duties that might be difficult to establish.[32] So, for instance, immunity-rights to prohibit humans from torturing or enslaving nonhuman animals need not alienate liberals who regard rights as legal shields that protect one individual from another or from the state. This approach might, for instance, meet Sionadh Douglas-Scott's concern that the best way to take the environment (and animals, we may extrapolate) seriously is *not* to accord it rights.[33] Her twofold opening premise is that rights are the legal fiction we use to mold society together and concern the enjoyment of goods by individuals separately. Rights do not apply to subhuman species. Consequently, she argues, rights claims in the neo-Kantian tradition are unable to provide the legal protections we must accord to the environment if the earth is to continue supporting us all. According legal rights to plants, trees, and animals would be impractical and the result of muddled thinking. In the liberal, neo-Kantian tradition obligations must be allocated to and/or accepted by a specific agent. Endlessly extending the modern notion of rights is not, she says, the most effective way of protecting the natural world.

The nub of Douglas-Scott's criticism (which is representative of the neo-Kantian view that the only real subject of a right is a citizen) is that rights attributed to animals or the environment would be ill defined in scope and unenforceable and would, consequently, do little to protect the environment and would damage the usefulness of rights in other contexts. Arguably, however, immunity-rights are practicable means of granting animals protection against individuals or corporations with respect to torture and cruelty when, otherwise, these individuals or corporations might have no concern for animals' claim-rights with respect to torture and cruelty. In other words, the specification of immunity-rights provides ways of saying what the more general claim-rights mean. It is difficult to say what an animal's claim to appropriate respect at law should mean without disaggregating this claim into liberties, powers, and immunities. Given that animals do not answer to the question "Who?" and are not, therefore, capable of certain powers, they cannot be the subject of certain rights reserved for humans. This much may be granted to liberal critics. Animals can, however, be the subject of immunity-rights that render them immune from the removal or alteration of the powers that they do hold; immunity-rights are a possible first step toward recognition for nonhuman animals as legal persons.

Humans would, of course, have to be empowered to bring cases to court on behalf of, or as representative of, the animal(s) subject to torture or cruelty. Cass R. Sunstein makes this point and outlines practicable ways in which it could happen.[34] As a first step, he adapts a definition of torture from the California Penal Code 599b to read "any act or omission 'whereby unnecessary or unjustified physical pain or suffering is caused or permitted.'"[35] Moreover, he is clear about the potential benefits of immunity-rights over current welfare legislation. Prohibitions against cruelty include, he suggests, the possibility for private individuals rather than public prosecutors to bring cases; a widened scope of protection from obligations to animals within a given individual's care or corporate oversight to the rights of animals on their own terms, that is, removal of the need to consider animal welfare through a particular relationship with a human; and more extensive coverage of protection to include animals currently excluded from legislation. In other words, there is a strong chance that immunity-rights could be used to protect animals more effectively than they are currently protected against torture and cruelty. Immunity-rights are potentially practicable and would have the symbolic function of denoting greater respect for animals than is common now.

What Levels of Protection? Working with a Capabilities Approach

There are, of course, obvious differences between species of nonhuman animals. This must give rise to some differences in the immunity-rights that each have. Arguably the best philosophical approach to date in response to these questions is Martha Nussbaum's "capabilities approach" adapted from work in collaboration with Amartya Sen on international human development. As noted in chapter 6, their central moral question regarding international development is: "What are individuals actually able to do or to be?" The underlying idea is that development policy should be linked to the most significant human capabilities (e.g., for life, bodily health, bodily integrity, thought, imagination, affiliation, and play).[36] When adapted to animals and immunity-rights at law, this question becomes: "What level of life does it enjoy?" Here the implication is that the legal protection due to animate things should be linked to its significant capabilities. Legal protection should be increased as significant capabilities (e.g., for pain and communication) increase. The protection due to animate things should increase according to the level of life that it enjoys—so that, for example, it might be deemed morally acceptable to perform procedures on a bacterium that would not be acceptable on a higher primate.

So far, so good. But to accept that the level of protection due to an animal should be decided according to the level of life that its species enjoys is to accept the need for much difficult and new moral reasoning. To illustrate the point, consider whether living beings, such as bacteria, should be patentable with reference to the now famous "Chakrabarty ruling." Before this ruling, a long-established convention in patent law excluded products of nature from patentability.[37] In the *Diamond v. Chakrabarty* ruling, the majority decided that Chakrabarty's bacterium was not found in nature before the application of his genetic engineering techniques. It is now widely acknowledged that the bacterium he "invented" resulted from naturally occurring bacteria and by naturally occurring processes.[38] The ruling was as follows:

> [Chakrabarty's] microorganism plainly qualifies as patentable subject matter. His claim is not to a hitherto unknown natural phenomenon, but to a nonnaturally occurring manufacture or composition of matter—a product of human ingenuity "having a distinctive name, character [and] use." (*Hartranft v. Wiegmann*, 121 US 609, 615 [1887]) . . . [T]he patentee has produced a new bacterium with markedly different characteristics from any found in nature and one having the potential for significant utility. His discovery is not nature's handiwork, but his own; accordingly it is patentable subject matter under §101.[39]

Hailed as a landmark decision, the *Chakrabarty* case opened the way for phenomenal growth of the biotechnology industry in the United States. In its wake, the U.S. Patent Office issued patents on other genetically engineered plants and animals, including the now famous Harvard "onco mouse."[40] Despite the consequences of the ruling, there is widespread consensus among religious leaders, Christian ethicists, and environmental campaigners that it blurred the distinction between discovery and invention and crossed an established ethical boundary.[41] The immunity-right appropriate to a bacterium might involve a prohibition against being treated as merely inanimate matter—the implication being that patenting of bacteria, as well as higher animal life-forms, is excluded on the grounds that they are products of nature and not inventions.[42]

Chief Justice Burger's citation of the congressional report that accompanied the 1952 Patent Act noted that Congress intended statutory subject matter to "include anything under the sun that is made by man." In other words, he thought that Chakrabarty's microorganism qualified as patentable subject matter because it had been "made" by the scientist—in a manner analogous to any other manufactured product. In a dissenting opinion, Justice Brennan, together with three other justices in the 5–4 split decision, said:

Patents on the processes by which he has produced and employed the new living organism are not contested. The only question we need decide is whether Congress, exercising its authority under Art. I, § 8, of the Constitution, intended that he be able to secure a monopoly on the living organism itself, no matter how produced or how used. Because I believe the Court has misread the applicable legislation, I dissent.[43]

Justice Brennan argued that Congress had never before intended to extend the scope of patenting legislation to living organisms, and that it was the role of Congress and not the Court to broaden or narrow the reach of the patent laws. He recognized the legitimacy of process patents in biotechnology but challenged the extension of patent law to living organisms.

We must surely agree with Brennan that simply extending the rules for inorganic materials to the biological sphere has encouraged inappropriate attitudes toward nature. The point here is simply that working with a capabilities approach is likely to be difficult and fraught with controversy. To my mind, the level of life enjoyed by a bacterium warrants immunity from treatment as an inanimate object, which would translate, in this instance, to nonpatentability. It is more difficult, however, to differentiate between animals of different species as the level of life enjoyed increases. Evidence suggests that cold-blooded animals such as fish, snakes, and frogs suffer pain and that cephalopods (such as octopus and squid) can learn complex tasks and appear to form social bonds. Recent advances in genetic science render the issues even more complex as biologists tell us that there may be very few genes expressing proteins that are unique to human beings. Most genes we use are also used in one form or another by other organisms but are regulated differently.[44] It would also be difficult to gain consensus on the types of tests for deciding where lines should be drawn between species. If, however, immunity-rights are to be recognized at law then a "capabilities approach" of some kind is surely the best way forward.

Why Legal Rights Should Be Accorded to Nonhuman Species

To summarize, our account of the claim-rights of animals suggests that it is inappropriate to regard animals as property, at least in the same sense that inanimate objects are regarded as such, and inappropriate also to regard animals as persons or entitled to legal personhood. Humans may not treat animals however they wish, nor are animals equal to humans in all moral and legal respects. Rather, the issue is what the claim-rights of animals should be deemed to entail and how these theologically derived rights might translate into law. We have argued that Christian ethics needs a differentiated understanding of rights that moves from *theological* claim-rights to legally enforceable rights in distinguishable steps—not based on an abstract principle of equality between human and nonhuman animals but on theologically derived claim-rights to appropriate respect and protection and legally recognizable immunity-rights from certain human behaviors. I cannot myself accept that some meat eating and use of animals in medical experiments, and so forth, is totally unacceptable. Arguably, however, immunity-rights correlate with the prohibition in Genesis 9:2-4 against lack of respect for the animal's life, offer practicable steps toward stronger legal recognition of the respect due to animals as animals, and recognize the peculiar ethical responsibilities that humans bear toward other animals.

❧ 7 ❧

War, Democracy, and the Retreat
from Human Rights

The most powerful democracy is detaining hundreds of suspected foot soldiers of the Taliban in a legal black hole at the United States naval base at Guantánamo Bay, where they await trial on capital charges by military tribunals. This episode must be put in context. Democracies must defend themselves. Democracies are entitled to try officers and soldiers of enemy forces for war crimes. But it is a recurring theme in history that in times of war, armed conflict, or perceived national danger, even liberal democracies adopt measures infringing human rights in ways that are wholly disproportionate to the crisis.

—Johan Steyn[1]

. . . when questions of policy and balance arise, the legislature and the executive are democratically accountable to the electorate, unlike the judiciary. . . . True enough, but we should recognize that the argument based on the democratic imperative may slide into a form of majoritarianism or moral populism.

—Anthony Lester[2]

For your own lifeblood I will surely require a reckoning; from every animal I will require it and from human beings, each one for the blood of another, I will require a reckoning for human life.

—Genesis 9:5

Guantánamo Bay: The Legal Black Hole

The quality of justice afforded to prisoners at Guantánamo Bay is widely recognized as falling below minimum international standards. Until July

147

2004. when the U. S. Supreme Court ruled that prisoners held at Guantánamo Bay could take their case of unlawful imprisonment to the American courts, detainees had no rights under the Geneva Conventions of 1949 as prisoners of war and were not subject to human rights norms under U.S. law because they were being held outside the territory of the United States on land leased from Cuba. In February 2002 President George W. Bush wrote in a memorandum entitled "Humane Treatment of al Qaeda and Taliban Detainees" that the provisions of the Geneva Conventions do not apply to the conflict with al Qaeda because inter alia the latter is not a High Contracting Party to Geneva.[3] The memorandum spoke of acting consistently with the principles of Geneva but, in effect, declared that the Geneva Conventions do not apply to al Qaeda detainees and that Taliban detainees should be regarded as neither prisoners of war nor civilians.[4] Condemned by many as "a monstrous failure of justice" the effect of "the blanket presidential order" was to deprive them all of any rights whatsoever.[5]

In describing the failure of justice at Guantánamo Bay, Lord Steyn (a retired British Law Lord, now president of the political action organization Justice) writes: "[T]he purpose of holding the prisoners at Guantánamo Bay was and is to put them beyond the rule of law, beyond the protection of any courts, and at the mercy of the victors."[6] How prisoners are treated at Guantánamo Bay we do not know. But, says Lord Steyn, detainees are held in 1.8 x 2.4 meter cells for up to 24 hours a day, and photographs have been published of prisoners being returned to their cells on stretchers after interrogation. Most nations have their own examples of attempts to put persons beyond reach of the law, but history has yet to judge these trials held in secret by the military, in which detainees are deprived of confidential communications with their lawyers and refused access to all relevant evidence, and where there is no possibility of judicial review. At least in Franz Kafka's *The Trial*, Joseph K. could talk confidentially with his (albeit incompetent) lawyer and there was a court to hear his case. For the moment, it looks as if the Guantánamo Bay regime put prisoners beyond the reach of the law in a gross violation of UNDHR Article 6, which states, "Everyone has the right to recognition everywhere as a person before the law," and Article 3 of the Third Geneva Convention.

As a counterargument, it may be noted that the regime was consistent (at least debatably so) with the so-called "Saboteurs' Case" (*Ex parte Quirin* [1942]), in which the U.S. Supreme Court authorized a congressional decision that military tribunals rather than the courts could try alleged violations of the laws of war. Those without prisoner of war status would not be tried and punished under the criminal legislation of the adversary but should be subject to prosecution and punishment by military tribunals for the acts that made their belligerency unlawful. In 1949, however, Article 3 of the Third Geneva Convention detailed minimum provisions relating to the treatment of prisoners prohibiting "outrages upon personal dignity, in particular humiliating and degrading treatment," and requiring the need to afford at trial "all the judicial guarantees which are recognized as indispensable by civilized people."[7] Regardless of prisoner of war status, unlawful combatants are not to be deemed beyond the ambit of the law and are still covered by this convention.[8] This has led many to suggest that the International Criminal Court would have been the most fitting place for Guantánamo Bay prisoners to have been tried.

Personhood before the Law

Terrorism is inimical to human rights and democracy. Indeed, it might appear offensive to associate the fight against terrorism with the defense of "rights" when the rights of many, including the right to life, have been ignored and violated. As the lawyer Clive Walker remarks, the expression of any viewpoint about defending the rights of those accused of terrorism is likely to raise more hackles than quality debate because of the depth of feeling involved.[9] Action to protect the rights of those threatened by terrorist attacks is needed as much as, if not more than, those who pose a threat to them. The suppression of terrorism has to be the goal of governments whose primary responsibility is the protection of citizens; national security weighs more heavily than a collection of individual rights. As Walker notes, however, there can be a confusion between national security used as a substantive legal argument and as a procedural defense.[10] The individual's defense must be treated on its own merits. The "new paradigm" of counter-terrorism is one in which the fair and effective administration of justice is at risk of compromise.[11] If the rights of access to the courts and a fair trial are denied, then voices of protest should be loud. In the meantime, if, as it would appear, Guantánamo Bay detainees lost the right to recognition as persons before the law, then injustice has been done to us all.

In the remainder of this chapter, we consider this kind of retreat from human rights with reference to what Anthony Lester (in the opening quotation above) calls the "majoritarianism or moral populism" of modern democracies. While a worldwide culture of human rights seems to be developing, some of the nations most involved with the 1948 United Nations Declaration of Human Rights have condoned egregious violations of human rights. We are interested in why and how this could have happened and what, if anything, about the framing of liberal, secularist human rights doctrines is prone to the kind of violation that, in effect, denies someone personhood before the law. Many factors could be taken into account, and multidisciplinary investigations of the kind not possible here are needed to arrive at anything approaching satisfactory answers. Our considerations are preliminary and brief. We hope, however, at least to frame questions that warrant further investigation. Our bottom-line questions are *why* the right to personhood before the law should be recognized, and what difference, if any, placing one's faith in God as the ultimate origin and guarantor of human rights makes to moral reasoning caught between absolutist rights and utility.

Individual Rights versus Utility

One possible response to the regime at Guantánamo Bay is that any injustice to detainees is more than outweighed by the likely reduction in terrorism. The threat of terrorism might be deemed to constitute the kind of supreme emergency in which individual rights have to be overridden if a greater, justifiable good is to be attained. Michael Walzer describes supreme emergencies as times when "our deepest values and our collective survival are in imminent danger"—for example, the struggle against Nazism, which, arguably, justified the decision in 1942 to bomb German cities.[12] The bombings were criminal, says Walzer, because the victims were innocent noncombatants. Yet, those who took the decision deemed there to be no other way of preventing a Nazi triumph. The emergency demanded the decision, and those who took it had to bear the guilt, along with recognition of the enormity of what had been done, for the rest of their days. If applied to Guantánamo Bay, the analogy would be that the unprecedented threat to the safety of millions of civilians demanded that the rights of a few be disregarded; we should thank rather than criticize those who compromise the rule of law for this end.

Ambivalence besets all human exercise of earthly governance. Here we see the tragic conflict of absolutist notions of individual rights with utilitarian maximization of welfare that characterizes much present-day moral reasoning. Walzer's reaction is to revert to the "communitarian foundation of emergency ethics."[13] While not wanting to turn the notion of community into an object of worship, he appeals to a nonfetishized idea of community as the basis for a response to this conflict with no resolution. Only a strong community, he says, will sustain both the discipline of soldiers and the restraint of leaders. Only strong communities can negotiate the conflict between absolutist notions of individual rights and utilitarian considerations by paradoxical means: moral communities make great immoralities morally possible! In the remainder of this chapter, we investigate this kind of response using Ronald Dworkin's version of political pragmatism as our main focal point. Dworkin shares fundamental assumptions with Walzer but offers a more developed ethic of human rights. He is aware of problems associated with legal positivism (law as a matter of historical fact) and selected natural law theories (general theories of legal practice that justify connections between past political decisions and present coercion).[14] More pertinent for our purposes, his work connects with wider social questions about what constitutes legitimate law in democratic societies, and the pressures on governments and legislators to decouple law and ethics.

In attempting to expose some moral problems inherent in democratic, human rights cultures, we do not intend to imply that reference to God's revealed will is always and almost automatically the answer to all moral questions. The chapter is not intended to be a simplistic, knee-jerk assertion that belief in God and appeal to his transcendent righteousness is the only answer that we need. Christian political comment can be naïve—and we do not mean in the Christ-like, childlike sense. Merely to appeal to God or religion is not a sufficient response to our modern failures to enforce human rights. Neither is the repetition of biblical passages that, yes, can set us in the right direction but require us to take up questions that cannot be answered directly by biblical teaching or scriptural categories alone. Nonetheless, we ask how theological arguments are peculiarly able to expose not only retreats from rights in the name of greater security but also increasing legal voluntarism and formalism—whereby the practice and doctrine of the law produce "ad hoc exercises in power," and meaning is made through the force of rhetoric.[15] In particular, we pick up issues raised in chapter 2 about the danger in democratic societies, where law is legitimated by consent, of the ethical worth of rights collapsing into democratic processes.

The Problem of Legitimacy in Modern Democracies

Where legitimacy no longer depends on an appeal to metaphysics or even to universal conceptions of justice, governments are required to evaluate options for action according to their consequences in relation to voter-choice. Law legitimates what Max Weber called "domination" *provided that* law is based on the agreement of the citizens of the state.[16] Weber gave classic expression in the mid-twentieth century to modern, liberal approaches to the legitimacy of law in his analyses of the beliefs, attitudes and willingness of individuals in a given society to assume the disciplines and burdens required for membership. Legitimate political power is that where citizens have consented freely to the exercise of such power, and is normally expressed through the ballot box. Legitimacy designates subjective attitudes and beliefs on the part of members of society rather than objective evaluation of a regime against external criteria. The legitimacy of an action is the probability that people will orient their action to it. Once attained, and when subject to the logic of reason and debate generating allegiance and loyalty, legitimacy is "the exclusive moral right of an institution to impose on some group of persons binding duties to be obeyed by those persons, and to enforce those duties coercively."[17] Modern states are legitimated by law insofar as law is legitimated by the consent of the people—or, as a skeptic might claim, by the ability of those in power to pacify the masses.

These issues were summarized in 1973 by Jürgen Habermas in *Legitimationsprobleme im Spätkapitalismus*, a book that popularized the term "legitimation crisis."[18] A response to the crises that shook advanced capitalist societies in 1968 and afterward, with the resurgence of neo-Marxist ideologies and industrial action, the book examined economic theories emerging from the Marxist tradition, together with the systems theories of Niklas Luhmann et al. trying to identify crisis tendencies within advanced capitalism: notably economic crises and crises of rationality, legitimation, and motivation. The term "legitimation" referred to the ways in which governments and legislators claim legal status or authorization for their existence and power, and the term "crisis" referred to situations in which various tensions and strains have reached such a point that the whole system is likely to implode. Briefly, Habermas denied any source of legitimacy outside the democratic procedure, and this commitment to democratic procedure has remained constant in his work. In his more recent *Between Facts and Norms: Contributions to a Discourse Theory of Law and Democracy* he argues that discourse constitutes the conceptual or inherent relation between the rule of law and democracy in postmetaphysical, sociologically disenchanted, democratic societies.[19] The crisis of legitimacy in lawmaking and legal interpretation—that is the lack of consensus on answers to questions such as "What is the relation between law and ethics?" and "By what criteria do we judge between good and bad law?"—claims Habermas, is overcome through discourse; the tension between legal "facts" and "norms," between positivity and various claims to normative recognition, is resolved in the practice of discursive reason.

If true, and supposing Habermas's account of liberal democracy to be a descriptively accurate account of contemporary Western societies, we are faced with a massive irony, not to mention the depressing and wretched spectacle, of governmental retreat from human rights and civil liberties in the name of law, order, and security. Access to the courts is denied for the sake of protecting human rights! Sacrifices of liberty of the kind witnessed at Guantánamo Bay undermine the very processes of legitimacy on which liberal democracies rest. Debate in the United States about the "tapping" of private telephone lines and e-mail accounts illustrates the point.[20] As Baroness Helena Kennedy writes of recent developments in the UK, the preemptive strike thinking that informed foreign policy in the 2003 war against Iraq is creeping into other policy areas:

> In the new thinking, the moral component of law is absent, and the very high risk of innocent people losing their liberty is simply "collateral damage." Our own prime minister showed disdain for the approach to justice that every mature democracy once respected, when, in 2002, he claimed that "the biggest miscarriage in today's system is when the guilty walk away unpunished." The premises on which our legal system is founded—the presumption of innocence, open trial, admissible evidence, access to lawyers of choice, rights of appeal and an onerous burden of proof—are now considered old hat.[21]

Her concerns extend beyond government responses to the challenge of terrorism to reductions in trial by jury and the right to silence, the introduction in court of previous convictions, the reduction of standards of proof, the unnecessary extension of police powers, and much more. Her central point is that when the legitimacy of states is derived from the continuation of practices and institutions that ascribe rights to individuals and protect them against infringement, the denial of fundamental human rights makes a mockery of the very processes by which rights are ascribed to individuals in community and protected by the force of law.

Habermas helps us to understand that, in the democratic majoritarianism of Western societies, the framing of human rights law is tied so closely to public opinion that no one can claim that a right should be recognized except on the grounds that condemnation of a violation could command a future majority.[22] Mindful of the tension between law as something exhibiting moral value or integrity and as an inherently value-free social phenomenon, something morally neutral and sociologically descriptive rather than morally substantive in nature because of an association with metaphysics, he looks to discursive proceduralism as a way out of the "vicious cycle" circumscribed by parochial justice and arbitrary democracy.[23] Alert to the vagaries of electorates and the gullibility of public opinion, his proceduralism does not transcend all substantive norms. This point must be noted with care. Every citizen is to be treated with dignity and respect, and the forms of procedural justice are to be oriented toward the attaining of just rather than unjust outcomes. In large part, however, his proceduralism is parasitic upon the substantive norms of other worldviews. The abuses at Guantánamo Bay are unjust, he might say, because violations of internationally agreed liberties have occurred. If these liberties command majority support, and if they have an established legal grounding, then the violations are to be denounced.

Despite these nuances, a frequent complaint against Habermas is that the fragile relations between law, ethics, and morality require more than the careful framing of the practice of discourse. Because Habermas leaves many substantive considerations to the processes of democratic deliberation and public debate, he cannot therefore give a strong account of the bonds that unite individuals one to another.[24] He puts his faith instead in the hope that the norms recognized by the liberal democratic legislatures will prove their "rationality" by means of due procedures and communicative presuppositions, or will be corrected by all relevant participants in the discourse.[25] For Habermas, the normative character of morality proceeds from rationality itself. The question posed by some critics is whether further account is needed of the various ways in which humans express and pursue their desire for truth, belong to communities, and draw on cultural and other resources with which to contest whether a law is just or unjust. For those less optimistic about the redemptive power of rationality and discourse, the question is whether more explicit attention is required to substantive beliefs because how one reasons is determined by the investment of one's faith. Robert Gascoigne puts it well when he asks if Habermas's understanding of autonomous rationality and discourse ethics could be expanded to include the recognition that humans have a fundamental orientation to the truth, or, at least, that the search for truth is something common to humanity: "Does the practice of discourse simply reflect a need for autonomous beings to negotiate their interests in communicative ways, or does it express a common orientation to truth?"[26] That humans seek after truth is as fundamental to their makeup as their ability to seek consensus. Heller gets even closer to the heart of the matter when she observes:

> The responsibility of men in postmodernity is essentially the responsibility for the investment of one's Faith and not of the exercises of Reason. One can put one's faith in the most incorrect (most absurd) end, and still argue for it splendidly. The Devil reasons well. But reasoning is no longer the work of the Devil, but is now the commonly assumed exercise of modern men and women.[27]

Different worldviews yield different approaches to moral reasoning and often irreconcilable conclusions. But we always put our faith in something. This is a fundamental phenomenon of the human makeup to which Habermas gives insufficient recognition. In our late-modern or postmodern world, many of us live without right or truth (defined with reference to a metaphysical source). Yet, we put our faith in other things—ourselves, the principle of respect for individual liberty, the saving power of technology, money, or celebrities. Either this or we submit to nihilism.

Dworkin pays more attention than Habermas to substantive considerations. He views society as an inclusive community of associative obligations that needs more than procedural majoritarianism to protect the vulnerable in times of crisis, and takes considered account of how human subjectivity and rationality are a form of participation in community life. His principled model of political community presupposes the substantive values of democracy, liberty, and equality and emphasizes the importance of creative interpretation of these values in new and demanding situations.[28] Dworkin claims to make no explicit use of social contract theory in order to achieve the impartial justification of norms and distinguishes the idea of a social contract from other arguments used to establish the character of justice.[29] He holds instead to a quasirealism, comprising liberal principles of individual liberty and autonomy, which allows him to assert that moral convictions are beliefs about facts (such as the fact that ethnic discrimination is morally wrong), and that these facts are independent of our own will or desire or motives.[30] We look briefly in the next section at how Dworkin frames the relations between law, ethics, and morality. This is important because he claims to offer a denser ethos of law than some liberal theorists. He demonstrates that the law sets out general moral principles about liberty, equality, and dignity that private citizens, lawyers, and finally judges interpret and apply. Individuals bring their own concrete moral questions to these principles as they come into contact with the law. Given this, a law is just when it resonates appropriately with the best written and unwritten principles, and when it describes the necessary "constructive interpretation" in the courts that must accompany the political structure and legal doctrine of those communities.[31] In the next section, we consider how he digs behind the practice of consensus seeking to consider how legitimacy is embedded in the subjective attitudes and beliefs of members of society.

Ronald Dworkin and Context-Determined Interpretive Pragmatism

Relevant background information to Dworkin's context-determined interpretive pragmatism includes debate in the 1960s about the relation between law and morality, notably the exchange between Lord Devlin and H. L. A. Hart, the professor of jurisprudence at Oxford University (1952–1968). Lord Devlin argued in *The Enforcement of Morals* (1965) that, in certain cases, the law should be used to enforce morals.[32] Morality is the cement of society because society is constituted in significant measure by the sharing of moral beliefs by its members. Consequently, Devlin argued, the law should condemn acts that society regards as immoral; the legal toleration of such acts would put society at risk of fragmentation. The law should be morally binding when it condemns acts that society regards as immoral. Hart disagreed and argued that the law should be morally binding only when it expresses rules that are necessary for a given society to exist. As a legal positivist, he argued that there is no inherent connection between law and morality because laws are simply rules made by humans. Moral judgments about right and wrong in behavior are not universal, he claimed: "[T]he development of law, at all times and places, has been profoundly influenced both by the conventional morality and ideals of particular social groups."[33] In a given society, he observed, both eating pork and stealing might be wrong, but only stealing should be punished at law. Moral and legal norms should be disentangled because a prohibition against stealing is a social rule that sociohistorical evidence will vindicate. A prohibition against eating pork is a moral notion that may or may not be dominant in a given society at a given time. Law is (or should be) a system of rules that give rise to normative duties or a sense of what ought to be done. Laws are social rules that every society must have to survive, such as laws that restrict violence, theft, and deception. Laws exist as social practice and are posited by those in authority.

Briefly, Devlin argued that if a society regards certain practices as damaging to the moral well-being of its members, then it should use the criminal law to establish minimum standards of conduct. "If at any point," he stated, "there is a lack of clear and convincing moral teaching, the administration of law suffers."[34] In a variation on J. S. Mill's harm principle, Hart opposed Devlin's view that immoral conduct was a ground for legal prohibition: "[V]ast numbers [may] be coerced by laws which they do not regard as morally binding."[35] Against this background we may attempt to understand Dworkin's insistence that morality is a community possession that concerns the benefits and values, relationships and obligations, mutual dependencies and expectations that characterize an ordered and peaceful society in which people live under the law. Dworkin succeeded Hart at Oxford and became a harsh critic of his predecessor, reacting against his "soft positivism" that separated law from societal assumptions and controversies about the character of a good life. The legitimacy of a particular law or judicial decision is deemed properly functional and rational, says Dworkin, when it expresses and respects the principles that shape this community. Employing Gadamerian hermeneutics, Dworkin seeks to demonstrate that individual judges work within particular paradigms of law and that, provided that each acts according to generally accepted notions of political community and virtue, the most powerful influences in each paradigm converge and press toward agreement.

In *Law's Empire*, Dworkin considers the "puzzle" of legitimacy within a wide-ranging treatment of "law as an interpretive concept." Law, he says, is a bit like courtesy in the sense that most of us recognize a duty to act courteously but what this means in a given situation must be worked out according to the best available interpretation of all relevant considerations at the time.[36] Judges, says Dworkin, are as "an author in the chain of the common law."[37] He does not (and cannot) prescribe ethical principles for the liberal community because he believes that liberalism is ethically neutral at relatively concrete levels, although he believes that the liberal community is (and must be) ethical before it is political. How one society prescribes its laws will depend on what its traditions and customs are like as well as the extent to which individuals possess the qualities needed to make policy and to judge wisely. In extreme forms, this radically interpretive type of approach claims that the law in a given community is a self-contained practice, like a game of chess or backgammon, in which decisions demand compliance as "ad hoc exercises in power."[38] In his own writings, this work of interpretation is embodied in Judge Hercules, the community personified, who illustrates the idea that law should be interpreted as if derived from a single will. Integrity is the political ideal that requires judges to treat the present system as an expression of a coherent set of principles and "to interpret these standards to find implicit standards between and beneath the explicit ones."[39] The essence of legitimacy depends on legislators enacting requirements that give citizens reasons to obey. Hercules has no vision into transcendental mysteries opaque to citizens. In everyday situations, judges must do their best to make decisions that have integrity when viewed as part of a long story of similar decisions by other judges, and they must be prepared to justify their conclusions by their "fit" within the system. The essence of legitimacy is temporal and context determined.

Moral Particularity and/or Ahistorical Appeals to Universality?

Critics have challenged Dworkin to spell out what this understanding of law as integrity would have meant under the Third Reich or in apartheid South Africa. For Dworkin, the essence of legitimacy is temporal and context determined in the sense that a law might have been legitimate yesterday but might no longer be such tomorrow if the particular requirements of justice and fairness in a given community change. The procedures that declare an action just or unjust have no external referent but reflect what a particular society has agreed is just. "Why," asks Habermas, "does it [the legal system] not merely reflect the moral intuitions of the average, male, middle-class member of a modern Western society?"[40] This kind of context-determined pragmatism places too much faith in the value of custom and morality in law making and risks omitting an explicit hermeneutic of suspicion with respect to interests that might remain unheeded or destructive powers that might remain unmasked. Dworkin's response is to remind readers that he does not write for judges under the Third Reich or in apartheid South Africa but for those under the United States Constitution and part of the story of English common law. The point remains, however, that, for Dworkin, a state and its laws are legitimate if its constitutional structure and practices are such that "its citizens have a general obligation to obey political decisions that purport to impose duties on them."[41] Justice rests on the best "constructive interpretation" of the political structure and legal doctrine of a given community.[42] He relies on transcendence from within, so to speak, for criticism of existing social values and decisions. Legitimation and legal integrity depend on the same set of substantive values for both the exercise of the law and its critique.

In other words, Dworkin's principle of legal integrity presupposes the substantive values that are already embedded in the legal traditions in question. His approach is intertextual in the sense that the values of the community are both the context in which legal interpretation is embedded and the source of innovation. Dworkin's world of meaning might provide an answer to the question of injustice but is at risk of self-enclosure and of not being open to new possibilities of ethical meaning beyond itself.

Against this backdrop, we should perhaps be surprised that Guantánamo Bay happened. But it did happen and the political climate is such that the right of personhood before the law continues to be under threat. All this raises urgent questions about the tension between the particular moral convictions of given communities over against ahistorical and universal notions of human nature. If the particular community of citizenship is viewed as the basis for the privileging of its members and/or of morality, then to what extent do states have moral responsibility other than that afforded by the electorate? What is to guard against "bad" forms of tribalism that exclude "the Other"?[43]

An Illustrative Detour

This tension may be illustrated practically with reference to one of the most difficult international political questions, namely, the kind of protection and assistance that nation-states owe to asylum seekers and refugees. We take a detour from matters peculiar to Guantánamo Bay to expound the issues at stake. Consider briefly how the UN Convention Relating to the Status of Refugees is being challenged and even "openly flouted by a growing number of states."[44] The continuing validity of the 1951 convention has been questioned publicly—especially as the number of refugees soared during the 1990s and the cost of managing asylum systems has risen. While the Convention Plus initiative, coordinated by the Office of the United Nations High Commissioner for Refugees, is an attempt to broker agreements between states for the management of refugees worldwide, there is still no global treaty right to asylum; the grant of asylum remains a discretionary act by a state, and, to date, the UN Commission on Human Rights has been cautious in finding state violations against noncitizen asylum seekers in its case law.[45] The interface between international refugee law and international human rights law is subject to diverse interpretation.[46] The need for authoritative interpretations by the International Court of Justice on the 1951 convention in relation to relevant human rights treaties is evident.[47] In other words, international provision for asylum seekers and refugees is mired in crisis. The interactions of the various dimensions of the problem are cross-cultural and complex. Few agree about what a morally acceptable response to refugees and asylum seekers might look like if states' obligations to these people are to be met with broad-based agreement from the citizens of those states.

Of interest for our purposes is how debate divides between those who work with an ideal of states as distinct cultural communities possessing a right to self-determination that justifies priority for the interests of citizens over refugees ("partialists") and those who work with an ideal of states as cosmopolitan agents that must take into equal account the interests of citizens and refugees ("impartialists").[48] We are interested in the weight given to the legal processes, customs, and culture of a given state over against ahistorical appeals to human rights. Using the broad descriptors "partialists" and "impartialists," Matthew J. Gibney observes how communitarian and contract liberals typically argue that a nation-state has the right and the responsibility to protect the moral unity between its people based on territory, language, association, history, and culture (Roger Scruton),[49] and consequently give a low weighting to the claims of refugees. Globalist liberals and utilitarians (Michael Dummett and Peter Singer)[50] argue that the requirements of equal consideration to every human being oblige states to accept refugees up to the point where the resident community has eliminated all luxuries, or to the point when tolerance in a multicultural society is breaking down. States do not have legitimate grounds for the exclusion of foreigners and should maintain open borders. Gibney's own humanitarianism exposes this conflict and is, to a limited extent, successful in cutting across it. What, he asks the partialists, gives a state the right to exclusive use of the territory it occupies?[51] What really is shared by citizens that distinguishes them from outsiders? Are you politically realistic, he asks the impartialists, given that there is no world government to administer justice in a world of open borders? Political discussion is under way about whether states are duty-bound to admit individuals applying for protection, and how the burden of these applications might be shared. Even so, the tension is considerable between those who argue from the moral particularity of a given community versus those who advocate asylum-seeker rights by appeal to ahistorical notions of universality.

How skeptical, then, should we be about Dworkin's construal of the relation between the judicial enforcement of human rights and democratic political structures? Dworkin himself is relatively unskeptical and describes the U.S. Supreme Court in ideal terms as an "exemplar of public reason."[52] His high view of the Supreme Court is linked to its role in governing the "higher law," or expression of the people's constituent power, as distinct from the ordinary law or expression of the power of the electorate. In his interpretation of the power of U.S. liberal democracy, the Supreme Court's role is to protect the higher law—where necessary in almost antidemocratic or antimajoritarian ways in order to ensure that its judgments fit with a coherent, constitutional view over a historical range of decisions. Its role is to effect judgments that belong to "the most reasonable understanding of the public conception and its political values of justice and public reason."[53] Mindful that there is more than one possible answer to any particular question within the scope of public reason, Dworkin places his faith in judges and citizens being able to explain their votes to one another and thereby to effect a reasonable balance of public political values. He hopes that each will have an understanding heart of the kind that will make it possible for us to bear with one another, and with the stranger in our midst.

Skepticism is easy as compared to long-term commitment to legal institutions, their workings, maintenance, and analysis. Dworkin draws our attention to this, as well as to the narrative coherence of legislative traditions in given democratic societies, and to internal systems of checks and balances. His point is that internal rectification of a legal system is always possible, at least in principle, if enough institutional checks and balances are in place. Such checks and balances include the role of the judiciary in ensuring the continuity of decision making within a given interpretive framework of legal history, as well as the values of liberty and equality, and the criterion of universalization. Worse investments of moral faith might be made, Dworkin suggests, than in democratic values and the moral duties and obligations of both regular citizens and the judiciary. His stance raises questions, however, about what institutional measures are needed to protect fundamental human rights, and whether we can place as much faith as Dworkin does in the processes of the law to meet the requirements of a political community to act in a coherent and principled manner toward all its members. We now look briefly at some of these issues in practical terms as they relate to Guantánamo Bay.

In December 2003 two U.S. federal courts ruled against President Bush's unilateral detaining of both U.S. citizens and non-U.S. citizens as enemy combatants without the protections offered by the due processes of law.[54] As reported by the American Civil Liberties Union (ACLU), Justice Stephen Reinhardt wrote: "Even in times of national emergency—indeed, particularly in such times—it is the obligation of the Judicial Branch to ensure the preservation of our constitutional values and to prevent the Executive Branch from running roughshod over the rights of citizens and aliens alike."[55] In other words, steps were taken by legal institutions set apart from the ordinary processes of politics to protect the detainees' fundamental right of personhood at law. In November 2005, however, the Senate voted 84–14 to limit federal court jurisdiction over cases filed by prisoners at Guantánamo Bay. An amendment to the 2006 Defense Appropriations Bill, filed by Senator Lindsey Graham, would have nullified the U.S. Supreme Court's decision in *Rasul v. Bush*, 542 U.S. 466 (2004), which held that non-U.S. citizen prisoners at GTMO (U.S. Naval Base at Guantánamo Bay) may file habeas corpus petitions challenging their imprisonment as well as claims under federal law concerning the conditions of their confinement. As reported by *Jurist: Legal News and Research*—a Web-based discussion site overseen by the University of Pittsburgh—a compromise amendment (brokered by Senator Carl Levin and backed by Graham) "permits some, albeit limited, federal appellate review over GTMO tribunals and military commissions. (There is no mention of prisoners held at CIA secret prisons in former Iron Curtain countries.) But the court review is too limited to provide any real benefits."[56] In other words, democratically elected politicians took steps to override court decisions in order further to delimit the legal recognition granted to detainees. For all the skepticism that some entertain about the history of judicial appeal in the United States, in this instance, the Supreme Court did file habeas corpus petitions thereby respecting the detainees' right to personhood before the law.[57] This runs us up, of course, against questions about how judges are appointed to courts and the relation between judicial enforcement of fundamental human rights and the political structure of the legislature.

To summarize, Dworkin's emphasis on the importance of the so-called soft moral matters of wanting our communities to respect fairness and decency, plus wanting our judiciary to be wise, is surely welcome—and especially so in a culture increasingly "outerregulated" by new forms of "soft positivism" and voluntarism. His hope is that "the leaden spirits of our age" that nurture these aspirations will soon lift.[58] Yet Guantánamo Bay is a wake-up call. Despite the merits of Dworkin's worldview, the inertia and indifference among typical Western electorates makes us wonder how well equipped this kind of approach is to identify and counter difficulties, and whether his own interpretive approach includes a strong enough hermeneutic of suspicion with respect to the interests that might remain unheeded.

Genesis 9:5: "I Will Require a Reckoning"

So far, then, we have attempted to expose some difficulties with contemporary liberal theorists in explaining *why* the right to personhood before the law should be recognized. These difficulties have centered around the arbitrariness of democracy and the tension between the moral particularities of a given community over against abstract notions of universal humanity. In this final section, we ask what a Christian ethic of rights might have to say about whether, and if so, why, the right to personhood before the law should be recognized. Does biblical witness to God's command bear upon the matter in hand? If so, how?

In asking these questions, I assume with Nicholas Wolterstorff, David Hollenbach, Michael J. Perry, and others that there is an important role for religious faith in the public life of nations. Wolterstorff, for instance, wrote brief but powerful essays in *Religion in the Public Square* in which he argued against "the liberal position" according to which "the role of the citizen in a liberal democracy includes a restraint on the use of reasons, derived from one's religion, for one's decisions and discussions on political issues, and a requirement that citizens instead use an independent source."[59] Restraint on religious reasoning, he argued, is in flagrant conflict with the idea of liberal democracy. As Perry argues, neither citizens nor their political representatives "contravene the morality of liberal democracy by relying on religiously grounded moral belief in public discussions."[60] Even from the perspective of liberal democracy, the outlawing or otherwise disfavoring of conduct merely because it is the outworking of religiously grounded belief is illegitimate.[61] Debate has moved *beyond whether* there is an important role for religious faith in the public life of nations *to the character and quality* of the contributions to debate.

We tread with caution because appeal to the sources of Christian faith for guidance should not be construed as an attempt to say directly what God's command is. "An ethics that thinks it can know and set forth the command of God, the Creator, plants itself upon the throne of God: it stops and poisons the wells and is . . . fraught with peril to the Christian life."[62] We cannot appeal to truths in this or the other text of the Bible as if we were judges of God's own command. Genesis 9:5-6 does not translate directly into respect for Article 6 of the UNDHR. But neither can we neglect to study and be doers of God's word. We can only try to heed God's commands at "stations on a road which we have to tread."[63]

> Between the arrogance of those who regard themselves as judges of what they will and do, and the false humility of those who take no notice of God's judgment because they cannot change it, there is the third possibility—the sense of responsibility of those who know that God alone is their Judge and not they themselves, and that because God is their Judge they have every reason to remember Him in all their willing and doing.[64]

God's revelation retains sovereignty over which humans cannot and may not have control, and Holy Scripture retains a special place in God's saving dealings with humankind (2 Tim 3:16-17). On the one hand, "the sacred and inspired Scriptures are sufficient to declare the truth" in matters of both doctrine and morals.[65] God's word comes to us continually, sometimes in the most concrete ways. On the other hand, we cannot set ourselves up as interpreters of the word of God's revelation to us. Christian ethics is not called on to determine the meaning of life in obedience to divine command; "for this is solely the business of God's Word."[66] John Webster puts it well: "Christian theology will only be worthy of the title 'Christian' if it allows itself to be led all along the line by the witness of Holy Scripture, and if it modestly and humbly, and yet also with courage and astonishment, tries to indicate what it finds there."[67] Our suggestion, however, is that a Christian ethic of rights may assert God's claim upon all humanity as the reason for the claims that humans have on one another. If God requires a reckoning for all human blood and has commissioned humanity to have a care for the exercise of judgment, then we must find ways of heeding this claim in obedience to the divine will.

Taking a lead once again from the covenant with Noah, we suggest that something like the claim to "personhood before the law" arises from God's own demand for a reckoning of the shedding of human blood and from his giving to human communities a role to play in exacting earthly justice because all persons bear his image. Moreover, God himself requires a reckoning for all human blood and this is sufficient reason to urge protection of the right to personhood at law. All persons are answerable before God, and all should therefore be respected as such before human judges too. Here, arguably, is reason enough to affirm that *all* have the right to respect as persons before the law. The human exercise of justice does not, of course, equate to divine justice. Genesis 9:5-6 does not translate directly into any particular form of earthly governance, legal code, or philosophy, or even the desirability of democratic human rights regimes across the globe. God's ways are different from ours, and the divine exercise of justice belongs to a radically different order of existence than that which we occupy.[68] Yet, divine and human justice are not unrelated. The very heart of the gospel precludes an isolationist stance that divorces Christian ethical reflection from the world to which Jesus Christ came.

More specifically, God directs that a system of retributive justice delimit the endemic tendency of humanity to violence and murder (Gen 9:6). This command does not transfer divine sovereignty over the lives of individual human beings to humanity as executor in his stead. God alone demands a reckoning for the shedding of human blood. Claus Westermann renders the assertion of God's lordship as follows:

> But: Your own blood   will I demand,
> from all animals   will I demand it,
> and from humans in turn
> the life of a person   will I demand.[69]

In a characteristic stylistic device, the author of these verses uses a three-fold repetition to emphasize the primary meaning: only God's lordship over all human and other created life is unconditional. The ultimate authority to exact punishment for bloodshed belongs to him alone. Animal blood may be shed but not eaten. Human blood may not be shed because God alone has the right to dispose of human life; all blood belongs to God. Indeed, the taking of life is both a crime against one's fellows and a sin against God. Hence, the community is allowed a limited share in divine authority by taking the life of a murderer.[70] There is no denying that capital punishment appears to serve in Genesis 6 as a reminder that life belongs to God and that "[n]o-one may dare to take the life of another as though they were God."[71] Commanded by God as a limit to human violence, it serves to assert God's unique right over both life and death.[72] Its central reminder, however, is that murder is a direct attack on divine dominion over human life, that all judgment belongs truly to God, and that God demands a reckoning for the blood of all created in his image. This answerability before God and one's fellows is, arguably, reason enough for everyone to be accorded the right to personhood before the law.

A similar stance from a Jewish perspective has been taken recently by David Novak with respect to other passages. In a fascinating account of biblical precedents for human rights, he roots rights discourse among humans in God's original rights over created beings. More specifically, the human right to have one's murder avenged is deduced from God's encounter with Cain immediately following his murder of Abel: "What have you done? Listen; your brother's blood is crying out [tso'aqim] to me from the ground!" (Gen 4:10).[73] Rabbinic teaching with respect to the destruction of Sodom and Gomorrah notes that the cities had "no law [din]" and "no judge [dayyan]."[74] Hence their destruction, in contrast to Ninevah, which believed in the God of justice and knew when and how to turn away from violence. Nathan's rebuke of King David could, today, be cast in terms of remonstration for his violation of the rights of Uriah (2 Sam 12:7-10). For Novak, the separation of church and state means that there can be no official requirements on citizens to recognize biblical revelations of divine truth, but for believers, biblical precedents translate readily into strong reasons for the defense of human rights. We have argued along comparable lines—the central claim being that no one be put beyond the reach of the law because God himself requires a reckoning for all human blood.

To summarize, our claim is that biblical teaching about divine command remains a stronger foundation for human rights than procedural approaches to discourse ethics or context-bound, democratic pragmatism. Personhood before the law is recognized in Christian ethics because the image of God in every living person is the personal representation of the true and living God, every person is an addressee of divine command, and God himself has given to humankind the responsibility for the maintenance of justice. Murder and failure to respect the imago Dei in others are an affront to the sovereignty of God, as well as an attack on human life. These are self-evidently theological reasons why human life and the processes of justice are valuable. The work of Christian ethics (and/or political theology) is to see life's value and the processes of human justice in terms of their relation to God rather than in any practice of democracy, social custom, or intrinsic human property. In contrast to secularist approaches, it is because of the relationship between God and humankind, and not for any other reason—at least not primarily—that Christian ethics affirms that personhood before the law should be respected. Even so, Christians are not forced into some kind of "split consciousness" or what Hegel calls the "frenzy of deceit" of those who experience an alienation between their own worldview and other ways of thinking about humanity. God's command "is the source of all ethical truth, and it determines not only the church, but all who are elected for the covenant of grace in Christ."[75] The Lord watches over frail mortals (Ps 144:3) and will exercise judgment over the nations (Jer 30:11). In the meantime, with respect to Guantánamo Bay, secularist lawyers and human rights campaigners cannot be expected to do all the shouting.

Afterword

Now the whole earth had one language and the same words. . . . Then they said,
"Come, let us build ourselves a city, and a tower with its top in the heavens,
and let us make a name for ourselves; otherwise we shall be scattered
abroad upon the face of the whole earth."

—Genesis 11:1-4

Now the word of the Lord came to Jonah son of Amittai, saying, "Go at once
to Nineveh, that great city, and cry out against it; for their wickedness has
come up before me."

—Jonah 1:1-2

"The truth is plain," wrote Alasdair MacIntyre, "there are no such rights, and belief in them is one with belief in witches and unicorns. . . . [E]very attempt to give good reasons for believing that there *are* such rights has failed. . . . Natural or human rights are fictions."[1] The benefits of MacIntyre's approach to moral reasoning are familiar to recent Christian ethics and need not be rehearsed here. Suffice it to cite the general editor's preface to David Fergusson's *Community, Liberalism and Christian Ethics*: "Alasdair MacIntyre's *After Virtue* has succeeded beyond most other recent books in setting an agenda which has challenged many philosophers and theologians alike."[2] The problematic consequences of his work are less frequently discussed—not least his eschewal on philosophical (not theological) grounds of the meaningfulness and validity of rights discourse. Against the kind of backdrop set by MacIntyre and those who take rights discourse to be essentially non-Christian, this book has argued that the Christian gospel can support a theologically valid discourse of rights that is different from and more meaningful than those dismissed by them. What we have called the command-rights dynamic is an attempt to describe the command of God given variously to humankind (not least in the covenant with Noah) and to suggest that believers' attempts to live obediently to God's word can be mediated by the language of rights without compromise to the primary claims of God on all humanity and his self-revealing and gracious goodness.

MacIntyre's now-famous eschewal of natural and human rights fits with the central thesis of his work that modern, political liberalism can give no coherent account of the moral life and that, instead, Western moral philosophy should seek a revival of neo-Aristotelian virtue theory, narrative ethics, and tradition-constituted inquiry. Charles Taylor summarizes nicely the kind of problem with which MacIntyre was concerned:

> Contemporary philosophers have been preoccupied with a rather narrow range of issues, which people often refer to today as "morality," in contrast to "ethics." The "moral" concentrates on issues of justice and inter-personal fairness, issues about rights or what is right in our treatment of others, over and against questions of the "good life," of what is a worthwhile way to live, what is fulfilling, valuable to be, and the like. As a consequence of this focus, political theory has often been led to make justice the supreme issue.[3]

For MacIntyre, questions about ethos and the common good do not follow automatically from a focus on procedural justice. Nor does the liberal fiction of the social contract amount to a vision of the good. As Paul Ricoeur also indicates: "When the just is subordinated to the good, it has to be discovered; when it is engendered by purely procedural means, it has to be constructed. . . . It is supposed to result from deliberation in a condition of absolute fairness."[4]

The central point is that modern citizens should not be satisfied with procedural-liberal theories of justice where reasonability is divorced from teleologically determined goods and the rationality of traditions within which persons may acquire and learn to exercise the virtues. And we must surely agree. In Christian ethics also, it is important to move debate about substantive human freedoms beyond the dichotomy of postmodern relativism and modern liberalism of the kind that prioritizes individual autonomy and personal choice above the social roles of embodied human beings, structural injustice, collective rights, and so forth.

A problem for Christian ethics is hidden, however, in the observation by Ricoeur cited above. While MacIntyre's dissatisfaction with humanly constructed notions of justice is probably shared by most Christian theologians and moralists, the priority given by him to the concept of "the good" over what is "right"—more specifically, his acceptance of Aristotle's designation of "the good" or "the supreme good" as "that at which all things aim"—is of more concern.[5] David Novak takes us quickly to the heart of the matter from a Jewish perspective: "A biblically based theology should never stretch the use of the term 'good' to function as a proper name, that is, 'the Good.'"[6] God's goodness and righteousness precedes any and all good that humans might recognize and designate as "good." In Jewish and Christian ethics, "good" is only the adjective that modifies the way humans respond to divine initiative.[7] There is no identifiable "good" apart from or prior to God. Thus, Aquinas was careful always to affirm that God is the supreme Good. Following Augustine, for instance, he speaks of the Trinity of the divine persons as "the supreme good, discerned by purified minds."[8] As a moral philosopher, MacIntyre has fewer qualms about adopting Aristotle's concept of "the good" along with his treatment of the virtues as those habitual dispositions that both facilitate and constitute human goodness. His concept of "the good" takes epistemological precedence over what is "right" because "the good" is that at which all things aim, and knowledge of "the good" is important for the conduct of all human life. This is problematic for Christian ethics to the extent that "the good" is given precedence not only over right(s) but potentially over God himself, as if, as Novak says, "to designate a state of being that names or qualifies the divine." In biblical ethics, "good" is a qualification not a ground; "the good" is never "the ultimate *telos* of the transaction."[9]

MacIntyre's neo-Aristotelian naturalism is thus not reason enough for Christian ethics to shun rights discourse. Nor is it enough merely to expose the problems inherent in much secularist rights discourse or to accept uncritically that "natural or human rights are fictions" on grounds influenced heavily by neo-Aristotelian naturalism, or other non-Christian sources. Far better, we have urged in this book, to investigate the kind of rights discourse that faith in the gospel can, or cannot, support. To this end, our approach has been primarily dogmatic and shaped especially by a tropological reading of Genesis 9:1-17 whereby God's mercy to humankind through Noah is renewed and fulfilled in Christ. To put the matter at its simplest, we have argued that the commands of God the Creator are restored to believers in Christ. Because of the gospel, Christian people have access to the resources of the law for guidance with respect to true human flourishing. Disjunctions between human modes of governance and the ways of God remain; the commands of God the Creator do not equate directly to either human accounts of natural or human rights; there is no direct analogy between divine and human being or thoughts (i.e., no analogia entis of the kind condemned by Barth). Yet, it is possible to seek an appropriate correspondence between God's gracious self-communication and human response: "Our human attempts at worldly justice can always correspond only indirectly to divine action."[10] Obedient action is demanded of believers, and their decisions may still by guided by God's law. This is *not* to suggest that the gospel of Christ is exhausted by a system of commands and responses. Those justified in Christ are called to exist in a new way, through faith alone (Rom 3:27-28), free from the bondage of the law. The sinner is not justified by his or her own obedience to the law but by grace alone. Yet, the law is fulfilled not overturned by Christ and remains a gift of divine righteousness for the ordering of human relations —both inside and outside of the church.

Contra MacIntyre, our claim has been that there *are* rights—or, more precisely, there are theological truths that may be expressed as rights—and that these may be discerned from the commands of God in Holy Scripture, not least the covenant with all humanity through Noah (Gen 9:1-17). We cannot go as far as David Novak with respect to construing the life of faith as a system of commands and rights responses.[11] Novak's magnificent study *Covenantal Rights* reconciles modern rights-talk with Judaism by showing that authentically Jewish polity comprises a system of correlative rights and duties "at all levels from top to bottom."[12] He finds close correspondence between rights discourse, God's law, Holy Scripture's language of the "cry" of the oppressed (Heb *tsa'aqah*), the rabbis' teaching about the claims of one person upon another (*ta'anah*), and so on.[13] His subtle reconceiving and restructuring of rights discourse on theological grounds aims to overcome the standoff between the theocratic principles of the Jewish tradition and the democratic principles of the societies in which many Jewish people live by locating the concept of human rights *within* the Jewish tradition.[14] Unlike Novak, our intention has not been to understand Christian polity in terms of rights. Much of his project concerns the ordering of rights and duties within the Jewish community, but we have not attempted to construe intraecclesial relations in terms of rights. Like Novak, however, we agree that rights can be construed as claims within the normative order established at creation, and that all such rights are originally God's as Creator.[15] God's power may be understood as a right to command all created beings; his goodness and righteousness always precedes the response that he expects from his creatures. Hence the priority of rights over goods and/or duties. Like Novak, we affirm that God's claims on humankind precede the goods or desirable ends that pertain to our flourishing, and/or the duties or responses to rights claims that others have upon us; "responses cannot generate the claims made prior to them for them."[16] God's righteousness and salvific goodness always precede what we can or should do. This is where a Christian ethic of rights also begins and ends.

In what sense, then, is a Christian ethic of rights an ethic of *human* rights? The answer is: *indirectly*. In a Christian ethic of rights, the origin of rights pertaining to humans is divine righteousness not human nature per se. "Ought" follows ultimately from the divine not human "is." The natural order is a result of divine command. Natural teleology is secondary to, and derivative upon, the voice of God. Right human claims must be justified originally with reference to what has been revealed of divine law. Subjective rights express the entitlements of creatures as creatures, and the claims that they might legitimately have against their fellows—and perhaps even against God himself.[17] As Jüngel observes, "That God is righteous means nothing less than that God is God."[18] Theological ethics is related integrally to doctrine. To speak of God's righteousness is to speak of God himself. His word demarcates the ground of moral action wherein human individuals and communities have freedom to accept or reject the negative and positive requirements of the law. His self-communication in Christ is the criterion by which Christian ethics affirms that each is to be given their due. God became human and, as a human, suffered and died for humanity. Here we learn that human attempts at worldly justice can only correspond indirectly to divine action. As Jüngel explains so well:

> It is in the humanity of God which not only allows us, but rather makes it nothing short of our duty, not only to demand human justice on the basis of the righteousness of God, but also to state criteria for that which in truth deserves to be called human justice, in order thereby to make existing worldly justice more just and more human . . . when . . . one makes the prevailing order better.[19]

Only the gospel of Christ justifies sinners because in it the righteousness of God is revealed (Rom 1:17). Only because the incarnate Son of God has endured the cup of death and has been raised from death is it possible for God's judgment to be accomplished without allowing injustice to go unmarked. The law accuses, judges, and condemns. But God would not be merciful if he were not also judge. His judgment in Christ, who died in our place (2 Cor 5:21), frees humanity from the punishment of death and directs the created order toward a new beginning. God's righteousness is not revealed in the law but in the gospel. Justified sinners live out of God's righteousness and "should risk earthly parables of heaven in this life."[20]

At the heart of a Christian ethic of rights is thus the belief that God is for us in Christ and through his commandments. That which God has commanded is life to us (Deut 6:24). Hence the priority of rights, or what is due to God and to neighbor because of God, over natural goods and/or duties that correlate to rights. The rights of the other and the respect due to the other are never merely because of his or her dignity as a human per se but because he or she is a person accepted by God. Apart from divine action, Christian ethics cannot speak of human rights, responsibilities, and/or duties. Only contemplation of the righteousness of God leads to consideration of "what the divine action which justified sinners means for our own efforts at worldly justice."[21] "Efforts at worldly justice" are ultimately for God's sake and not ours. Similarly with respect to nonhuman animals and the environment. Theologically considered, subjective rights make sense only as an integral part of an account of divine righteousness—namely what God's graciousness establishes is due to persons and other created beings. "If . . . human righteousness is to correspond to divine righteousness without misunderstanding itself as a prolongation of the latter, then it will have to orient itself by the above criterion [i.e., that which divine justice establishes is due]."[22] Prior to any effort with respect to worldly justice is always the question of God himself and how Holy Scripture speaks of God.[23] Regardless of the language used, what matters is whether a person (or other living creature) has their due within the ordering of divine providence. This sense of "what is due" should not be confused with quasi-feudal notions of positions within a social hierarchy. Rather, that Christ died for all is the measure of God's abundant generosity to all that he has created, and the reason to heed what he has commanded of all humanity.

The disjunction between theologically conceived notions of right(s) and secularist ethics, ideologies, politics, and modes of moral reasoning is not likely to go away. It is not a dialectic to be synthesized, nor a tension to be resolved, but a separation or disconnection that lacks unity. Nor can it be denied that the term "rights" is subject in secularist discourse to all kinds of reification that tempt projects of self-realization at the expense of others. "Sinners . . . are characterized by a belief that they must and can seize their own right."[24] In some sense at least, human rights are like a mask that certain societies choose to put on when declaring what they stand for, and how they want to live.[25] In this sense, MacIntyre is correct. Human rights are fictions that individuals and groups choose to inhabit because they express some things that they hold to be true. This does not mean, however, that Christian people need be either indifferent about or hostile to secular(ist) notions of human rights. Christ is our victory over both false denials and false affirmations of the world. "For when we find ourselves in God, we find ourselves committed to the task of affirming him in the world as it is and not in a false transcendent world of dream."[26] In Christ, believers may affirm the world as it is before denying it. The aforementioned disjunction between theologically conceived notions of right(s) and secularist ethics, is not a reason for Christian people to abstain from seeking and affirming God in the midst of human rights advocacy. While human rights still serve as an important vehicle for the guarantee and enforcement of legal standards, there is work to do in considering similarities and differences between theological notions of divine law and international human rights law.

Appeals to divine providence and/or divine law as a reason for action are vulnerable always to arbitrariness, or worse. Perverted notions of reward and punishment can easily distort accounts of divine command. The danger that the catchphrase "*Deus volente*" can become an excuse for inhumanity perpetrated in the name of God is ever close.[27] As the Dutch moral theologian Jan Jans notes, brief mention of the persecution of heretics, the Crusades, the Inquisition, witch trials, racial and sexual apartheid, and more besides, reminds us of atrocities in Christian history perpetrated in the name of God and with seeming assurance of knowledge of his will.[28] From history, we can learn how many accounts of divine law have run counter to the gospel and God's redeeming love, and the evangelical command to love. There is a particular danger that, as Jans puts it, those who "officiate" in neo-Barthian divine command theory are vulnerable always to seeming arbitrariness when venturing from theological exposition to the drawing of practical conclusions.[29] Divine command "theory" is also vulnerable to the charge that morality becomes nothing but blind obedience to a divine command without any other or further point of reference; humans cannot know with certainty what the divine commandments are and/or what obedience requires in the present day, and there is no guarantee against pharisaical claims to knowledge of the requirements of God's law.[30]

Yet, to reduce contemplation of the commands of God to the notion of a "theory" is to have missed something vital. The phrase "*theory* of divine command" should perhaps be expunged from Christian ethics. It suggests something formulaic rather than the deeply existential demands of practical reasonableness that faith entails, and offers no way out of the false dilemma between blind obedience and failure to respond in love to God's word. What we have instead called the command-rights dynamic is intended to express the responsive nature of all human action, and awareness that faith does not translate directly into convictions about the rightness or wrongness, acceptability or repugnance, of, indeed, any natural or human right. (Hence the contingency of human rights legislation and provisional nature of moral judgments.) As the postdiluvian covenant with Noah makes clear, nothing of human ontology or teleology occupies an autonomous, natural sphere outside the order of salvation. All human action is a response of some kind to the deliverance that God has already wrought. Even so, the divine command to live in freedom is an odd thing. It borders on the absurd but is, says Bonhoeffer, the center and fullness of human life. God's command not only prohibits but also liberates for authentic life. It exists in the solemn form of God's covenant with Noah and the Decalogue as well as "in the form of everyday words, admonitions, and requests for some kind of concrete behavior and activity."[31] It does not merely guard boundaries that must not be crossed but calls to responsible living in love of God and neighbor, with ways that have clear direction and an internal steadiness. In Christian ethics, response to God's word—which is the fragile business of moral reasoning—is rooted in the hope that divine accompanying and prevenience is not restricted to within the walls of the church and in the belief that God's command of life still speaks to all humanity. This is the reason that, even in a human rights culture, believers are called to be "doers of the word" (Jas 1:22 *AV*) in ways that correspond with and witness to the love of God in Christ.

Notes

Introduction

1. Vigen Guroian, "Human Rights and Modern Western Faith: An Orthodox Christian Assessment," in *Journal of Religious Ethics* 26, no. 2 (1998), reprinted in and cited from Elizabeth M. Bucar and Barbra Barnett, eds., *Does Human Rights Need God?*, Eerdmans Religion, Ethics, and Public Life (Grand Rapids: Wm. B. Eerdmans, 2005), 44.

2. Johan Steyn, *Democracy through the Law: Selected Speeches and Judgments* (Aldershot, UK: Ashgate, 2004), 133, 171.

3. As Mark Engler reports, Juan Luis Segundo warned in 1976 of the ideological trap that human rights posed for those struggling in the developing world. For a useful summary article, see Mark Engler, "Toward the 'Rights of the Poor': Human Rights in Liberation Theology," *Journal of Religious Ethics* 28, no. 3 (2000): 339–65.

4. Juan Luis Segundo, *Liberation of Theology*, trans. John Drury (Maryknoll, N.Y.: Orbis, 1976), 64. Segundo, Bonino, Assmann et al. argue that priority given to social and political rights, notably the right to property, effectively deprioritizes social and economic rights. In addition, they argue that human rights, of themselves, are not sufficient to protect the poor; the "juridical limits of human rights closely coincide with the concerns of élites." Engler, "Rights of the Poor," 345.

5. Engler, "Rights of the Poor," 347.

6. George Newlands, *Christ and Human Rights* (Aldershot, UK: Ashgate, forthcoming), promises a Christology that centers on a Christ of the vulnerable and the marginal, that is, precisely the kind of theological engagement with the topic that Protestant Christian ethics and moral reasoning needs.

7. Karl Barth, *Ethics,* Lectures at Münster (1928) and Bonn (1930), trans. Geoffrey W. Bromiley (Edinburgh: T&T Clark, 1981), 25.

8. Barth, *Ethics,* 381.

9. This description of ecumenism as "gift exchange" is taken from Margaret O Gara, *The Ecumenical Gift Exchange* (Collegeville: Minn.: Liturgical Press, 1998).

10. Carl E. Braaten, "Protestants and Natural Law," *First Things* 19 (1992): 20–26.

11. Braaten, "Protestants and Natural Law," 20–26.

12. Jean Porter, *Nature as Reason: A Thomistic Theory of the Natural Law* (Grand Rapids: Wm. B. Eerdmans, 2005), 325.

13. Fergus Kerr, *After Aquinas: Versions of Thomism* (Oxford: Blackwell, 2002), 163. See also how Aquinas argues clearly that Jesus Christ's assumption of human nature was not in any sense abstract, nor an assumption of only the human intellect. Either of these would have made his humanity a sham: "[I]f he did not assume it in reality, this would be a false understanding; nor would this assumption of the human nature be anything but a fictitious Incarnation, as Damascene says (*De fide orth.* iii, 11)." *Summa Theologia* (*S.T.*), III q. 4 a. 5, argues equally clearly that Jesus Christ did not assume human nature as a species but as the "firstborn among many brethren" (Rom 8:29 *AV*). Thomas Aquinas, *S.T.*, trans. the Fathers of the English Dominican Province (New York: Benziger Bros. Edition, 1947), III q. 4 a. 4. *S.T.* III q. 4 a. 6 repeats the teaching of Hebrews 2:17 that Jesus Christ had to become like us in every respect so that he might make atonement for our sins, and notes that his genealogy is traced back to Adam (Luke 3:23-38). Furthermore, Aquinas wrote many tomes and chose diverse structures for them. Their ordering principles were different and sometimes had a more explicitly Trinitarian shape than at other times. In other words, as Kerr argues, it would be wrong to assume that Aquinas speaks of God apart from the truth of revelation. For a similar perspective on Aquinas's Christology, see Michael Dauphinais and Matthew Levering, *Knowing the Love of Christ: An Introduction to the Theology of St. Thomas Aquinas* (Notre Dame, Ind.: University of Notre Dame Press, 2002), esp. chaps. 4–5.

14. Aquinas, *S.T.* III q. 19 a. 1.

15. Kieran Cronin, *Rights and Christian Ethics* (Cambridge: Cambridge University Press, 1992), 250.

16. David Hollenbach S.J., *The Common Good and Christian Ethics* (Cambridge: Cambridge University Press, 2000), 112. See also Hollenbach, *Claims in Conflict: Retrieving and Renewing the Catholic Human Rights Tradition* (New York: Paulist Press, 1979).

17. Hollenbach, *Common Good*, 165–66.

18. David Hollenbach S.J., *The Global Face of Public Faith: Politics, Human Rights, and Christian Ethics* (Washington, D.C.: Georgetown University Press, 2003), 147.

19. Porter, *Nature as Reason*, 345.

20. Porter, *Nature as Reason*, 345.

21. Porter, *Nature as Reason*, 357.

22. John Webster, *Word and Church: Essays in Church Dogmatics* (Edinburgh: T&T Clark/Continuum, 2001), 192.

23. "He wills therefore the excellence of order in the universe in reference to Himself, and the excellence of order in the universe in mutual reference of its parts

to one another." Thomas Aquinas, *Summa Contra Gentiles* (*S.C.G.*), trans. Vernon J. Bourke (Notre Dame, Ind.: Notre Dame University Press, 1976), bk. 1, chap. 78.

24. Aquinas, *S.C.G.*, bk. 3a, chaps. 22, 69. "[T]he particular good is directed to the common good as its end: for the being of the part is on account of the whole: therefore the good of the nation is more godlike than the good of one man." Aquinas, *S.C.G.*, bk. 1, chap. 77. See also O. J. Brown, *Natural Rectitude and Divine Law in Aquinas: An Approach to an Integral Interpretation of the Thomistic Doctrine of Law* (Toronto: Pontifical Institute of Medieval Studies, 1981), 74–84.

25. Jean Porter, *Natural and Divine Law* (Grand Rapids: Wm. B. Eerdmans, 1999), 170.

26. John Nurser, *For All Peoples: Christian Churches and Human Rights* (Washington, D.C.: Georgetown University Press, 2004), esp. chap. 1.

27. Nurser, *For All Peoples,* 1.

28. Nurser, *For All Peoples,* 172.

29. "Statement on Religious Liberty," in *The New Delhi Report: The Third Assembly of the World Council of Churches,* 1961 (New York: Association Press, 1962), 159. On similarities with Roman Catholic teaching at the time, see James E. Wood Jr., "An Apologia for Religious Human Rights," in *Religious Human Rights in Global Perspective: Religious Perspectives,* ed. John Witte Jr. and Johan D. van der Vyver (The Hague: Martinus Nojhoff, 1996), 455–83, esp. 466.

30. For relevant Roman Catholic teaching, see *Dignitatis Humanae: On the Right of the Person and of Communities to Social and Civil Freedom in Matters Religious,* promulgated by His Holiness Pope Paul VI, December 7, 1965.

31. These statements included Jürgen Moltmann, "A Definitive Study Paper: A Christian Declaration on Human Rights," in *A Christian Declaration on Human Rights: Theological Studies of the World Alliance of Reformed Churches,* ed. Allen O. Miller (Grand Rapids: Wm. B. Eerdmans, 1977), vol. 129 (hereafter cited as WARC), 142–43; World Baptist Congress, "Declaration on Human Rights," in *Baptist World Alliance Official Report of the Fourteenth Congress: Celebrating Christ's Presence through the Spirit* (Nashville: Published for the Baptist World Alliance by Broadman Press, 1980); Presbyterian Church in the United States, *Minutes of the General Assembly* 187 (1978); Lutheran World Federation, *Theological Perspectives on Human Rights 12–14* (Geneva: Lutheran World Federation, 1977).

32. Martin Shupack, "The Churches and Human Rights: Catholic and Protestant Human Rights Views as Reflected in Church Statements," *Harvard Human Rights Journal* 6 (1993): 127–57, esp. 130.

33. Shupack, "Churches and Human Rights," 131.

34. Shupack, "Churches and Human Rights," 135, citing WARC, 61.

35. Shupack, "Churches and Human Rights," 152.

36. Paul Tillich et al., *To Live as Men: An Anatomy of Peace* (Santa Barbara, Calif.: Center for Democratic Institutions, 1965), 13.

37. See also Paul Tillich, "Beyond Religious Socialism," *Christian Century,* June 15, 1949, <http://www.religion-online.org/showarticle.asp?title=475> (date accessed: 07/24/06).

38. Tillich, *To Live as Men,* 14.

39. Tillich, *To Live as Men*, 13.
40. Max Stackhouse, "Why Human Rights Need God: A Christian Perspective," in Bucar and Barnett, *Does Human Rights Need God?*, 36.
41. Michael J. Perry, *Under God? Religious Faith and Liberal Democracy* (Cambridge: Cambridge University Press, 2003), 124.
42. Michael J. Perry, *The Idea of Human Rights* (Oxford: Oxford University Press, 1998), 11.
43. Perry, *Under God?*, 125.
44. Tillich, *To Live as Men*, 13.
45. Bucar and Barnett, *Does Human Rights Need God?*, 3.
46. Jean Bethke Elshtain, afterword to Bucar and Barnett, *Does Human Rights Need God?*, 294.
47. Stanley Hauerwas, "Abortion, Theologically Understood," in *The Church and Abortion: In Search of New Ground for Response*, ed. Paul T. Stallsworth (Nashville: Abingdon, 1993), 50.
48. Kevin Maguire, "Hewitt Plots Union Rights for Clergy," *Guardian*, July 12, 2002.
49. Ruth Gledhill, "Clergy May Win Workers' Rights," *The Times*, July 12, 2002.
50. According to the Amicus national secretary Chris Ball, "Reverend Owen alleges that not only have his fundamental rights not been respected in the course of the process, but that European Directives have been either breached or not properly applied by the UK authorities. In his petition, he refers in particular to the fact that he has been discriminated against, contrary to Article 13 of the Amsterdam Treaty, and contrary to Articles 48(2) and 112 of the Treaty of Rome. He furthermore claims that Council Directive 91/533/EEC of October 1991 has not been properly incorporated into UK law." Posted to the Web by Chris Ball on July 16, 2002, http://www.3rdsectorunion.org.uk/cgi-bin/dbman/db.cgi?db=default&uid=default&ID=138&view_records=1&ww=1 (date accessed: 07/20/2002).
51. Other relevant considerations include arrangements for disciplinary and grievance procedures within the church itself, including the Draft Clergy Discipline Measure 2000, which appears to have been prepared with the possibility in view that statutory employment protection might be extended to the clergy.
52. R (on application of Amicus and others) v Secretary of State for Trade and Industry [2004] EWHC 860 (Admin), reported at [2004] IRLR 430.
53. For more on this, see Esther D. Reed, "Labour Law and the Employment Status of Clergy," *Crucible* 3 (2003): 429–35.
54. Canon 9 of the Council of Chalcedon expressly forbade the clergy to do this: "If any Clergyman have a matter against another Clergyman, he shall not forsake his Bishop and run to secular courts; but let him first lay open the matter before his own Bishop, or let the matter be submitted to any person whom each of the parties may, with the Bishop's consent, select." Commenting on this canon and the Constitutions of the Holy Apostles, Jeremy Taylor said that "the bishop is the judge; the bishop is to inflict censures: the presbyters and deacons are either to obey or be deposed." Taylor, "Of the Sacred Order of Episcopacy," in *The Whole Works of the Right Rev. Jeremy Taylor* (London: Longman, Orme, Brown, Green, & Longmans, 1839), 161.

55. *Clergy Discipline Measure 2003: Code of Practice* (London: Church House, 2005).
56. Elie Wiesel, "A Tribute to Human Rights," in *The Universal Declaration of Human Rights: Fifty Years and Beyond*, ed. Yael Danieli et al. (Amityville, N.Y.: Baywood), 3.
57. Karl Barth, "The Christian's Place in Society," in *The Word of God and the Word of Man*, trans. Douglas Horton (London: Hodder & Stoughton, 1928), 289.
58. Karl Barth, "Christian's Place in Society," 288.
59. Karl Barth, "Christian's Place in Society," 281.
60. Karl Barth, "Christian's Place in Society," 290.
61. Aquinas, *S.T.*, I–II, q. 61 a. 4, *sed contra*.
62. Barth, *Ethics,* 376.
63. Miroslav Volf, *Work in the Spirit: Toward a Theology of Work* (Eugene, Ore.: Wipf & Stock, 2001; previously published by Oxford University Press, 1991), 76–79. An inductive approach falls foul of at least three problems: the occasional or indirect manner in which the Bible makes mention of the topic; the historico-cultural gap between biblical times and our own; and the problem of attributing significance to those biblical statements that appear relevant.
64. "'The Wall behind Which Refugees Can Shelter': UNHCR Comments at the 50th Anniversary of U.N. Refugee Convention," <http://www.unhcr.org/cgi-bin/texis/vtx/protect?id=3c0762ea4> (date accessed: 08/11/06).

Chapter 1

1. *The Devil's Advocate* (1997), directed by Taylor Hackford, based on the novel by Andrew Neiderman.
2. Howard Zinn, "The Modern Era of Law," in *Declarations of Independence: Cross-Examining American Ideology* (New York: Harper Perennial, 1991), 49.
3. William Shakespeare, *Henry VI*, pt. 2, act 4, sc. 2.
4. The meaning of "human rights" for our purposes is understood with reference to documents such as the Universal Declaration of Human Rights (1948) (UDHR) and the European Convention on Human Rights (1950) (EHCR) as freedoms and claims on others that are recognized at law. The term "human rights" can be used indescriminantly to refer to various moral claims and liberties, but we resrict our usage to rights enshrined in national legislation, international treaties, covenants, and the like. So, for instance, when talking about a "right to life" we mean the right recognized by Article 3 of the UDHR and/or Article 2 of the EHCR, or similar legislative or constitutional documents. When talking about the right to just conditions of work, we mean the right recognized by Article 2 of the European Social Charter (1965), or similar documents.
5. Agnes Heller, *A Theory of Modernity* (Oxford: Blackwell, 1999), 54.
6. Francesca Klug, *Values for a Godless Age: The Story of the United Kingdom's New Bill of Rights* (London: Penguin, 2000), 200n6. Klug was director of the Human Rights Act Research Unit at King's College Law School, London, and, at the time she wrote, a member of the Labour Government's Human Rights Task Force.

7. Klug, *Values for a Godless Age*, 32.
8. Klug, *Values for a Godless Age*, 13n6.
9. Kathleen Marshall, in Kathleen Marshall and Paul Parvis, *Honouring Children: The Human Rights of the Child in Christian Perspective* (Edinburgh: St. Andrew Press, 2004), §1.2.1.
10. This is a familiar claim. See, for instance, United States Embassy, Bogotá, Colombia, "The Noble Endeavor: The Creation of the Universal Declaration of Human Rights," <http://bogota.usembassy.gov/wwwshr01.shtml> (date accessed: 11/19/05).
11. See Abdullahi Ahmed An-Na'im, ed., *Human Rights in Cross-Cultural Perspectives: A Quest for Consensus* (Philadelphia: University of Philadelphia Press, 1992), 19–43. For a rigorous study of the compatibility of Islamic law and human rights, see Mashood A. Baderin, *International Human Rights and Islamic Law* (Oxford: Oxford University Press, 2003).
12. Conor Gearty and Adam Tomkins, eds., *Understanding Human Rights* (1996; Reprint, London/New York: Pinter, 1999); Tom Campbell, K. D. Ewing, and Adam Tomkins, eds., *Sceptical Essays on Human Rights* (Oxford: Oxford University Press, 2001).
13. K. D. Ewing, "The Unbalanced Constitution," 103.
14. Martin Loughlin, "Rights, Democracy, and Law" in Campbell, Ewing, and Tomkins, *Sceptical Essays*, 45.
15. Mark Tushnet, "Living with a Bill of Rights," in Gearty and Tomkins, *Understanding Human Rights*.
16. Helena Kennedy, *Just Law: The Changing Face of Justice and Why It Matters to Us All* (London: Vintage, 2005), 4.
17. See, for instance, Richard Ford and Frances Gibb, "Blair Leads the Attack on His Own Human Rights Laws," *The Times*, May 16, 2006. Article 3 of the European Convention on Human Rights is non-derogable.
18. Jürgen Habermas, *Autonomy and Solidarity: Interviews with Jürgen Habermas*, ed. Peter Dews (London and New York: Verso, 1992), 158.
19. Peter Novick, *That Noble Dream: The "Objectivity" Question and the American Historical Profession* (Cambridge: Cambridge University Press, 1988), 16.
20. On this, see Philippe Sands, *Lawless World: America and the Making and Breaking of Global Rules* (London: Penguin, 2005), 66.
21. Michel Rosenfeld, *Just Interpretations: Law between Ethics and Politics* (Berkeley/Los Angeles: University of California Press, 1998), 173–80.
22. Richard Rorty, "Human Rights, Rationality, and Sentimentality," in Belgrade Circle and Obrad Savic, *The Politics of Human Right* (London/New York: Verso, 1999), 73.
23. Rorty, "Human Rights, Rationality, and Sentimentality," 79–81. We might note that historically *Uncle Tom's Cabin* has also been viewed as having done much in the U.S. to deepen mutual antipathies and misunderstandings.
24. Oliver O'Donovan asks similar questions and makes this latter point with respect to the imperfectibility of politics in *The Ways of Judgment* (Grand Rapids: Wm. B. Eerdmans, 2005), 13.
25. O'Donovan, *Ways of Judgment,* 15.
26. O'Donovan, *Ways of Judgment,* 20.

27. See Campbell, Ewing, and Tomkins, *Sceptical Essays on Human Rights*, 2–3, for their definition of skeptics as those who do not believe all they are told and who want to continue searching for a better way.

28. Stanley Hauerwas, *Suffering Presence: Theological Reflections on Medicine, the Mentally Handicapped, and the Church* (Notre Dame, Ind.: University of Notre Dame Press, 1986), 130.

29. Stanley J. Grenz, *The Moral Quest: Foundations of Christian Ethics* (Downers Grove, Ill.: InterVarsity, 1997), 262–66.

30. Joan Lockwood O'Donovan, "Historical Prolegomena to a Theological Review," *Studies in Christian Ethics* 9, no. 2 (1996): 53.

31. See, e.g., Gordon R. Dunstan's involvement with the ethical committees of the Royal College of Obstetricians and Gynaecologists, Royal College of Physicians, the Medical Research Council, and the Royal College of Paediatrics and Child Health. Consider how, for instance, the "Ethical Assumptions" articulated in *A Consideration of the Law and Ethics in Relation to Late Termination of Pregnancy for Fetal Abnormality* are stated in the following: "The ethical question falls to be discussed in terms of what duties are owed to, and what liberties may be taken with, the fetus living in the womb." Report of the RCOG Ethics Committee (London: Royal College of Obstetricians & Gynaecologists Press, 1998), 8.

32. HE Msgr. Celestino Migliore, *Intervention by the Holy See at the 58th Session of the General Assembly of the United Nations Organization on the Occasion of the Fifty-fifth Anniversary of the Universal Declaration of Human Rights*, December 10, 2003, <http://www.vatican.va/roman_curia/secretariat_state/2003/documents/rc_seg-st_20031210_human-rights_en.html> (date accessed: 04/03 /04). Msgr. Migliore was citing addresses by Pope John Paul II to the United Nations in 1979 and 1995.

33. Migliore, *Intervention by the Holy See.*

34. Max L. Stackhouse, director of Princeton Seminary's Project on Public Theology and a minister in the United Church of Christ, writes: "[A]fter the church joined biblical ideas to philosophical insights to form theology, and carved out a new kind of social space in society on that basis, subsequent theorists set forth the implications of these developments in a way that allowed widespread recognition of human rights that people ought not be tortured, that they had a right to freedom of worship, speech and press, etc. The spreading of such ideas allowed those influenced by them and the social changes they entail to pass human rights provisions into law. It was an enormous contribution by the faith to the world. . . . Modern, secular theorists kept the flower but threw out the root ideas, a development that made human rights appear more groundless than they were" ("In the Company of Hauerwas," *Journal for Christian Theological Research*, 2, no. 1 [1997], available at <http://apu.edu/~CTRF/articles/1997_articles/stackhouse.html> [date accessed: 03/18/04]).

35. *Centesimus Annus*, Encyclical Letter of the Supreme Pontiff John Paul II on the Hundredth Anniversary of *Rerum Novarum*, includes several affirmations of human rights. With particular reference to the condition of workers, John Paul II calls Christian people "to proclaim the truth and to communicate the life which is in Christ (cf. John 14.6)" (§3); "Peace is built on the foundation of justice in the economic and social situation of the

time" (§5); bearing witness to Christ as Savior entails the exposure of injustice and, where necessary, reforms to restore "a certain equality" such that no party is so powerful as to "reduce the other to subservience" (§15).

36. John Finnis, *Natural Law and Natural Rights* (Oxford: Clarendon, 1980), 221. Chapter 3 below treats Finnis's work in more detail.

37. Consideration of Human Rights Act Commons Amendments, October 29, 1998, col. 2090.

38. Statements on human rights were made at the Fifth Assembly of the World Council of Churches, Nairobi, 1975; the Seventh Assembly, Canberra, 1991; Morges, Switzerland, June 1998 (entitled *Human Rights and the Churches*); and the Eighth Assembly, Harare, Zimbabwe, December 1998 (entitled *A Statement on Human Rights*).

39. See Newlands, *Christ and Human Rights*.

40. See Finnis, *Natural Law and Natural Rights,* 206.

41. Finnis, *Natural Law and Natural Rights,* 198. John Finnis's work, along with that of Germain Grisez, has made a significant contribution in recent years to debate about what practical reason entails. Finnis's *Natural Law and Natural Rights* is arguably the most substantial attempt in recent years to develop a natural law-based conception of human rights. His rehabilitation of Aquinas's theory of natural law makes the strong claim that human rights institutionalize the conditions necessary for human flourishing, and his restatement of natural law is one of the few to warrant serious interdisciplinary attention by thinkers outside Christian theology and ethics.

42. Brian Tierney, *The Idea of Natural Rights: Studies on Natural Rights, Natural Law, and Church Law, 1150–1625*, Emory University Studies in Law and Religion, no. 5 (Atlanta: Scholars Press, 1997).

43. Tierney, *Idea of Natural Rights*, 25.

44. See esp. Tierney, *Idea of Natural Rights*. Tierney's own proposal is to develop "permissive," as compared to "prescriptive," natural law, as the more plausible ground for convergence between medieval and modern rights talk. While no developed sense of subjective right can be derived from Aquinas's objective definition of *ius*, there is another aspect of medieval and early modern natural law teaching found elsewhere than in the writings of Aquinas, namely, the idea of permissive natural law—that is, the idea that all things are permitted except those prohibited by biblical precept or human statute. The idea was developed in connection with private property: the law of nature permits something to be mine and something else to be yours, but does not command it. Tierney's major sources are the *Decretum* of Gratian and the writings of the great canonist Huguccio. His convincing claim is that, from the twelfth century to the age of Hobbes and Locke and beyond, the idea of permissive natural law was persistently invoked as a ground of natural rights, especially the right to property.

45. Aquinas, *S.T.* I–II q. 96 a. 3 c.

46. Tierney, "Natural Law and Natural Rights: Old Problems and Recent Approaches," *Review of Politics* 64, no. 3 (2002): 392.

47. For good accounts see Micheline R. Ishay, *The History of Human Rights: From Ancient Times to the Globalization Era* (Berkeley: University of California Press, 2004); Michael J. Perry, *The Idea of Human Rights: Four Inquiries* (New York:

Oxford University Press, 1998); Richard Tuck, *Natural Rights Theories: Their Origin and Development* (Cambridge: Cambridge University Press, 1979); Jeremy Waldron, *Theories of Rights* (New York: Oxford University Press, 1984).

48. Hugo Grotius, *Hugonis Grotii: De jure belli et pacis (On the Law of War and Peace),* ed. J. B. Scott (1913; repr., Oxford: Oxford University Press, 1646), bk. 1, chap. 1, §10.

49. "*Et haec quidem quae jam diximus, locum aliquem haberent etiamsi dare*mus, *quod sine summo scelere dari niquit, non esse* Deum, *aut non curari ab eo negotia humana.*" Grotius, *De jure belli et pacis, Prolegomena,* (no page numbers given).

50. Ernst Cassirer makes the point as follows: "Law is in this respect like pure arithmetic; for the teachings of arithmetic concerning the nature of numbers and their relations imply an eternal and necessary truth which would not be affected, even if the whole empirical world were destroyed" (*The Philosophy of the Enlightenment,* trans. Fritz C. A. Koelln and James P. Pettegrove [Princeton: Princeton University Press, 1979], 237).

51. John Locke, "The Second Treatise of Government" (first published 1689), *Political Writings,* ed. David Wootton (Harmondsworth, UK: Penguin, 1993), chap. 6, 289.

52. Jean-Jacques Rousseau, *The Social Contract,* trans. Maurice Cranston (Harmondsworth, UK: Penguin, 1968; first published 1762), bk. 1, chap. 8, 65.

53. Rousseau, *Social Contract,* bk. 1, chap. 8, 65.

54. Rousseau, *Social Contract,* bk. 2, chap. 6, 80–81.

55. Rousseau, *Social Contract,* bk. 1, chap. 2.

56. Immanuel Kant, *The Metaphysics of Morals,* trans. Mary Gregor (Cambridge: Cambridge University Press, 1991), 56.

57. Kant, *Metaphysics of Morals,* 57.

58. Further details are available from Martin Dixon, *Textbook on International Law,* 4th ed. (London: Blackstone Press, 2001), 331, 334.

59. Karl Marx, "On the Jewish Question," in David McLellan, ed., *Karl Marx: Selected Writings* (Oxford: Oxford University Press, 1977), 53.

60. Oliver O'Donovan makes this point in *The Desire of the Nations* (Cambridge: Cambridge University Press, 1999), 247. By "subjective sense of 'right'" he understands powers, qualities, or entitlements pertaining to individuals as such; individuals are deemed to have a primitive endowment such that their rights become the basis on which the law entitles them to demand performance.

61. Jeffrey Stout, "The Emergence of Modern Democratic Culture," in *Democracy and Tradition* (Princeton: Princeton University Press, 2004), 205.

62. Agnes Heller, "Rights, Modernity, Democracy," in *Can Modernity Survive?* (Cambridge: Polity Press, 1990), 149.

63. Consider, for instance, Aquinas's twofold definition of law, as given in *S. T.,* I–II q. 90 a. 1, for what it says about the created order's participation in the divine wisdom. Human law never ceases to be *human* law because the operation of human reason never becomes divine; it may never be pronounced God. The capacity to reason is given by God and may be drawn toward faith, mingling with God's self-disclosure. Human law is both proper to reason and potentially at least a participation in the divine understanding.

64. Aquinas, *S.T.*, II–II q. 57 a. 1, ad. 2.
65. Dietrich Bonhoeffer, *Ethics. Dietrich Bonhoeffer Works*, vol. 6, ed. Ilse Tödt et al., trans. Reinhard Krauss et al. (Minneapolis: Fortress, 2005), 184.
66. Bonhoeffer, *Ethics,* 186–87.
67. Bonhoeffer, *Ethics,* 183.
68. John Milbank, *Theology and Social Theory* (Oxford: Blackwell, 1990), 381.
69. John Webster, *Barth's Moral Theology: Human Action in Barth's Thought* (Edinburgh: T&T Clark, 1998/2004), 121, citing Karl Barth, *Church Dogmatics (CD)* (Edinburgh: T&T Clark, 1956–1977), IV.3, §69, 234, 212.
70. Barth, *C.D.*, III.3, §48, 52–53.
71. I draw on John Webster's summary of Eberhard Jüngel's treatment of analogy as that which facilitates the drawing of appropriate distinctions between God's action and human action while recognizing that humankind has been made God's covenant partner in bringing his purposes to fruition. Webster, *Barth's Moral Theology*, chap. 9. I draw also on Battista Mondin's demonstration that differences between Aquinas and Barth with respect to analogy are more of emphasis than substance. "It is true that Barth insists more than Aquinas on the *sola gratia* but not to the point of eliminating nature and reason. On the other hand, it is true that Aquinas insists more than Barth on the relative autonomy of nature but not to the point of forgetting its subordination to revelation and grace" (Battista Mondin, S.J., *The Principle of Analogy in Protestant and Catholic Theology* [The Hague: Martinus Nijhoff, 1963], 171). The function of analogy for Aquinas is less to ascertain true representations of God's goodness and being than to consider how judgments can be made about the relation between God and humankind. So, too, for moral theologians schooled by Barth: "Ohne Analogie keine Theologie." Eberhard Jüngel, "Vorwort," in *Entsprechungen: Gott–Wahrheit–Mensch: Theologische Erörterungen* (Munich: Kaiser, 1980), 7, cited in Webster, *Barth's Moral Theology*, 199.
72. Cited in Donald Wigal, ed., *The Wisdom of Eleanor Roosevelt* (New York: Citadel Press, 2003), xiv.
73. Guroian, "Human Rights and Modern Western Faith," 47.
74. For an accessible account of how the most powerful nations of the world have undermined the law-based international order that developed after World War II, see Sands, *Lawless World*.
75. John Milbank, *The Word Made Strange: Theology, Language, Culture* (Oxford: Blackwell, 1997), 1.

Chapter 2

1. Heller, *Theory of Modernity*, 54.
2. Aquinas, *S.T.*, I–II q. 61 a. 4, *sed contra*.
3. This image is used in Heller, *Can Modernity Survive?*, 148.
4. These issues were summarized in 1973 by Jürgen Habermas in *Legitimations probleme im Spätkapitalismus* (*Legitimation Crisis*, trans. Thomas A. McCarthy [London: Heinemann, 1976]).
5. As theorists at the Society for Social Research, University of Chicago, summarize: "The validity of an order is the probability that people will orient their action to it." Available at <http://www.src.uchicago.edu/ssr1/PRELIMS/

Theory/weber.html>. According to Max Weber, the legitimacy of any given social order may be upheld by either disinterested or self-interested motives, and submission to a particular regime is almost always determined by a variety of motives that map onto three broad bases of legitimacy: rational (including legal), traditional, and charismatic. Weber, *Economy and Society: An Outline of Interpretive Sociology,* ed. Guenther Roth and Claus Wittich (New York: Bedminster, 1968), 1:212ff.

6. Hooker, *Of the Laws of Ecclesiastical Polity: An Abridged Edition,* ed. A. S. McGrade and Brian Vickers (London: Sidgwick & Jackson, 1975), I.iv.1, 69. Joan Lockwood O'Donovan speaks of a separation in Hooker's work between the law of nature and the law of reason: "Hooker's non-Thomistic separation between nature's law and the law of reason flows from his sharp division of natural from voluntary agents, according as God is the efficient cause or the final cause of their motion." Lockwood O'Donovan, *Theology of Law and Authority in the English Reformation,* Emory University Studies in Law and Religion, no. 1 (Atlanta: Scholars Press, 1991), 137. Hooker, she says, regards human law as having its origin in the law of reason rather than divine law or natural law, and thinks that the need for human law originates in the sinful depravity of individuals. Lockwood O'Donovan thus places a question mark over the extent to which Hooker sees human law as having its origin in the divine law.

7. Christopher J. Insole, *The Politics of Human Frailty: A Theological Defense of Political Liberalism* (Notre Dame, Ind.: University of Notre Dame Press, 2005), chap. 2, esp. 77.

8. Insole, *Politics of Human Frailty,* 159–60.

9. Jeffrey Stout, *Ethics after Babel: The Language of Morals and Their Discontents* (Princeton: Princeton University Press, 2001; first published by Beacon Press, 1988), 124.

10. Aquinas, *S.T.,* I–II q. 100 a. 8 c.

11. Hooker, *Of the Laws,* I.iii.1, 63.

12. A. S. McGrade, introduction to Richard Hooker, *Of the Laws,* 18.

13. Hooker, *Of the Laws,* I.vii.2, 78.

14. Lockwood O'Donovan, *Theology of Law and Authority,* 137.

15. Lockwood O'Donovan, *Theology of Law and Authority,* 138.

16. Insole, *Politics of Human Frailty,* 34.

17. ALMIGHTY God, whose kyngdom is everlasting, and power infinite, have mercy upon the whole congregacion, and so rule the heart of thy chosen servant Elizabeth our Quene and governoure that she (knowing whose minister she is) may above all thinges, seke thy honoure and glorye: and that we her subjectes, (duly considering whose authority she hath) may faithfully serve, honour, and humblye obey her in the and for the, according to thy blessed worde, and ordinance, through Jesus Christ our Lord, who with the and the holye ghost, lyveth and reygneth ever one God, worlde without ende. Amen. "Book of Common Prayer," 1559.

18. Hooker, *Of the Laws,* I.xvi.2, 136.

19. Hooker, *Of the Laws,* VIII.vi.8, 381.

20. Jeremy Taylor, "Of Obedience to Our Superiors," *The Rule and Exercises of Holy Living* (Philadelphia: J. W. Bradley, 1860), chap. 3, §1.

21. Taylor, "Of Obedience," chap. 3, §1, 15.
22. Taylor, "Of Obedience," chap. 3, §1, 9.
23. Thomas Cranmer, *A Short Instruction into Christian Religion: Being a Catechism set forth by Archbishop Cranmer in 1548*, ed. E. Burton (Oxford: Oxford University Press, 1829), 142.
24. "So God doth ratify the works of that sovereign authority which kings have received by men" (Hooker, *Of the Laws*, VIII.ii.6, 346).
24. Hooker, *Of the Laws*, I.ii.1, 58.
26. On this see McGrade, introduction to Richard Hooker, *Of the Laws*, 17–19.
27. Hooker, *Of the Laws*, I.xvi.5, 138.
28. Hooker, *Of the Laws*, I.i.3, 58.
29. This is noted by W. J. Torrance Kirby, who provides a useful summary of such attacks on Hooker and their interpretations in "Richard Hooker's Discourse on Natural Law in the Context of the Magisterial Reformation," in *The Theology of Richard Hooker in the Context of the Magisterial Reformation*, Studies in Reformed Theology and History (Princeton: Princeton Seminary Press, 1999), <http://www.mun.ca/animus/1998vol3/kirby3.htm> (date accessed: 03/20/04).
30. "A Christian Letter of certaine English Protestantes, unfayned favourers of the present state of religion, authorized and professed in England: unto that Reverend and Learned man Mr. R. Hoo[ker] requiring resolution in certayne matters of doctrine (which seeme to overthrowe the foundation of Christian Religion, and of the Church among us) expreslie contayned in his five bookes of Ecclesiasticall Policie" (Middelburg, Neth.: R. Schilders, 1599; reprinted in *The Controversy with Travers*, in the *Folger Library Edition of the Works of Richard Hooker*, vol. 4, ed. John Booty [1982], 1–79, cited in Kirby, *The Theology of Richard Hooker*, n. 3.
31. Hooker, *Of the Laws*, I.xii.3, 121.
32. Hooker, *Of the Laws*, I.xii.3, 121.
33. Hooker, *Of the Laws*, I.xvi.5, 138.
34. Hooker, *Of the Laws*, I.xvi.5, 139.
35. Richard Hooker, "A Learned Discourse of Justification, Works, and How the Foundation of Faith Is Overthrown," cited from the Christian Classics Ethereal Library at Calvin College, available at <http://www.ccel.org/ccel/hooker/just.viii.html> (date accessed: 11/02/05).
36. Cranmer, *Short Instruction into Christian Religion*, 142.
37. William Laud, "Concerning the Church, the Ornaments Thereof, and the Church's Possessions," cited in Paul E. More and Frank L. Cross, *Anglicanism: The Thought and Practice of the Church of England* (Harrisburg, Pa.: Morehouse Publishing, 1935), 702.
38. Anthony Sparrow, *A Rationale upon the Book of Common-Prayer* (London, 1725), 5.
39. Cranmer, *Short Instruction into Christian Religion*, 83.
40. "For after our justification only begin we to work as the law of God requireth. Then we shall do all good works willingly, although not so exactly as the law requireth by mean of infirmity of the flesh. Nevertheless, by the merit and benefit of Christ, we being sorry that we cannot do all things no more exquisitely and duly, all our works shall be accepted and taken of God, as most

exquisite, pure, and perfect." Cranmer, an extract from annotations to *The King's Book*, which was the popular title for "A Necessary Doctrine and Erudition for Any Christian Man; Set Forth by the King's Majesty of England" (1538). Electronic edition scanned and edited by Shane Rosenthal from the Parker Society edition of Cranmer's writings (Cambridge: Cambridge University Press, 1840), <http://www.ccel.org/c/cranmer/doctrine/doctrine.html> (date accessed: 03/20/04).

41. John Bradford, Letter 46, in Works by John Bradford, from the Christian Classics Ethereal Library at Calvin College, <http://www.ccel.org/b/bradford/> (date accessed: 03/20/04).

42. Cranmer, *Short Instruction into Christian Religion*, 113.

43. Hugh Latimer, "Thou Canst Make Me Clean," a sermon available from The Anglican Library, <http://www.anglicanlibrary.org/latimer/clean.htm> (date accessed: 03/20/04).

44. Hooker, *Of the Laws*, I.ii.5, 62.

45. Brevard S. Childs, *Biblical Theology of the Old and New Testaments* (London: SCM Press, 1992), 554.

46. Hooker, *Of the Laws*, I.xiii.1, 122.

47. Hooker, *Of the Laws*, I.xiv.5, 129.

48. Hooker, *Of the Laws*, I.iii.2, 65.

49. Hooker, *Of the Laws*, I.ii.1, 58.

50. John S. Marshall, *Hooker and the Anglican Tradition: An Historical and Theological Study of Hooker's Ecclesiastical Polity* (London: Adam & Charles Black, 1963), x.

51. Hooker, *Of the Laws*, I.vii.2, 78.

52. Hooker, *Of the Laws*, I.xii,2, 121.

53. Hooker, *Of the Laws*, I.viii.5, 85.

54. Hooker, *Of the Laws*, I.viii,10, 91.

55. Hooker, *Of the Laws*, I.xii.1, 119, and I.xiii.1, 122.

56. Hooker, *Of the Laws*, I.xv.4, 34.

57. Hooker, *Of the Laws*, I.x.7, 101–2.

58. Hooker, *Of the Laws*, I.x.8, 102–3.

59. Arthur J. Jacobson, "The Idolatry of Rules: Writing Law according to Moses, with Reference to Other Jurisprudences," in *Deconstruction and the Possibility of Justice*, ed. Drucilla Cornell, Michel Rosenfeld, and David Gray Carlson (New York/London: Routledge, 1992), 135.

60. I am indebted in this reading of Hooker to Arthur J. Jacobson's work on "writings" of the law in biblical accounts of God's giving of the law to Moses and the people of Israel. In his essay "The Idolatry of Rules," Jacobson considers Moses' "writing" of the law, "writing" about writing the law, and "erasing" the law in the smashing of the tablets. For our purposes, Jacobson's superb essay is helpful when reading Hooker because it provides a way of expressing the dynamism and inherent dialogism that characterizes his theology of law. More specifically, it provides a means of demonstrating that, as for the biblical accounts, his theological ethic of law involves multiple writings. One of the essay's central observations is that naturalistic and positivistic jurisprudences entail only two "writings" of the law: initial inscriptions (whether in nature or at the word of a ruler) and subsequent nondialogic application. Moses'

understanding of the law entailed at least three "writings." The first is God's "writing"—namely "the world, along with the laws of the world, as a finished, created product" (130–31). The second is God's collaborative "writing" with Moses at Sinai. The third is Moses' later "writing" that is characterized by struggle, "erasure," delay, the need for sanctions to ensure compliance, rewriting, and the constant need for recourse to God in prayer. Natural law, says Jacobson, is part of God's first "writing," inscribed once by God without delay at the moment of creation. But natural law is not Moses' later "writing" of the law that poses rules as instruments to assist humans to realize Elohim's propositions (110). The challenge to Moses and his successors is to write laws as collaborators and friends of Yahweh, not as the direct representative of Elohim or a pharaonic-type God. (NB: According to Jacobson, Moses calls God "Elohim" when referring to him as the all-knowing, all-powerful Creator who rules the earth by right and "Yahweh" when referring to the God who interacts with the world he has created as collaborator and friend [Exod. 33:11].)

61. Hooker, *Of the Laws*, I.viii.3, 84.
62. Hooker, *Of the Laws*, I.viii.3, 84.
63. Hooker, *Of the Laws*, I.x.12, 107.
64. Hooker, *Of the Laws*, I.x.8, 102–3.
65. Hooker, *Of the Laws*, I.viii.3, 83.
66. Hooker, *Of the Laws*, I.x.1, 96, and I.x.2, 97.
67. Aquinas, *S.T.*, II–II q. 184 a. 1, *sed contra*.
68. Aquinas, *S.C.G.* bk. III, chap. 17. I follow Hollenbach's adaptation of the translation to use "God" rather than "Him" as contained in *Basic Writings of Saint Thomas Aquinas*, ed. Anton C. Pegis (New York: Random House, 1945), 2:27.
69. Hooker, *Of the Laws*, I.ii.3, 60.
70. Hooker, *Of the Laws*, I.ii.4, 61.
71. Hooker, *Of the Laws*, I.viii.3, 83.
72. Hooker, Of the Laws, I.viii.3, 84.
73. Hooker, *Of the Laws*, I.viii.5, 86.
74. Hooker, *Of the Laws*, I.viii.8, 88.
75. Hooker, *Of the Laws*, I.x.6, 101.
76. Hooker, *Of the Laws*, I.x.10, 105.
77. Hooker, *Of the Laws*, I.x.8, 102.
78. This useful summary is given by Arthur Ripstein in his review of *Rights and Responsibilities* (Toronto: University of Toronto Press, 1999) by Leon Trakman and Sean Gatien, in *University of Toronto Quarterly* 70, no. 1 (2000–2001).
79. Hooker, *Of the Laws*, I.viii.6, 86.
80. Max L. Stackhouse, "A Premature Postmodern," *First Things* 106 (2000): 19.
81. Stanley Hauerwas and William H. Willimon, *Resident Aliens: Life in the Christian Colony* (Nashville: Abingdon, 1989), 41.
82. John Milbank makes the similar point that Troeltsch's work may have descriptive power historically but should not be allowed to lock theologians into a self-confirming hermeneutic circle. Milbank, *Theology and Social Theory*, 75.
83. Ernst Bloch, *Natural Law and Human Dignity*, trans. Dennis J. Schmidt (Cambridge: MIT Press, 1986), 277.
84. Hooker, *Of the Laws*, VIII.v.8, 381.

85. Robert Sanderson, *Bishop Sanderson's Lectures on Conscience and Human Law* (Lincoln: James Williamson, 1877), 152.

86. This is cited on the official Web site of HRH The Prince of Wales, <http://www.princeofwales.gov.uk/about/princeswork/religion.html> (date accessed: 07/01/02).

87. Aquinas, *S.T.*, II–II, q. 184 a. 1, *sed contra*.

88. Michel Rosenfeld, *Just Interpretations*, 127.

89. We may illustrate with the topic of marriage and polygamous marriage. Consider the following statement from a recent UK Immigration and Nationality Directorate Instruction (IMMIGRATION, 2000: Annex D): "All marriages which take place in the United Kingdom must, *in order to be recognized as valid*, be monogamous and must be carried out in accordance with the requirements of the Marriage Act 1949, as amended by the Marriage Acts of 1970, 1983 and 1994, the Marriage Regulations of 1986 and other related Acts (eg; the Children Act 1989)." Polygamous marriages are recognized in England and Wales only if they took place in a country that allows marriages of this kind and if both parties were legally free to marry in this way. In such cases, UK law (Social Security and Benefits Act 1992) allows for income-related benefits (income support, housing benefit) to be payable to people in polygamous marriages. ("Under s.11d of the Matrimonial Causes Act 1973, polygamous marriages contracted abroad can only be valid in English law if the conditions outlined at 2.1 above are met. The marriage will not be valid if either party is domiciled in the UK or in any other country whose law does not permit polygamous marriage.") However, Section 2 of the Immigration Act 1988 gave effect to Parliament's decision that the formation of polygamous households in the United Kingdom should be prevented. It provided that a woman would no longer be granted entry clearance on the basis of marriage where entry clearance had previously been granted to another wife of the same man. My concern is that the supposed neutrality of human rights legislation organized around liberal democratic principles can hide indifference to the differences between people and communities. On these principles, monogamy is likely to be regarded in the public square as necessary for the equality of women. Where legitimacy turns only on consent, we risk a split between law, ethics, and morality in a "public square" where values other than individual liberty and democracy (e.g., Muslim values attaching to polygamy) are not recognized. (For more on this see Esther D. Reed, "Reform of the House of Lords and Christian Responsibility in a Plural Society," in Elaine Graham and Anna Rowlands, eds., *Pathways to the Public Square: Practical Theology in an Age of Pluralism* [Münster: Lit-Verlag, 2005], chap. 9.)

90. Hooker, *Of the Laws*, V.i.2, 17.

91. Jürgen Habermas, *Between Facts and Norms* (Cambridge: Polity Press, 1997), 414.

92. Habermas, *Between Facts and Norms*, xlii.

93. Heller, *Can Modernity Survive?*, 155.

94. Heller, *Can Modernity Survive?*, 155.

95. John Rawls, *Political Liberalism* (New York: Columbia University Press), 379.

96. Compare Habermas, *Between Facts and Norms*, 453, with John Rawls, *The Law of Peoples* (Cambridge: Harvard University Press, 2001), 132, 138.

97. As Oliver O'Donovan maintains, this totalizing of human reason and speech "destroys its own point and collapses under its own weight" thereby failing to bring us to decision. *Desire of the Nations*, 283–84. In Habermas's defense, it must be said that he recognizes the importance of a presumption in democratically accountable public discourse that participants will be oriented to the common good, even if the meaning of "common good" is allowed to remain ambiguous because too close a definition might cause the consensus to disintegrate. Discourse is constitutive of the free association of parties and is realized through the medium of law, which then acquires legitimate organizing and coercive power. It is also worth noting that what Habermas calls "discursive redemption" does not necessarily mean the "liquidization without trace" of the idea of God, though he thinks that the idea of a personal God is not salvageable: "The idea of God is transformed [*aufgehoben*] into the concept of a *Logos* that determines the community of believers and the real life-context of a self-emancipating society. 'God' becomes the name for a communicative structure that forces men, on pain of the loss of their humanity, to go beyond their accidental, empirical nature to encounter one another indirectly, that is, across an objective something that they themselves are not" (*Legitimation Crisis*, 121).

Chapter 3

1. Barth, *Church Dogmatics*, II.2, §37, 579–80.
2. Bonhoeffer, *Ethics*, 174.
3. "The *primum ius* [the First Right, i.e., God's] vanished from consideration, so that the act of human foundation ceased to depend upon divine foundation, and began to look like a repetition of it. The sovereign arbitrariness of God's creative decree was taken into the human act of founding a society, so that it appeared rather like a creation *ex nihilo*, presupposing no prior law, no preexisting social rationality, a new beginning not merely relatively and politically but absolutely and metaphysically. Legislation thereby became the *foundation of a social rationality*" (Oliver O'Donovan, "Government as Judgment," in Oliver O'Donovan and Joan Lockwood O'Donovan, *Bonds of Imperfection: Christian Politics, Past and Present* [Grand Rapids: Wm. B. Eerdmans, 2004], 212).
4. Barth, *Ethics*, 262.
5. These terms are used by John Milbank, *The Suspended Middle: Henri de Lubac and the Debate Concerning the Supernatural* (Grand Rapids: Wm. B. Eerdmans, 2005), 21. His treatment of de Lubac's understanding of Christianity as a humanism is informative for our purposes.
6. Barth, *C.D.*, II.2, §36, 509.
7. Webster, *Barth's Moral Theology*, 202.
8. Barth, *C.D.*, III.4, §52, 5.
9. I have written elsewhere about Christian ethics as the response in freedom of human persons to the divine work of salvation (*The Genesis of Ethics: On the Authority of God as the Origin of Christian Ethics* [London: Darton, Longman, and Todd, 2000]) and shall not repeat those arguments here. So we are not concerned especially with why an ethic of divine command is not

heteronomously controlling of human actions and/or overly constraining of human freedom. We investigate instead how divine command, which speaks to the innermost being of every human, both determines and requires moral reasoning.

10. This concern is voiced by Timothy J. Gorringe in *Karl Barth: Against Hegemony* (Oxford: Oxford University Press, 1999), 153.

11. The phrase "grammar of doing" is used by Webster in *Barth's Moral Theology*, chap. 8, during a comparison of the moral theology of Calvin and Barth.

12. This phrase is particularly associated with Nigel Biggar, *The Hastening That Waits: Karl Barth's Ethics* (Oxford: Oxford University Press, 1993).

13. Webster, *Word and Church*, 234.

14. Gorringe, *Karl Barth*, 156–57.

15. Bonhoeffer, *Ethics*, 82. This is also noted by Michael L. Westmoreland-White in "Contributions to Human Rights in Dietrich Bonhoeffer's *Ethics*," *Journal of Church and State* 39 no.1 (1997): 67–83, esp. 69.

16. Bonhoeffer, *Ethics*, 96.

17. Dietrich Bonhoeffer, *Sanctorum Communio: A Theological Study of the Sociology of the Church*, ed. Clifford J. Green, trans. Reinhard Krauss and Nancy Lukens (Minneapolis: Fortress, 1998), 169-70.

18. Dietrich Bonhoeffer, *Discipleship, Dietrich Bonhoeffer Works*, vol. 4, ed. Martin Kuske and Ilse Tödt, trans. Barbara Green and Reinhard Krauss (Minneapolis: Fortress, 2003), 95.

19. Bonhoeffer, *Ethics*, 244.

20. As an end in itself, "the natural" is from God and oriented toward God though not necessarily recognized as "creaturely." As the means to an end, it is the penultimate directed toward the ultimate, the created oriented toward the end times when Christ will come again. Bonhoeffer, *Ethics*, 173.

21. Bonhoeffer, *Ethics*, 186–87.

22. Bonhoeffer, *Ethics*, 184.

23. Bonhoeffer, *Ethics*, 184.

24. Bonhoeffer, *Ethics*, 180.

25. Bonhoeffer, *Ethics*, 183.

26. Dietrich Bonhoeffer, *Letters and Papers from Prison* (London: SCM Press, 1967), 360.

27. This is not surprising, of course, given Barth's influence on Bonhoeffer. See Andreas Pangritz, *Karl Barth in the Theology of Dietrich Bonhoeffer* (Grand Rapids: Wm. B. Eerdmans, 2000), see esp. chap. 9.

28. Barth, *Ethics*, 380.

29. Barth, *Ethics*, 380.

30. Barth, *Ethics*, 380. Karl Barth, *Ethik* II 1928–29 (Zürich: Theologische Verlag, 1978), 219–20.

31. Barth, *Ethics*, 380. Barth, *Ethik* II, 219–20.

32. Barth, *Ethics*, 271.

33. Barth, *Ethics*, 377.

34. Barth, *Ethics*, 384.

35. Barth, *Ethics*, 385.

36. Barth, *Ethics*, 377.

37. Bonhoeffer, *Ethics,* 198. This point is made both generally and with reference to self-murder.
38. Karl Barth, *The Holy Spirit and the Christian Life: The Theological Basis of Ethics,* trans. R. Birch Hoyle, Library of Theological Ethics (Louisville: Westminster, John Knox Press, 1993), §78, 205.
39. Barth, *Ethics,* p. 376.
40. Barth, *Christian Life,* §78, 213.
41. Barth, *C.D.,* II.1, §26, 173.
42. Barth, *C.D.,* II.2, §36, 519.
43. Barth, *C.D.,* II.2, §36, 520.
44. It is interesting to note that, for instance, John Locke's association of labor and property rights support theories of self-ownership that allow sale of body parts, reproductive tissue, and so on. C. A. Cohen, a political philosopher at Oxford, writes: "Each person is the moral and rightful owner of himself and, in effect, has all those rights that a slaveholder has over a complete chattel slave as a matter of legal right, and he is entitled morally speaking, to dispose of himself in the way such a slaveholder is entitled, legally speaking, to dispose over his slave" ("Self-Ownership, World-Ownership, and Equality," in F. Lucash, *Justice and Equality Here and Now* [Ithaca: Cornell University Press, 1986], 109, cited in Hillel Steiner, "Property in the Body: A Philosophical Perspective" in *Property Rights in the Human Body* [London: King's College, 1998], 1). Cohen suggests that a Lockean-based relationship between labor and the entitlement to property provides an appropriate philosophical basis for rights of ownership in the body. These rights are deemed necessary and useful protections against exploitation and abuse. Similar points might be made about the supposed "right to die" or the right to abort a postimplantation fetus. For more on the last point, see chap. 6 below.
45. Sonia Harris-Scott writes: "If human rights are to be truly universal and moreover effective, what is required is the consent of those on whom the obligation is really imposed: the people. If that consent is not obtained and international human rights are imposed against the will and consent of the internal populations of states—international human rights remain at their core culturally illegitimate—they remain a tool of the imperialist." She expresses the unease among many that much human rights discourse remains deeply entrenched within the imperialist mind-set. Harris-Scott, "Imperialist, Inept, and Ineffective? Cultural Relativism and the UN Convention on the Rights of the Child," in *Human Rights Quarterly* 25, no. 1 (2003): 130–81.
46. This last point is made effectively by Johan Galtung, "The Third World and HR: Post-1989," in *Human Rights Fifty Years On: A Reappraisal,* ed. Tony Evans (Manchester: Manchester University Press, 1998), 219–27.
47. Bonhoeffer, *Ethics,* 59.
48. Barth, *C.D.,* III.3, §49, 92.
49. Bonhoeffer, *Ethics,* 171.
50. Bonhoeffer, *Ethics,* 57.
51. Bonhoeffer, *Ethics,* 58.
52. Gustaf Wingren wrote in *The Flight from Creation* (Minneapolis: Augsburg, 1971) of the neglect of the doctrine of creation resulting from superficial readings of Barth and Bultmann.

53. Colin E. Gunton, A *Brief Theology of Revelation*—the 1993 Warfield Lectures (Edinburgh: T&T Clark, 1995), ix.
54. Gunton, *Brief Theology of Revelation*, 59n31.
55. Gunton, *Brief Theology of Revelation*, 41.
56. Gunton, *Brief Theology of Revelation*, 59.
57. Gunton, *Brief Theology of Revelation*, 41.
58. Gunton, *Brief Theology of Revelation*, 122.
59. Gunton, *Brief Theology of Revelation*, 123.
60. Plato, *The Republic*, ed. John M. Cooper, in *Plato: Complete Works* (Indianapolis: Hackett, 1997), 517b.
61. Gunton, *Brief Theology of Revelation*, 63.
62. Gunton, *Brief Theology of Revelation*, 61–62.
63. Gunton, *Brief Theology of Revelation*, 18.
64. Gunton, *Brief Theology of Revelation*, 63.
65. Colin E. Gunton, *The One, the Three and the Many: God, Creation and the Culture of Modernity* (Cambridge: Cambridge University Press, 1993), 189.
66. Michael Welker, *God the Spirit*, trans. John F. Hoffmeyer (Minneapolis: Fortress, 1994), 275. See Mark 16:17; Luke 24:49; Acts 2:38-39; Titus 3; Heb 2:4.
67. Gunton, *Brief Theology of Revelation*, 62.
68. Gunton, *Brief Theology of Revelation*, 61.
69. Bonhoeffer, *Ethics*, 71.
70. See Finnis, *Natural Law and Natural Rights*, 206.
71. Finnis, *Natural Law and Natural Rights*, 221n12.
72. Finnis, *Natural Law and Natural Rights*, 198. John Finnis's work, along with that of Germain Grisez, has made a significant contribution in recent years to debate about what practical reason entails. Finnis's *Natural Law and Natural Rights* is arguably the most substancial attempt in recent years to develop a natural law-based conception of human rights. His rehabilitation of Aquinas's theory of natural law makes the strong claim that human rights institutionalize the conditions necessary for human flourishing.
73. Finnis, *Natural Law and Natural Rights*, 207.
74. Finnis, *Natural Law and Natural Rights*, 198.
75. For a brief account of relevant debate about differences between Aquinas's objective sense of "right" and modern subjective senses, see Brian Tierney, "Natural Law and Natural Rights," 390.
76. Finnis, *Natural Law and Natural Rights*, 221.
77. John Finnis, *Fundamentals of Ethics* (Oxford: Oxford University Press, 1983), 1.
78. For a full list, see Germain Grisez, Joseph Boyle and John Finnis, "Practical Principles, Moral Truth, and Ultimate Ends," *American Journal of Jurisprudence* 32 (1987): 107-8.
79. Finnis, *Natural Law and Natural Rights*, 387.
80. John Finnis, "Natural Law and the Ethics of Discourse," *Ratio Juris* 12, no. 4 (1999): 354.
81. Tierney, "Natural Law and Natural Rights," 390.
82. Porter, *Nature as Reason*, 129.

83. Anthony Lisska, *Aquinas's Theory of Natural Law: An Analytical Reconstruction* (Oxford: Oxford University Press, 1996), 155.

84. McInerny questions whether Aquinas taught that basic human goods equate to the concept of the good or, more specifically, whether human goods were understood by Aquinas as a fundamental component of the common good. McInerny holds that Aquinas had a less formulaic sense of the directing power of reason within divine providence. "Grisez [and Finnis] thinks that the form of such particular precepts is 'X should be done, pursued, protected,' where X takes as its value one or the other of the basic goods. . . . For Thomas, the form of a particular precept is 'X should be pursued as reason directs the pursuit to one's overall good,' where values of X are the ends of natural inclinations." Ralph McInerny, "Grisez and Thomism," in *The Revival of Natural Law: Philosophical, Theological, and Ethical Responses to the Finnis-Grisez School*, ed. Nigel Biggar and Rufus Black (Aldershot, UK: Ashgate, 2000), 69.

85. An important exchange between Michael Villey, John Finnis, and Brian Tierney is worth mentioning for several reasons. First, Villey draws our attention to the objective meaning of "right" in Aquinas's theology of law. Second, Finnis supposes a sharply contrasting and self-standing conception of natural law that is independent of God and in which human nature as such gives rise to ethical principles, a grasp of basic human goods, and notions of the common good. Third, Tierney mediates between the interpretations of Aquinas offered by Villey and Finnis, drawing our attention to the multiplicity of meanings, or polysemy, that characterized classical and medieval uses of the term "right." Aquinas, he says, might have recognized little if any subjective sense of "right" residing in individuals or resulting from exchange agreements (commutative justice), but there is no reason to suppose that he would have excluded this development, and his successors rapidly came to conceive of natural rights as spheres wherein humans are permitted or free to act as they choose rather than objective states of affairs that exist externally to individuals. Moreover, Tierney demonstrates that examples of (what we call) modern language and concepts of subjective rights can be found as early as the thirteenth century. See Tierney, *The Idea of Natural Rights*; Brian Tierney, "Author's Rejoinder," *Review of Politics* 64, no. 3 (2002): 417.

86. A standard textbook in jurisprudence describes him as offering "a boot-strap argument" with respect to the definition of basic goods; that is, that he fails to explain how the goods of knowledge, play, or aesthetic experience should give rise to natural or human rights, or indeed, that they should. (See M. D. A. Freeman, *Lloyd's Introduction to Jurisprudence*, 6th ed. [London: Sweet & Maxwell, 1994], 86.) Despite not asserting God's existence, Finnis is charged with presupposing a "God's-eye standpoint" from which reality can be viewed and a notion of objective truth that is equivalent to believing in religion.

86. Finnis, *Natural Law and Natural Rights*, 198.

87. Finnis, *Natural Law and Natural Rights*, 49.

88. Barth, *C.D.*, II.1, §37, 567.

89. Webster, *Barth's Moral Theology*, 214.

90. Rowan Williams, "Making Moral Decisions," in *Cambridge Companion to Christian Ethics*, ed. Robin Gill (Cambridge: Cambridge University Press, 2001), 4.

91. Barth, *Christian Life*, 200.
92. Barth, *Christian Life*, 201.
93. Barth, *Christian Life*, 202.
94. Barth, *Christian Life*, 276.
95. Karl Barth, "Gospel and Law," in *Community, State, and Church* (New York: Anchor Books, 1960), 80.
96. Insole, *Politics of Human Frailty*, 70.
97. Insole, *Politics of Human Frailty*, 63.
98. Insole, *Politics of Human Frailty*, 87.
99. Samuel P. Huntington, *Who Are We? America's Great Debate* (London: Simon & Schuster, 2004), 104.
100. Huntington, *Who Are We?*, 106.
101. Barth, *Christian Life*, 198.
102. Bonhoeffer, *Ethics*, 329.
103. Eberhard Jüngel, "Barth's Theological Beginnings," in *Karl Barth: A Theological Legacy* (Philadephia: Westminster, 1986), 96.

Chapter 4

1. Alekandr Solzhenitsyn, *Rebuilding Russia* (New York: Farrar, Straus, & Gioux, 1991), 54.
2. John Cassian, "First Conference of Abbot Nesteros: On Spiritual Knowledge," in *Nicene and Post-Nicene Fathers,* 2nd Series, trans. Philip Schaff and Henry Wace (Edinburgh: T&T Clark, 1988–1991), conference 14, §13.
3. American Declaration of Independence (1776).
4. John Webster, *Holy Scripture: A Dogmatic Sketch* (Cambridge: Cambridge University Press, 2003), 84.
5. This paraphrases a sentence from Bonhoeffer, *Ethics,* 58–59.
6. Peter Novick, for instance, calls rights "regulative fictions," whose illusion or pretense is swallowed as long as it remains socially useful in *That Noble Dream,* 16. The political philosopher Agnes Heller makes this latter point when describing with typical eloquence how Western democracies disconnected their legal systems from cosmic visions of divine governance as subjective rights became an object of faith. Heller, *Theory of Modernity,* 14.
7. Noam Chomsky, interviewed by Jeff Sellers, "On Human Rights and Ideology," in *Forerunner*, October 13, 1979, <http://www.chomsky.info/interviews/19791013.htm> (date accessed: 05/05/06).
8. Dietrich Bonhoeffer, *Creation and Fall: A Theological Exposition of Genesis 1–3,* trans. D. S. Bax (Minneapolis: Fortress, 2004), 82.
9. J. Robert Nelson, "Human Rights in Creation and Redemption," in *Journal of Ecumenical Studies: Human Rights in Religious Traditions* 19, no. 3 (1982): 10.
10. Gary Younge, "God Help America," *The Guardian*, August 25, 2003, <http://www.guardian.co.uk/religion/Story/0,2763,1028830,00.html> (date accessed: 08/28/03).
11. BBC News, "U.S. Commandments Monument Removed," <http://news.bbc.co.uk/1/hi/world/americas/3185795.stm> (date accessed: 08/29/03).

These were reported as the words of Robert Schenck president of the National Clergy Council, a Washington, D.C.–based Christian group.

12. James Bone, "Thou Shalt Not See This," <http://www.timesonline.co.uk>; report dated August 28, 2003 (date accessed: 08/29/03).

13. Fr. John Romanides, "Leo and Theodoret, Dioscorus and Eutyches," in *Orthodox Unity*, <http://www.orthodoxunity.org/article05.html> (date accessed: 05/09/05).

14. Sheila Greeve Davaney, *Pragmatic Historicism: A Theology for the Twenty-first Century* (New York: State University of New York Press, 2000), 117.

15. Davaney, *Pragmatic Historicism*, 149.

16. Davaney, *Pragmatic Historicism*, 187.

17. Manlio Simonetti, *Biblical Interpretation in the Early Church: An Historical Guide to Patristic Exegesis* (London/New York: Continuum, 2002), esp. chap. 1.

18. For an authoritative account of biblical exegesis in the patristic and medieval church, see Henri de Lubac, *Medieval Exegesis: The Four Senses of Scripture*, vol. 2, trans. Mark Sebanc (Edinburgh: T&T Clark, 1998).

19. Augustine, *On Christian Doctrine*, bk. 3, chap. 5.

20. Stephen C. Barton, "Biblical Hermeneutics and the Family," in *The Family in Theological Perspective*, ed. Stephen C. Barton (Edinburgh: T&T Clark, 1996), 6. Barton's challenge (made in the context of a discussion about the family, divorce, etc.) is as follows: "[W]e should read the bible with a view to discerning more clearly how the biblical testimony to the love and justice of God *is* reflected and *ought to be* reflected in our life together" (22). To pay attention only to "what the bible says" might lead to improper adherence to the *sensus litteralus* of Scripture, and to a dubious form of "prooftexting" to justify one's own prejudices. Yet, communities of faith seek to discern God's word. Liberationist readings that seek to interpret its message in situations of hardship and oppression represent one way of seeking the direct meaning of Holy Scripture. Similarly, narrative readings retell the Bible's story of God's salvation with the intention of hearing the normative claims that the Bible mediates to the community of faith. Strands of modern biblical research such as the historical contextualizing of Jesus' teaching in ancient Judaism and/or reading the Bible through social scientific lenses offer yet further ways of seeking "literal" meanings.

21. C. R. Seitz, *Figured Out: Typology and Providence in Christian Scripture*, (Louisville, Ky.: Westminster John Knox, 2001), 10.

22. John Cassian, *Conferences*, bk. 14, chap. 8, <http://www.newadvent.org/fathers/350814.htm> (date accessed: 12/21/06)

23. *The Laws of Kings* 8:11.

24. See Michael Ellias Dallen, *The Rainbow Covenant: Torah and the Seven Universal Laws* (Springdale, Ark.: Lightcatcher Books, 2003); Rabbi Yirmeyahu Bindman, *The Seven Colours of the Rainbow: Torah Ethics for Non-Jews* (San Jose, Calif.: Resource Publications, 1995).

25. Aquinas, *S.T.*, I–II q. 100 a. 8 c.

26. Clifford J. Green, editor's introduction to Bonhoeffer, *Ethics*, 22.

27. On this point see Gerhard von Rad, *Genesis: A Commentary*, rev. ed. (Philadelphia: Westminster, 1972), 126. For a fuller account see Lubac, *Medieval*

Exegesis, vol. 1 and vol. 2, trans. E. M. Macierowski (Edinburgh: T&T Clark, 2000).

28. Peter J. Harland, *The Value of Human Life: A Study of the Story of the Flood* (Gen. 6–9), Supplements to Vetus Testamentum (Leiden: E. J. Brill, 1996), 166.

29. Aquinas, *S.T.*, II–II. q. 163 c.

30. von Rad, *Genesis*, 129–30.

31. Bonhoeffer, *Sanctorum Communio*, 120.

32. Dan G. Johnson, *From Chaos to Restoration: An Integrative Reading of Isaiah 24–27*, Journal for the Study of the Old Testament Supplement 61 (Sheffield, UK: JSOT Press, 1988), 27–28. Johnson's discussion of Isaiah 24 includes comment on its allusions to Genesis 6–9.

33. Bonhoeffer, *Sanctorum Communio*, 110–13.

34. John Chrysostom, "Homilies on the Epistle to the Romans," Homily 10 on Romans 5:12, *NPNF* 1st series, vol. 11, 401–3.

35. Consider debate surrounding the desirability of enforcing international labor standards. Established by the Treaty of Versailles in 1919, the International Labor Organization (ILO) has, since then, addressed the problem of labor conditions involving "injustice, hardship and privation." ILO Convention no. 138 incorporates the Minimum Age Convention of 1973, which specifies that full-time workers shall not be younger than fifteen years old. National laws may permit the employment of persons thirteen to fifteen years of age on light work that is (a) not likely to be harmful to their health or development or (b) not such as to prejudice their attendance at school. Convention no. 182 incorporates the Worst Forms of Child Labour Convention of 1999. It prohibits child slavery (including the sale and trafficking of children, debt bondage, and forced recruitment for armed conflict), child prostitution and pornography, the use of children for illicit activities (such as drug trafficking), and any hazardous work that is likely to harm the health, safety, or morals of children. The arguments for signing seem overwhelming. Initially surprising, therefore, is the warning sounded by organizations such as Third World Network, an India-based think tank devoted to development issues, and CentreSouth (see <http://www.twnside.org.sg> [date accessed: 07/27/03]). Both take issue with any linking of labor standards to aid or trade agreements, arguing that trade and social arrangements should be kept separate. Compulsory labor standards, they argue, quickly become protectionist and not altruistic measures. Even if such measures are intended to establish a global "social floor," the potential damage to developing economies is great. It is better for higher labor standards to be achieved in developing countries via evolutionary methods, and this cannot be done at a speed required by external bodies. According to these organizations, international measures to enforce compliance with labor standards in developing countries (by means of sanctions or other punitive measures), as part of efforts to establish a global "social floor," are neither desirable nor feasible.

36. Robert Wright, *The Moral Animal: Why We Are the Way We Are: The New Science of Evolutionary Psychology* (London: Vintage, 1995), 9.

37. Wright, *Moral Animal*, 217.

38. Jonathan Glover, *Humanity: A Moral History of the Twentieth Century* (New Haven: Yale University Press, 2001).
39. Harland, *Value of Human Life,* 32–40.
40. H. Haag, "Smh," in G. J. Botterweck and H. Ringen, eds., *Theologisches Wörterbuch zum Alten Testament* (Stuttgart, 1970–1994), 1056, cited in Harland, *Value of Human Life,* 34.
41. Harland, *Value of Human Life,* 34.
42. Harland, *Value of Human Life,* 37.
43. Harland, *Value of Human Life,* 156.
44. Perhaps the most well known such criticism is Duncan B. Forrester, *Beliefs, Values, and Policies* (Oxford: Clarendon, 1989), chap. 7. For a recent defense of Preston's method, see William F. Storrar, "Scottish Civil Society and Devolution: The New Case for Ronald Preston's Defence of Middle Axioms," in *The Future of Christian Social Ethics: Essays on the Work of Ronald H. Preston, 1913–2001,* ed. Elaine L. Graham and Esther D. Reed, special issue of *Studies in Christian Ethics* 17, no. 2 (London: Continuum/ T&T Clark, 2004), 37–39.
45. Storrar, "Scottish Civil Society and Devolution," 38.
46. Francis Watson offers a fine account of the *imago Dei* in christological perspective in "In the Image of God," *Text and Truth: Redefining Biblical Theology* (Edinburgh: T&T Clark, 1997), 277–88.
47. Watson, "Image of God," 288.
48. Witness Brevard Childs's new translation of the book of Isaiah which contains the following: "Cease to do evil, / Learn to do good. / Seek justice, / aid the oppressed, / support the rights of the orphans. / Plead the widow's cause" (Isa 1:16-17). "Woe to those who are champions at drinking wine, / And heroes in mixing drinks, / who acquit the guilty for a bribe, / and deprive the innocent of his right!" (Isa 5:22-23). "Woe to those who execute evil writs / and issue oppressive decrees, / to deprive the poor of their rights. / and rob the needy of my people of justice / making widows their prey, the fatherless their booty" (Isa 10:1-2). Childs, *Isaiah: A Commentary,* Old Testament Library (Louisville, Ky.: Westminster John Knox, 2001), 14, 39, 82. Of interest is how Childs's use of the term "rights" conveys a dynamic equivalence in meaning rather than a strict translation of the Hebrew *shiphetu yathom* (often translated as "judge the fatherless"). Verse 17, for instance, comprises four sets of verbs and objects that may be translated as "seek justice; relieve the oppressed; judge the fatherless; contend for the widow." The Hebrew is terse, and the text does not have a direct equivalent for the English-language phrase "support the rights of the orphans." Childs has responded by introducing a concept that has resonance in our own day, where we are familiar with abstract concepts to describe the human condition, but which would have been unknown to ancient Hebrew. Arguably, the force of the verse is its contrast to the last line of verse 16, "Cease to do evil"—the implication being that merely to refrain from doing evil is not enough; constructive acts of righteousness are also required. To this extent, Childs's leaning in meaning toward "judge for" or "on behalf of" captures something important. We should not forget, however, that the subjective sense of "rights" implied in his translation is not found in the Hebrew text. As throughout this book, the term "rights" represents a theological effort to

find terms that convey the imperative to act with and on behalf of the weakest members of society, albeit at the risk of innovation. (I am grateful to Christopher R. Seitz for insight concerning this verse.)

49. Barth, *Ethics*, 9.
50. Barth, *Ethics*, 45.
51. John Cassian, "First Conference of Abbot Nesteros," conference 14, §8, referring to 1 Cor 11:4.

Chapter 5

1.   von Rad, *Genesis*, 133.
2.   Barth, *C.D.*, III.4, §54, 268.
3.   Harland, *Value of Human Life*, 147.
4.   John Calvin, *Commentary on Genesis* vol. 1 (cited from Christian Classics Ethereal Library at Calvin College, <www.ccel.org/ccel/calvin/calcomol.xv.html> [date accessed: 12/21/06], chap. 9, v. 1, 7).
5.   Bonhoeffer, *Ethics*, 185.
6.   In "Rethinking the Right to Reproduce," Harvard Center for Population and Development Studies Working Paper no. 98.05, Bonnie Steinbock provides a useful summary of recent debate (available at <http://www.hsph.harvard.edu/hcpds/wpweb/reproright9805.html> [date accessed: 07/11/06]).
7.   Onora O'Neill, *Autonomy and Trust in Bioethics: The Gifford Lectures*, University of Edinburgh, 2001 (Cambridge: Cambridge University Press, 2002), 61–65. See also Onora O'Neill and William Ruddick, eds., *Having Children: Philosophical and Legal Reflections on Parenthood* (New York: Oxford University Press, 1979).
8.   Genesis 9 does not say much about families, and the right to found a family per se cannot be derived from it. Nor is this the place for detailed study of families in the Old Testament—which included polygamous families (Abraham, Sarah and Hagar; Jacob, Leah and Rachel plus servant women by whom he had children; Solomon and his seven hundred princess-wives plus three hundred concubines) as well as accounts of monogamous relationships (the story of Ruth perhaps implies monogamy). John Rogerson warns readers of the Old Testament not to draw conclusions for present-day ethics too readily: "[T]he family in ancient Israel was a natural social mechanism that developed initially to meet particular circumstances." The Old Testament family will not serve as a model for today. Instead, as Rogerson argues, if the Old Testament says anything to us today, it is that we need to devise theologically driven "structures of grace" appropriate to our situation that will sustain those aspects of family life that, from a Christian perspective, we deem to be most valuable, and that may be most under threat. Rogerson, "The Family and Structures of Grace in the Old Testament," in Barton, *Family in Theological Perspective*, 40.
9.   Charles Norchi, "Human Rights: A Global Common Interest," in *The United Nations: Confronting the Challenges of a Global Society*, ed. Jean E. Krasno (Boulder: Reinner, 2004), 79.
10. Mashood Baderin et al., eds., *Muslim World Journal of Human Rights* (Berkeley Electronic Press), <http://www.bepress.com/mwjhr/> (date accessed: 12/21/06).

11. Steinbock puts this question in "Rethinking the Right to Reproduce" when discussing work by Onora O'Neill.

12. John Harris, "Clones, Genes, and Human Rights," in *The Genetic Revolution and Human Rights: The Oxford Amnesty Lectures, 1998*, ed. Justine Burley (Oxford: Oxford University Press, 1999), 72–78.

13. Garrett Hardin, *Living within Limits: Ecology, Economics, and Population Taboos* (Oxford: Oxford University Press, 1993). See also "Living on a Lifeboat," *BioScience* 24, no. 10 (1974).

14. For a contrasting position to that of Hardin, see Peter Singer, *One World: The Ethics of Globalization* (New Haven: Yale University Press, 2002), in which the dominant metaphor is that of a global village in which everyone who can has a duty to help those who are less fortunate.

15. For a review of relevant literature see Steinbock, "Rethinking the Right to Reproduce," <http://www.hsph.harvard.edu/hcpds/wpweb/reproright 9805.html> (date accessed: 08/09/06).

16. Steinbock, "Rethinking the Right to Reproduce."

17. Antonio Cassese, "Are Human Rights Truly Universal?" in Belgrade Circle and Savic, *Politics of Human Right*, 152.

18. O'Neill, *Autonomy and Trust in Bioethics*, 74–75.

19. Michael Ignatieff, *Human Rights: Politics and Ideology* (Princeton: Princeton University Press, 2001), 77.

20. Ignatieff, *Human Rights*, 54.

21. Ignatieff, *Human Rights*, 76.

22. Ignatieff, *Human Rights*, 53.

23. Charles Taylor, "Conditions of an Unforced Consensus on Human Rights" in Belgrade Circle and Savic, *Politics of Human Right*, 118. For Taylor, the "goal" is practical not metaphysical. The metaphor is not "many roads up the same mountain" to one religious truth; not a single, supreme, spiritual reality at the convergence of diverse religious paths, but deeper theological engagement across the religious traditions.

24. Philip Alston, "The Fortieth Anniversary of the United Nations Declaration of Human Rights: A Time More for Reflection than Celebration," in Jan Berting et al., *Human Rights in a Pluralistic World* (London: Meckler, 1990), 7.

25. Lisa Sowle Cahill, "Justice for Women," in *Transforming Unjust Structures: The Capability Approach*, ed. Séverin Deneulin et al. (Dordrecht: Springer, 2006), 85.

26. John Milbank, "Materialism and Transcendence," in *Theology and the Political: The New Debate*, ed. Creston Davis et al. (Durham: Duke University Press, 2005), 400.

27. Bonhoeffer, *Ethics*, 378.

28. Bonhoeffer, *Ethics*, 379.

29. William Shakespeare, *The Merchant of Venice*, act 2, sc. 1.

30. Bonhoeffer, *Ethics*, 181.

31. O'Donovan, *Ways of Judgment*, 41.

32. O'Donovan reminds us that when Jesus confronted the woman caught in the act of adultery (John 7:53–8:11), he did not challenge the moral categories of his peers, merely their application to the accused woman. Were that community to carry out that judgment on that woman, the line between innocence

and guilt would have been wrongly drawn. Accommodation to human weakness is sometimes appropriate when passing and implementing judgment. "[T]he truth of a law must also be a truth about the society in which the law will function" (O'Donovan, *Ways of Judgment,* 19). To extrapolate, the implementation of minimum standards should surely be the default position, but absolute enforcement might not be appropriate in every situation. "The principle must be uniformly upheld but [perhaps] not uniformly implemented" (O'Donovan, *Ways of Judgment,* 20).

33. O'Donovan, *Ways of Judgment,* 40.

34. BBC News, "Childless Couples 'Self-indulgent'" March 8, 2000, available at <http://news.bbc.co.uk/1/hi/uk/669847.stm> (date accessed: 07/11/06).

35. Vitalism, writes Bonhoeffer, "arises from the false absolutizing of an insight that is essentially correct, that life, both individual and communal, is not only a means to an end but also an end in itself." Bonhoeffer, *Ethics,* 178.

36. Barth, *C.D.,* II.2, §36, 550.

37. Paul Ricoeur, "Capabilities and Rights," in Deneulin et al., *Transforming Unjust Structures,* 17.

38. World Health Organization, "Facts and Figures," *World Health Report 2005: Make Every Mother and Child Count* (Geneva: WHO, 2005), <http://www.who.int/whr/2005/media_centre/en/index.html> (date accessed: 06/23/05).

39. These recent and terrible figures have been recorded despite the fact that The Convention on the Elimination of All Forms of Discrimination against Women (CEDAW) was adopted in 1979 by the UN General Assembly and is one of the most widely ratified of all the UN Conventions (along with the Convention on the Rights of the Child). An introduction to the CEDAW is available at <http://www.un.org/womenwatch/daw/cedaw/text/econvention.htm#article16> (date accessed: 06/23/05). We note in passing that the CEDAW affirms the reproductive rights of women irrespective of marital status. The Preamble affirms equality between women and men and sets the tone by stating that "the role of women in procreation should not be a basis for discrimination." The link between discrimination and women's reproductive role is a matter of recurrent concern throughout the CEDAW. As Womanwatch—an organ of the UN interagency network on women and gender quality—explains, provisions for maternity protection and child care are proclaimed as essential rights and incorporated into all areas of the CEDAW, whether dealing with employment, family law, health care or education. See WHO, "Facts and Figures."

40. O'Donovan, *Ways of Judgment,* 44.

41. Séverin Deneulin, introduction to Deneulin et al., *Transforming Unjust Structures,* 2.

42. Deneulin, "Introduction," 6.

43. Martha C. Nussbaum, *Women and Human Development: The Capabilities Approach* (Cambridge: Cambridge University Press, 2000), 35.

44. Nussbaum, *Women and Human Development,* 100.

45. Nussbaum draws on John Rawls's sense of "overlapping consensus" to mean that people "may sign on to this conception as the free-standing moral core of a political conception, without accepting any particular metaphysical view of the world." See Nussbaum, *Women and Human Development,* 76.

46. Nussbaum, *Women and Human Development*, 78. Indeed, the United Nations Development Programme (UNDP) has drawn heavily in recent years on the concepts of "capacity development" or "capacity building" across its range of operations.

47. Nicholas Sagovsky, "'Capable Individuals' and Just Institutions" in Deneulin et al., *Transforming Unjust Structures*, 76.

48. Séverin Deneulin, "Necessary Thickening: Ricoeur's Ethic of Justice as a Complement to Sen's Capability Approach," in Deneulin et al., *Transforming Unjust Structures,* chap. 2, esp. 9. See also Cahill, "Justice for Women," 86.

49. On the concept of "social capability," see Sagovsky, "'Capable Individuals' and Just Institutions," esp. 77–78.

50. Sagovsky, "'Capable Individuals' and Just Institutions," 101.

51. See <http://www.hfea.gov.uk/PressOffice/Archive/1123751318> (date accessed: 08/19/05). NB: After launching the consultation, and before its completion, the HFEA awarded a license to screen for the retinoblastoma gene to a London clinic. This was reported in "Designer Babies May Put End to Cancer Blindness," *The Times*, August 19, 2005.

52. President's Council on Bioethics, *Beyond Therapy: Biotechnology and the Pursuit of Happiness* (Washington, D.C., 2003), <http://www.bioethics.gov/topics/beyond_index.html> (date accessed: 11/07/06), chap. 2.

53. New techniques such as preimplantation genetic haplotyping allow medics to spot increasing numbers of mutations in genes. A team of doctors at the Center for Preimplantation Genetic Diagnosis at Guy's and St. Thomas' NHS Foundation Trust in London developed this technique that includes testing parents, siblings, and other relatives for any signs of genetically passed diseases. A cell is then extracted from the embryo to check whether it contains telltale markers.

54. President's Council on Bioethics, "Executive Summary," in *Reproduction and Responsibility: The Regulation of New Biotechnologies* (Washington, D.C., 2004), <http://www.bioethics.gov/reports/reproductionandresponsibility/exec_summary.html> (date accessed: 07/03/06). In 2003, the PCB report entitled *Beyond Therapy: Biotechnology and the Pursuit of Happiness* reminded readers not only of the benefits of the new reproductive technologies but also of the need to consider broader ethical issues affecting life in an age of biotechnology when the modern cult of health and of the body-perfect threatens to obscure moral and spiritual considerations.

55. CNN.International.com, "Wealthy Couples Travel to U.S. to Choose Baby's Sex," June 15, 2006, <http://edition.cnn.com/2006/HEALTH/06/14/sex.selection.ap/index.html> (date accessed: 07/03/06).

56. CNN.International.com, "Wealthy Couples Travel to U.S. to Choose Baby's Sex."

57. This was the view of Julian Savulescu as presented to the House of Commons Science and Technology Committee Fifth Report of Session 2004–2005, *Human Reproductive Technologies and the Law* HC 491 (London: HMSO, 2005), 65, <http://www.publications.parliament.uk/pa/cm200405/cmselect/cmsctech/cmsctech.htm> (date accessed: 12/03/05).

58. Ronald Dworkin, *Life's Dominion* (London: HarperCollins, 1993), 166–67.

59. Human Genetics Advisory Commission and the Human Fertilisation and Embryology Authority, *Cloning Issues in Reproduction, Science and Medicine* (December 1998), 6. 2. iii.

60. Hilary Putnam, "Cloning People," in Burley, *Genetic Revolution and Human Rights*, 13.

61. Witness Ronald Dworkin's stance that procreative choices concern intrinsic values and are like religion in the sense that they should not be made a matter of collective decision rather than individual choice. Freedom to express these values should be protected, he says, by the First Amendment to the U.S. Constitution (Dworkin, *Life's Dominion*, 26; *Freedom's Law* [Oxford: Oxford University Press, 1996], 104–5). Despite Dworkin's focus on community and tradition (see chap. 8 below), more is required if adequate mutual or reciprocal recognition of future generations is to be preserved.

62. John Milbank, *Being Reconciled: Ontology and Pardon* (London: Routledge, 2003), 199.

63. Those who hold a so-called gradualist position with respect to "phases" of fetal development (e.g., the phase of fertilization, the phase of implantation, the phase of neural development) might conclude that doing something to a human embryo before implantation is not the ethical equivalent of doing it to a human person. If it is held, for instance, that individual human life begins at implantation, then PGS might be regarded as an acceptable way of preventing a genetic disease from developing. Selecting a four-cell embryo that will not develop a disease such as cystic fibrosis, Tay-Sachs disease, thalassemia, sickle-cell anemia, or Duchenne muscular dystrophy might be morally tolerable or desirable even at the cost of destroying embryos.

64. Milbank, *Being Reconciled*, 200.

65. The essence of the Christian story, says Amy Laura Hall, is the vulnerability and weakness of the child in a manger who offers a new gift of life to humanity for acceptance in humility and gratitude. Without compromising the difference between the activity of God and that of creatures, she draws our attention to similarities between the vulnerability and weakness of Christ and that of the embryo—every one of which challenges us to accept a new gift of life. See Hall, "Public Bioethics and the Gratuity of Life: Joanna Jepson's Witness against Negative Eugenics," *Studies in Christian Ethics* 18, no. 1 (2005): 15–31, esp. 21.

66. "To know good and evil, to be able to distinguish and therefore judge between what ought to be and ought not to be, between Yes and No, between salvation and perdition, between life and death, is to be like God, to be oneself the Creator and Lord of the creature." Barth, *C.D.*, III.1, §41, 258.

67. Rowan Williams, "Why Abortion Challenges Us All," *Sunday Times*, March 20, 2005.

68. Jürgen Habermas, *The Future of Human Nature* (Cambridge: Polity Press, 2003), 93–94.

69. Habermas, *Future of Human Nature*, 115.

70. This point is made by Alan Meisel about litigation and end-of-life issues in "The Role of Litigation in End of Life Care: A Reappraisal," *Hastings Center Report Special Report* 35, no. 6 (2005): S47–S51.

71. Meisel, "Litigation in End of Life Care," S48.

72. G. R. Dunstan, "Gene Therapy, Human Nature, and the Churches," *Journal of Bioethics* 2, no. 4 (1991): 237.
73. Dietrich Bonhoeffer, *Sanctorum Communio*, 110–13.
74. Barth, *C.D.*, III.3, §49, 74.
75. Chrysostom, "Epistle to the Romans," 401–3.
76. Bonhoeffer, *Sanctorum Communio*, 108.
77. Bonhoeffer, *Sanctorum Communio*, 121.
78. Bonhoeffer, *Sanctorum Communio*, 108.
79. Bonhoeffer, *Sanctorum Communio*, 109.
80. Barth, *Ethics,* 335.
81. Milbank, *Being Reconciled*, 153.
82. Milbank, *Being Reconciled*, 148.
83. I borrow this phrase from Hugh Connolly, *Sin*, New Century Theology (London: Continuum, 2002), viii.

Chapter 6

1. For a discussion of this "caring," see Umberto Cassuto, *From Noah to Abraham: A Commentary on the Book of Genesis, VI–XI*, trans. Israel Abrahams (Jerusalem: Magnes Press, 1964), 125.
2. Tom Regan, *Defending Animal Rights* (Chicago: University of Illinois Press, 2001), 127–29.
3. Augustine, *The Confessions*, bk. 8, chap. 23, §33, cited in Andrew Linzey, *Animal Theology* (London: SCM Press, 1994), 19. See also Andrew Linzey and Tom Regan, eds., *Animals and Christianity: A Book of Readings* (London: SPCK, 1989), 167, 176.
4. Sean E. McEvenue, *The Narrative Style of the Priestly Writer* (Rome: Biblical Institute Press, 1971), 67–71. For discussion see Harland, *Value of Human Life,* 152–54.
5. Harland, *Value of Human Life,* 155.
6. von Rad, *Genesis*, 132.
7. Harland, *Value of Human Life,* 156.
8. See Andrew Linzey, *Animal Rights: A Christian Assessment* (London: SCM Press, 1976), and *Christianity and the Rights of Animals* (London: SPCK, and New York: Crossroad, 1987).
9. By "*theos*-rights," Linzey means the moral right given by God to animals to be animals. Animals, he observes, have life as a gift from God and for humans to take over and domineer this life for their own purposes is a sinful perversion of God's purposes.
10. Aquinas, *S.C.G.*, bk. 3, pt. 1, chap. 81.
11. Linzey, *Christianity and the Rights of Animals*, 94–98.
12. Linzey, *Animal Theology*, 81.
13. Linzey, *Animal Theology*, 82.
14. Barth, *C.D.*, III.1, §41, 209.
15. Barth, *C.D.*, III.4, §55, 354.
16. Barth, *Ethics,* 142.
17. Barth, *C.D.*, III.4, §69, 356.
18. Bonhoeffer, *Ethics,* 152.

19. Bonhoeffer, *Ethics,* 160.

20. Cass R. Sunstein, introduction to Cass R. Sunstein and Martha C. Nussbaum, eds., *Animal Rights: Current Debates and New Directions* (Oxford: Oxford University Press, 2004), chap. 3, esp. 5.

21. In support of this see Tom Regan, "The Struggle for Animal Rights," in Linzey and Clarke, *Animal Rights,* 176.

22. Peter Singer, *Animal Liberation* (New York: Random House, 1975; revised 1990 and reissued 2001); Tom Regan and Peter Singer, *Animal Rights and Human Obligations* (Englewood Cliffs, N.J.: Prentice-Hall, 1976).

23. Raymond G. Frey, *Rights, Killing, and Suffering: Moral Vegetarianism and Applied Ethics* (Oxford: Blackwell, 1983), 196–97, 202.

24. See Peter Singer, "Ethics beyond Species and beyond Instincts," in Sunstein and Nussbaum, *Animal Rights,* 78–92, esp. 90.

25. A useful summary is given by Lindsay Wilson, "Human Beings—Species or Special? A Critique of Peter Singer on Animals," in *Rethinking Peter Singer: A Christian Critique,* ed. Gordon Preece (Downers Grove, Ill: InterVarsity, 2002). See esp. 111–19, where Wilson compares Singer's view of animals with biblical teaching.

26. See Cora Diamond, "Eating Meat and Eating People," in Sunstein and Nussbaum, *Animal Rights,* 93–106, esp. 105.

27. Curiously, this is argued, albeit on different grounds, by feminists wary of defining rights in terms that favor those doing the defining. Catharine Mac Kinnon, for instance, recognizes that most relations between humans and animals will be unequal, which means that any framing of animal rights on a "like-us" basis is fraught with what she describes as "dishonesty" from the outset. Better, she says, to look more carefully at relations among animals and learn appropriate patterns of behavior for animals there rather than from human law courts. Her challenge, with which I agree (albeit for different reasons), is not to seek justice for nonhuman animals on precisely the same terms as for human animals but with more careful attention to species differences between animals and in ways that confront the power relations that undeniably exist between humans and other animals. Catharine A. MacKinnon, "Of Mice and Men: A Feminist Fragment on Animal Rights," in Sunstein and Nussbaum, *Animal Rights,* 263–76, esp. 270.

28. Regan, *Defending Animal Rights,* 43.

29. On this, see Carl Cohen, "Reply to Tom Regan," in *The Animal Rights Debate,* ed. C. Cohen and T. Regan (New York: Rowan & Littlefield, 2001), 246–48.

30. Harland, *Value of Human Life,* 156.

31. In May 2002 Germany became the first European nation to guarantee animal rights in its constitution. It was agreed by a majority of the Bundestag that Article 20a of the German Basic Law would read: "The state takes responsibility for protecting the natural foundations of life and animals in the interest of future generations."

32. Steven M. Wise, "Animal Rights, One Step at a Time," in Sunstein and Nussbaum, *Animal Rights,* 19–26.

33. Sionadh Douglas-Scott, "Environmental Rights," in Gearty and Tomkins, *Understanding Human Rights.*

34. Cass R. Sunstein, "Can Animals Sue," in Sunstein and Nussbaum, *Animal Rights*, 251–62.
35. Sunstein, "Can Animals Sue," esp. 253.
36. On this see Martha Nussbaum, "Animal Rights: The Need for a Theoretical Basis," review of *Rattling the Cage: Toward Legal Rights for Animals* (Cambridge, Mass.: Perseus Books, 2000), by Steven M. Wise, in *Harvard Law Review* 114 (2001): 1506–47. For an earlier account of the capabilities approach developed with respect to human capabilities, see Martha C. Nussbaum, *Sex and Social Justice* (Oxford: Oxford University Press, 1999), 41–42.
37. In the United States, the Patent Act of 1952 specified four basic statutory requirements that must be met to obtain a patent: (1) the claimed invention must be statutory subject matter and have utility; (2) it must be novel; (3) it must not have been obvious to a person having ordinary skill in the art at the time the invention was made; and (4) it must be fully and unambiguously disclosed in the text of the patent application, so that the skilled practitioner would be able to practice the claimed invention. In 2001 new utility guidelines required patent applicants to identify explicitly, unless already well established, a specific, substantial, and credible utility for all inventions; the U.S. Patent and Trademark Office Guidelines for Determining Utility of Gene-Related Inventions (January 4, 2001) raised the utility threshold. For more on this see Esther D. Reed, "Thinking Liturgically," in Celia Deane-Drummond, *Brave New World: Theology, Ethics, and the Human Genome Project* (London: T&T Clark/Continuum, 2004).
38. This is argued by Mark Sagoff in "DNA Patents: Making Ends Meet," in *Perspectives on Genetic Patenting: Religion, Science, and Industry in Dialogue*, ed. Audrey Chapman (Washington, D.C.: American Association for the Advancement of Science, 1999), 254–57.
39. I have deliberately cited this information from the statement of Dennis J. Henner, senior vice president, research, Genentech, Inc., before the Subcommittee on Courts and Intellectual Property of the Committee on the Judiciary, U.S. House of Representatives, July 13, 2000, <http://www.house.gov/judiciary/henn0713.htm> (date accessed: 02/10/02).
40. I cite the statement of Q. Todd Dickinson, undersecretary of commerce for intellectual property and director of the U.S. Patent and Trademark Office, before the Subcommittee on Courts and Intellectual Property of the Committee on the Judiciary, U.S. House of Representatives, July 13, 2000, <http://www.house.gov/judiciary/dick0713.htm> [date accessed: 02/10/02]. Note Dickinson's wording regarding the granting of patents on plants and animals. NB: The "onco mouse" was genetically engineered to be more susceptible to tumor growth.
41. Audrey Chapman provides a useful summary in Chapman, *Perspectives on Genetic Patenting*, 17–21.
42. Related debates are needed about gene patenting and whether novel gene sequences should be subject to proprietary patent rights that could be used to prevent others from publishing research or marketing tests based on DNA as it occurs in the body. For preliminary discussion see Esther D. Reed, "Property Rights, Genes, and Common Good," *Journal of Religious Ethics* 34, no.

1 (2006): 41–67. I reserve discussion of plant patents for another time and place.

43. Justice Brennan's ruling, < http://www2.law.cornell.ecu/cg> (date accessed: 04/12/02).

44. I am indebted at this point to Mr. Dan Wood. See also Lesley J. Rogers and Gisela Kaplan, "All Animals Are *Not* Equal: The Interface between Scientific Knowledge and Legislation for Animal Rights," in Sunstein and Nussbaum, *Animal Rights*, 175–202.

Chapter 7

1. Johan Steyn, twenty-seventh F. A. Mann Lecture, November 25, 2003, "Guantánamo Bay: The Legal Black Hole" in *Democracy through the Law,* at <http://www.fairgofordavid.org/pubdocs/LordSteynlecture.pdf> (date accessed: 11/08/05).

2. Anthony Lester, "The Human Rights Act 1998: Five Years On," November 25, 2003, <http://216.239.59.104/search?q=cache:anX1PUDOFsJ:www.hrla.org.uk/LesterHRA5.pdf+lord+steyn+human+rights&hl=en&ie=UTF-8> (date accessed: 11/08/05).

3. PDF download of memo available from *The Crimes of War Project* <http://www.crimesofwar.org/news-CIA.html> (date accessed: 11/10/05).

4. For the Fact Sheet issued by the White House, February 7, 2002, see "Status of Detainees at Guantanamo," <http://www.us-mission.ch/press2002/0802detainees.htm> (date accessed: 11/08/05).

5. Steyn, *Democracy through the Law,* 201.

6. Steyn, *Democracy through the Law*, 202.

7. Third Geneva Convention (III), Art. 103. In 1977 Article 75 of the First Protocol Additional to the Geneva Conventions of August detailed fuller provisions regarding treatment of prisoners of war and is widely held to be an expression of customary international law (Y. Dinstein, *The Conduct of Hostilities under the International Law of Armed Conduct* [Cambridge: Cambridge University Press, 2004], 33). The conditions of lawful combatancy were drawn stringently with clear requirements regarding the carrying of arms openly and the wearing of a uniform or distinctive emblem. These conditions seem not to have been met by Taliban fighters in Afghanistan, but Lord Steyn, and others, draw our attention to Article 75(4), which states: "No sentence may be passed and no penalty may be executed on a person found guilty of a penal offence relating to the armed conflict except persuant to a conviction pronounced by an impartial and regularly constituted court respecting the generally recognized principles of regular judicial procedure."

8. Dinstein, *Conduct of Hostilities,* 32.

9. Clive Walker, "The Governance of Special Powers: A Case Study of Exclusion and the Treatment of Individual Rights under the Prevention of Terrorism Acts," in Gearty and Tomkins, *Understanding Human Rights*; Campbell, Ewing, and Tomkins, *Sceptical Essays*, chap. 27, esp. 611.

10. Walker, "Governance of Special Powers," 622.

11. Bush, "Humane Treatment of al Qaeda and Taliban Detainees"; see note 3 above.

12. M_chael Walzer, *Arguing about War* (New Haven: Yale Univerity Press, 2004), 33.

13. By "communitarianism" I understand the view that qualifies, or in some instances rejects, the liberal concern for individual choice in favor of the recognition of common moral values and virtues, thus emphasizing duties over rights and often the social importance of the family unit. For a similar definition see Allen Buchanan et al., *From Chance to Choice: Genetics and Justice* (Cambridge: Cambridge University Press), 371–72.

14. Ronald Dworkin, *Law's Empire* (Oxford: Hart Publishing, 1998), 9 and 98, respectively.

15. Rosenfeld, *Just Interpretations*, 38.

16. Max Weber, *Economy and Society: An Outline of Interpretive Sociology*, ed. Günther Roth and Claus Wittich (New York: Bedminster, 1968), pt. 1, chap. 3, 212ff.

17. John A. Simmons, *Justification and Legitimacy: Essays on Rights and Obligations* (Cambridge: Cambridge University Press, 2001), chap. 7. According to Simmons, a leading political philosopher, "justification" is a defensive concept that applies when the person advancing the justification feels pressed to vindicate their existence or argument against a background presumption of possible objection. The threshold of justifiability depends on particular circumstances, personalities, and other vagaries. Essentially, however, "justification" of this kind is a practice or strategy that shows itself to be reasonable, prudent, and morally acceptable to interested parties. It entails a willingness to rebut possible objections and to show how such a rebuttal might be achievable in practice, and attempts to meet those with whom we disagree on common ground. By contrast, legitimacy applies to legal right or status or, "in extended use, to a right or status supported by tradition, custom, or accepted standards" (124). Simmons writes about the "justification and legitimacy" of the state; I reapply his meaning in this context.

18. Habermas, *Legitimation Crisis*.

19. Jürgen Habermas, *Between Facts and Norms* (Cambridge: Polity Press, 1997), 449.

20. For instance, see Peter Baker, "Surveillance Disclosure Denounced," June 27, 2006, <http://www.washingtonpost.com/> (date accessed: 09/09/06); Slashdot, "State and Federal Governments Clash on NSA Snooping," August 7, 2006, <http://yro.slashdot.org/article.pl?sid=06/08/07/2014255> (date accessed: 09/09/06).

21. Helena Kennedy, "Take No Comfort in This Warm Blanket of Security: Terrorism Is Being Used to Justify a Retreat from Legal Principle," *The Guardian*, March 15, 2004, <http://www.guardian.co.uk/comment/story/0,3604,1169277,00.html> (date accessed: 05/26/06).

22. Agnes Heller, "Law, Ethos, and Ethics: The Question of Values," in *Theory of Modernity*, 206.

23. This is noted by Rosenfeld, *Just Interpretations*, 115.

24. Habermas, *Between Facts and Norms*, xlii. On the latter point, see Robert Gascoigne's critique of Habermas's neo-Kantianism in *The Public Forum and Christian Ethics* (Cambridge: Cambridge University Press, 2001), esp. 77.

25. Habermas, *Between Facts and Norms*, xlii.

26. Gascoigne, *Public Forum and Christian Ethics,* 78.

27. Heller, *Theory of Modernity,* 232.

28. Ronald Dworkin, *Sovereign Virtue: The Theory and Practice of Equality* (Cambridge: Harvard University Press, 2000), 4.

29. Dworkin, *Law's Empire,* 192–93.

30. Dworkin, "Objectivity and Truth: You'd Better Believe It," *Philosophy and Public Affairs* 25, no. 2 (1996): 87–139.

31. Dworkin, *Law's Empire,* 255.

32. Patrick Devlin, *The Enforcement of Morals* (Oxford: Oxford University Press, 1965).

33. H. L. A. Hart, *The Concept of Law,* 2nd ed. (Oxford: Clarendon, 1997), 185.

34. Devlin, *The Enforcement of Morals,* 23.

35. Hart, *The Concept of Law,* 203.

36. Dworkin, *Law's Empire,* 87.

37. Dworkin, *Law's Empire,* 239.

38. This critique is made by Michael Rosenfeld of Stanley Fish's new legal formalism but is relevant here; see *Just Interpretations,* 38.

39. Dworkin, *Law's Empire,* 217.

40. Habermas, *Autonomy and Solidarity,* 158.

41. Dworkin, *Law's Empire,* 191.

42. Dworkin, *Law's Empire,* 255.

43. On "bad" forms of tribalism, see Jonathan Sacks, *The Dignity of Difference: How to Avoid the Clash of Civilizations,* rev. ed. (London/New York: Continuum, 2003), 46.

44. UNHCR Press Release, July 17, 2006, "UNHCR Marks 50th Anniversary of U.N. Refugee Convention," <http://www.unhcr.org/cgi-bin/texis/vtx/ news/ opendoc.htm?tbl=NEWS&page=home&id=3b6027264> (date accessed: 06/17/06).

45. Tom Clark, "Rights Based Refuge, the Potential of the 1951 Convention and the Need for Authoritative Interpretation," *International Journal of Refugee Law* 16, no. 4 (2004): 599.

46. Witness the problem in the UK that section 9 of the Asylum and Immigration (Treatment of Claimants) Act of 2004 runs counter to the government's established welfare duties and practice under the Children Act of 1989 and the Human Rights Act of 1998. A report by the children's charity Barnardo's paints a picture of confusion and concern and is bitterly critical of section 9 of the Asylum and Immigration Act, which gives officials the right to stop all benefits for those who do not return voluntarily to their home countries. See Barnardo's, *The End of the Road: The Impact on Families of Section 9 of the Asylum and Immigration (Treatment of Claimants)* Act 2004 (London: Barnardo's, 2005), esp. 30.

47. Clark, "Rights Based Refuge," 586.

48. I borrow terms developed by Matthew J. Gibney in *The Ethics and Politics of Asylum: Liberal Democracy and the Response to Refugees* (Cambridge: Cambridge University Press, 2004), 36ff.

49. Roger Scruton, *The Philosopher on Dover Beach: Essays* (Manchester: Carcanet, 1990), 320; *The Need for Nations* (London: Civitas, 2004), 2.

50. Michael Dummett, *On Immigration and Refugees* (London: Routledge, 2001); Peter Singer and Renata Singer, "The Ethics of Refugee Policy," in *Open Borders? Closed Societies? The Ethical and Political Issues*, ed. Mark Gibney (Westport, Conn.: Greenwood Press, 1988).

51. Gibney, *Ethics and Politics of Asylum*, 36.

52. Ronald Dworkin, *Political Liberalism*, 2nd ed. (New York: Columbia University Press, 1996), 231.

53. Dworkin, *Political Liberalism*, 236.

54. On the latter see the decision in *Gherebi v. Bush et al.* CV-03-01267-ANM. In a 2–1 decision by the Court of Appeals for the 9th Circuit, in response to a petition from the relative of a Libyan held in Cuba, the court decided that the 660 detainees should be afforded some minimal access to the U.S. legal system. Also relevant is *Rasul v. Bush*, 542 U.S. 466 (2004).

55. In *Gherebi v. Bush et al.*, ACLU, "Federal Court Decision Granting Guantánamo Bay Detainees Judicial Review Caps Red-Letter Day for Checks and Balances," <http://www.aclu.org//safefree/general/16920prs20031218.html> (date accessed: 11/23/05).

56. The Jurist, <http://jurist.law.pitt.edu/forumy/2005/11/graham-levin-amendment-and-due-process.php> (date accessed: 11/23/05).

57. Mark Tushnett argues in "Skepticism about Judicial Review: A Perspective from the United States" that the Supreme Court's actions have rarely deviated significantly from the positions taken by the political forces controlling the political process, and that when those decisions have deviated from what the political process produces, the implications of the decisions for protecting fundamental human rights have frequently been ambiguous. In Campbell, Ewing, and Tomkins, *Sceptical Essays on Human Rights*, 359–73.

58. Dworkin, "Objectivity and Truth," 139.

59. Robert Audi and Nicholas Wolterstorff, *Religion in the Public Square: The Place of Religious Convictions in Political Debate* (Lanham, Md.: Rowan & Littlefield, 1997), 77.

60. Perry, *Under God?*, chap. 3, esp. 35.

61. I borrow wording from Perry, *Under God?*, 45.

62. Barth, *Christian Life*, 10.

63. Karl Barth, *C.D.*, II.2, §36, 551.

64. Karl Barth, *C.D.*, II.2, §38, 636.

65. In the opening pages of Athanasius, *Against the Heathen*, in *Nicene and Post-Nicene Fathers*, 2nd ser., vol. 4, §1.

66. Barth, *Christian Life*, 9–10.

67. Webster, *Word and Church*, 201.

68. There is no *analogia entis* between divine and human justice. Nor are we suggesting a source of ethical knowledge apart from the self-revelation of God in Jesus Christ (see chap. 3). Doctrinal truth does not give rise to universal and categorically binding politico-legal judgments to which all persons have access by virtue of their natural reason, nor do affirmations of every person's creation *imago Dei* translate directly into human rights.

69. Claus Westermann, *Genesis 1-11: A Commentary*, trans. John J. Scullion, S.J. (London: SPCK, 1974), 466.

70. Capital punishment is not the topic of this chapter—though, if it were, I should attempt to draw attention to the many failings cf criminal justice systems that impose death, with a view to arguing against the viability of the death penalty today in all but the most exceptional of circumstances.

71. Harland, *Value of Human Life,* 163.

72. Westermann, *Genesis 1–11,* 469.

73. David Novak, "God and Human Rights in a Secular Society: A Biblical Talmudic Perspective," in Bucar and Barnett, *Does Human Rights Need God?,* 51.

74. Novak, "God and Human Rights," 55, citing *Targum Yerushalmi*: Genesis 4:8; also *Palestinian Talmud*: Kiddushin 4.1/65b.

75. This point is made by David Fergusson, *Community, Liberalism, and Christian Ethics* (Cambridge: Cambridge University Press, 1998), 27.

Afterword

1. Alasdair MacIntyre, *After Virtue* (Notre Dame, Ind. University of Notre Dame Press, 1981), 67.

2. Robin Gill, general editor's preface to Fergusson, *Community, Liberalism, and Christian Ethics,* ix.

3. Charles Taylor, review of *Rethinking Multiculturalism,* by Bhikhu Parekh, in *Times Literary Supplement,* April 20, 2001, 4.

4. Paul Ricoeur, *The Just* (Chicago: University of Chicago Press, 2000), 40.

5. Aristotle, *Nichomachean Ethics,* trans. H. Rackham, Loeb Classical Library (London: Heinemann, 1926), bk 1, §1, 3.

6. David Novak, *Covenantal Rights: A Study in Jewish Political Theory* (Princeton: Princeton University Press, 2000), 19.

7. This point is made by Novak, *Covenantal Rights,* 21.

8. Aquinas, *S.T.,* I q. 6 a. 1.

9. Novak, *Covenantal Rights,* 20.

10. Eberhard Jüngel, "Living Out of Righteousness," in *Theological Essays,* vol. 2, trans. Arnold Neufeld-Fast and John B. Webster (Edinburgh: T&T Clark, 1995), 259.

11. Note Novak's description of his own work in this field: "Covenantal Rights is a study of Judaism itself as a full system of rights and correlative duties. In principle, that full system is the everlasting covenant (berit) between God and Israel" (*Covenantal Rights,* ix).

12. Novak, *Covenantal Rights,* x.

13. Novak, *Covenantal Rights,* 28.

14. Novak, *Covenantal Rights,* 29.

15. Novak, *Covenantal Rights,* 77.

16. Novak, *Covenantal Rights,* 25.

17. A particularly interesting aspect of Novak's *Covenantal Rights* is its discussion (chap. 2) of the claims that humans have on God as Creator.

18. Jüngel, "Living Out of Righteousness," 243.

19. Jüngel, "Living Out of Righteousness," 260.

20. Jüngel, "Living Out of Righteousness," 260.

21. Jüngel, "Living Out of Righteousness," 259.

22. Jüngel, "Living Out of Righteousness," 261.
23. Jüngel, "Living Out of Righteousness," 243.
24. Jüngel, "Living Out of Righteousness," 252.
25. Conor Gearty uses the idea of human rights as a "mask" in *Can Human Rights Survive? The Hamlyn Lectures 2005* (Cambridge: Cambridge University Press, 2006), 143.
26. Barth, "Christian's Place in Society," 299.
27. I borrow Jan M. N. E. Jans's presentation of the Euthyphro dilemma as given in "Divine Command and/or Human Ethics? Exploring the Maieutical Dialectics between Christian Faith in God and Responsibility," in *Für die Freiheit verantwortlich. Festschrift für Karl-Wilhelm Merks zum 65. Geburtstag*, ed. J. Jans (Freiburg: Academic Press Freibourg, 2004)," 38.
28. See Jan M. N. E. Jans, "Christian Ethics: On the Difficult Dialectic between Faith and *Ethics*," *Australian E-Journal of Theology*, Issue 2, February 2002, <http://dlibrary.acu.edu.au/research/theology/ejournal/aejt_2/Jan_Jans.htm> (date accessed: 07/27/06).
29. Jan M. N. E. Jans, "Neither punishment nor Reward: Divine Gratuitousness and Moral Order" *Concilium* 40 (2004): 83–92.
30. This question is put by Jans in "Divine Command and/or Human Ethics?" 38.
31. Bonhoeffer, *Ethics,* 381. He also addressed the issue by interpreting God's commandment to be free by subordinating the concept of "ethics as command" (*Ethik als Gebot*) to that of "ethics as formation" (*Ethik als Gestalt*), 99–100.

Indices

Scripture Index

Index of Names

Index of Subjects